U0459425

江西省高校人文社会科学研究 2021 年度项目 (YY21213)；
江西省教育科学“十四五”规划 2022 年度课题 (22YB351)；
2023 年江西省高等学校教学改革研究省级立项课题 (JXJG-23-36-2)

学术论文的语类复杂性研究

Exploring Generic Complexity in Research Articles

邱 敏 著

吉林大学出版社
·长春·

图书在版编目(CIP)数据

学术论文的语类复杂性研究 / 邱敏著. -- 长春 : 吉林大学出版社, 2024. 9. -- ISBN 978-7-5768-3694-3

Ⅰ. H315

中国国家版本馆 CIP 数据核字第 2024N45E46 号

书　　名：学术论文的语类复杂性研究
　　　　　XUESHU LUNWEN DE YULEI FUZAXING YANJIU

作　　者：邱　敏
策划编辑：邵宇彤
责任编辑：刘　丹
责任校对：崔吉华
装帧设计：寒　露
出版发行：吉林大学出版社
社　　址：长春市人民大街4059号
邮政编码：130021
发行电话：0431-89580036/58
网　　址：http://www.jlup.com.cn
电子邮箱：jldxcbs@sina.com
印　　刷：河北万卷印刷有限公司
成品尺寸：170mm×240mm　　16开
印　　张：19.5
字　　数：374千字
版　　次：2024年9月第1版
印　　次：2024年9月第1次
书　　号：ISBN 978-7-5768-3694-3
定　　价：98.00元

版权所有　　翻印必究

前言

FOREWORD

宏观语类指为实现复杂目的，将多种基础语类实例化的大型语篇（Martin, 1994, 2002; Martin and Rose, 2008; Zhang and Pramoolsook, 2019）。语类复杂性指形成宏观语类所需基础语类的数量和种类（Jordens et al., 2001）。学术论文作为一种宏观语类 （Hood, 2010），其语类复杂性特征未受到学界深入关注。然而，为了有效传播研究成果，学术论文作者需要掌握运用基础语类构成宏观语类的技巧。有鉴于此，本书探究学术论文的语类复杂性特征。

本书首先提出探讨英语学术论文语类复杂性的框架。接着从跨学科及跨文化的角度，探讨学术论文的语类复杂性。一方面，本书运用该框架分析物理、语言学、文学三个学科英文学术论文的语类复杂性，揭示学科特征对学术论文语类复杂性的影响。 另一方面，本书对比分析了汉英语言学期刊论文的语类复杂性特征，并试图从文化差异的角度对汉英学术论文语类复杂性特征进行分析。

本书共分为八章。第一章为引言，介绍本书的研究背景、研究目标及研究问题、研究方法、研究意义，以及全书的整体架构。

第二章为文献回顾，主要从语类研究、语类复杂性研究、从语类角度对学术论文的研究三方面梳理相关文献，引出研究问题。通过评述相关文献，指出关于学术论文语类复杂性研究三方面可改进之处，为研究框架的确立提供理论和实践支撑。

第三章介绍语类复杂性分析框架及研究方法，详述其理论动因及描写基础。首先，本书提出学术论文语类复杂性研究框架。该框架包括两个维度，即基础语类的分布以及基础语类在论文各主要语类阶段形成宏观语类的机制。一方面，本书借鉴有关基础语类的研究，提出基础语类的分类框架。该框架包含五大基础语类族，共计 24 种基础语类。另一方面，依据 Martin（1994, 1995）关于语类连接策略的观点，本书分析基础语类构成宏观语类的方式，包括延伸、详述、增强、投射和内嵌。本研究在此基础上从语类层、语域层和语篇语义层分析了具有学科特色的基础语类。与此同时，本书还借鉴 Maton（2014）对知识结构和知者结构的论述，分析三个学科学术论文语类复杂性异同的原因。接着，本书从功能语言学的理论概念出发，详细介绍语类复杂性分析框架的理论动因，包括语境、语类、逻辑语义关系、层次化、体现，以及实例化。然后，本书按照功能语言学自上而下的顺序，阐明了语类复杂性分析框架的主要描写指标，包括基础语类、语类连接策略、语场和语篇语义资源。最后，本章说明数据收集、处理和分析工具及方法。

第四章呈现学术论文的基础语类布局特点。主要从宏观语类结构、新兴基础语类、基础语类整体及分阶段布局三方面阐述三门学科学术论文基础语类布局的特征。

第五章分析基础语类的连接策略。本书分析比较了三门学科研究论文在语类延伸、详述、增强、投射、内嵌方面的相似性和差异性。

第六章分析特定基础语类。基于基础语类分布的数据分析，本书从三门学科论文中选取了八种具有学科特色的基础语类进行调查。调查从语类、语场和语篇语义层展开。

第七章选取了汉英语言学期刊论文，分析其在基础语类整体和分阶段布局方面的异同。

第八章为全书结论，首先从主要语类结构、新兴基础语类、基础语类布局、基础语类连接策略、具有学科特色的基础语类、学科特征六个方面概括研究发现；接着阐述研究的理论、方法、实践意义；最后指出研究局限及后续研究方向。

本书的研究发现总结如下：

第一，三门学科英语论文的语类结构各具特色。语言学论文最常见的语类结构型式是ILMRDC，物理学和文学论文的最常用语类型式分别为IM[RD]C和(I)A。

第二，语料中出现了语类分类框架原来未包含在内的六种语类，它们分别是说明评论文、阐释文、图形说明文、直接公式描写文、条件公式描写文以及序列公式描写文。

第三，对于基础语类的分布情况，本书分析了三门学科学术论文在语类整体分布以及各宏观语类阶段基础语类分布方面的异同。

分析结果表明，各学科论文在基础语类的总体布局方面呈现各自特点。物理学英文论文可能由于偏重陈述知识，更多使用公式描写文、图形说明文和过程描写文。文学英文论文的作者试图说服读者接受其对文学作品的判断，广泛应用论辩说明文和说明评论文。语言学英文论文呈现知识语码和知者语码的混合特性。

一方面，较之文学英文论文，语言学英文论文更频繁使用过程描写文和图形说明文。另一方面，与物理学论文相比，语言学英文论文使用更多的论辩说明文和说明评论文。

在各主要宏观语类阶段的基础语类分布方面，三个子语料库也表现出差异。物理学论文与语言学论文相比，在论文的“方法”“结果”“结果和讨论”，以及“讨论”部分使用更多的序列解释文、图形说明文和直接公式描写文，而在论文的“结果”以及“结果和讨论”部分，语言学学术论文比物理学学术论文使用更多的说明评论文。这一结果可以从两个学科知识结构取向的差异进行解释。

第四，语类延伸是三门学科论文最常用的语类连接策略。与此同时，各学科论文也具有各自偏好的语类连接型式。物理学子语料库常用“描写报告文 × 因素解释文”的连接组合，用于解释产生实验或计算结果的原因。此外，文学学术论文出现更多的显性语类内嵌。

第五，基于基础语类分布的数据分析，本研究从三门学科论文中选取了八种具有学科特色的基础语类进行调查。调查从语类、语场和语篇语义层展开。在语言学子语料库中，分类报告在语场资源方面主要由项目体现。论辩说明和过程描写文可以由项目和活动体现。在物理学子语料库中，事物实体和符号实体建构图形说明文，直接公式描写文在语义层由符号实体（如不同的公式参数）体现。在文学子语料库里，说明评论文和论辩说明文常用文学评论家作为来源实体，并使用较多评价资源，明确表达作者观点。

第六，学科特点构成本书探讨语类复杂性的一条主线。具体而言，学科特点可以影响基础语类布局与语类连接策略。此外，学科特性会影响基础语类的建构。这一点表现为具有学科特色的语场和语篇语义资源识解某些基础语类。

第七，汉英语言学期刊论文的语类复杂性特征存在共性和差异。在基础语类整体布局方面，两个子语料库中，数量排名前三的基础语类族一致。在基础语类的分阶段布局方面，汉语语言学期刊论文在各主要语类阶段呈现更多的报告文和论辩文。

本书具有理论和教学意义。在理论方面，本书有三方面价值。其一，本书提出了分析英语学术论文语类复杂性的框架，扩大了语类理论的解释力。其二，本书丰富了对学术论文的研究。本研究通过分析基础语类整体布局与语类连接策略，对学术论文的语类复杂性展开了较深入的研究。其三，本研究拓展了人们对不同学科论文语类复杂性的认识。本研究表明，某些基础语类在特定学科具有统计学上的显著分布。即使在同一宏观语类阶段，不同学科论文的基础语类分布也存在差异。此外，不同学科论文具有不同的基础语类连接型式。上述发现有助于加深人们对三门学科学术论文语类复杂性特征的理解。

在教学方面，本书的研究结果可以给学术写作教学和教材编写提供很好的参考。研究表明，不同学科的英语研究论文呈现不同程度的语类复杂性。因此有必要提高学生进行学术写作时的语类复杂度意识。此外，在编写学术写作教学材料时，需要强调语类复杂性的学科差异、文化差异，给学生提供运用基础语类撰写不同学科汉英论文的详细指导。

本书得以出版，我首先要感谢我的导师厦门大学杨信彰教授。书稿确立选题、拟定框架到完成初稿，其间老师不辞辛劳，一章一章一遍一遍逐词逐句修改。杨老师严谨治学的精神、渊博的学识、敏锐的洞察力，引领我走入学术研究的大门，也成为我今后学习的榜样。

其次，我要感谢我在厦门大学读博期间的老师和同学们，他们引导我走进功能语言学与语篇分析领域。

最后，我要感谢我的父母。他们在我读博期间，悉心照料我年幼的女儿。正是他们的全力支持，我才得以完成学业。

尽管历经数轮修改，但由于本人能力有限，书中的不足之处，恳请各位专家学者批评指正。

在此特别感谢赣南科技学院对本书出版的资助。

目 录

CONTENTS

List of Figures

List of Tables

List of Abbreviations

CARS	Create a research space
CRA	Chinese research articles
ERA	English research articles
ESP	English for specific purposes
GSP	Generic structural potential
LRA	Literature research article
RA	Research articles
RAI	Research article introduction
RQ	Research questions
SFL	Systemic functional linguistics

Chapter 1 Introduction

The present study aims to explore generic complexity in research articles (henceforth abbreviated as RAs) from the perspective of Systemic Functional Linguistics (henceforth abbreviated as SFL). The main concern is with the examination of generic complexity in two dimensions: the elemental genre deployments and the genre combining strategies. The identification of the two major dimensions is carried out through the genre, register, and discourse semantics strata. The current chapter consists of seven sections, dealing respectively with the research background, research objectives and research questions, methodological preview, research significance, and organization of the whole book.

1.1 Why generic complexity?

Research articles (henceforth abbreviated as RAs), have long gained attention as a vital route for researchers to communicate their research findings within the academic community. Scholars either explore the macro rhetorical structures (e.g., Swales, 1990, 2004) or the micro lexicogrammatical resources (e.g., Hyland, 2005; Hyland&Zou, 2020) of RAs. However, as a macrogenre, RAs are understudied.

Generic complexity was originally proposed by Jordens et al. (2001), referring to the number and variety of elemental genres used for forming macrogenres. Genre, according to Martin and Rose (2008:20), is a configuration of meanings. It is also a staged goal-oriented social process (Martin, 1992:505).

A macrogenre, as reported by Martin (1994, 2002), Martin and Rose (2008), and Zhang and Pramoolsook (2019), is a large-scale text that instantiates more than one elemental genre to accomplish complicated purposes. In this sense, a research article, as seen by Hood (2010:6), is by nature a macrogenre, containing a series of linked segments and each segment has its own generic structure.

This section presents the background of the current study, explaining the motivations for studying generic complexity, RAs, and generic complexity in RAs.

The motivation for analyzing generic complexity in RAs lies in two aspects. Theoretically, this study presents a framework for describing generic complexity in RAs, which can enrich the SFL-based exploration of this phenomenon. Practically, the application of the framework into the analysis of RAs in physics, linguistics, and literary studies can check the explanatory power and feasibility of the theoretical model.

The examination of related literature on generic complexity lends weight to these motives. From the theoretical perspective, three strands of scholars are devoted to analyzing the phenomenon. Researchers of the first strand are represented by Martin (1994, 1995, 2002, 2008), who creates the concept of macrogenre and discusses the strategies through which elemental genres are combined to form a macrogenre. It is worthy of mentioning that Martin's (1994, 1995) and Martin and Rose's (2008) discussion on elemental genres are mainly derived from the observations on textbooks of primary and secondary schools. In addition, Zhang and Guo (2019) proposes an analytical framework for genre hybrid, which include mixeds genre and fused genre.

The second strand of researchers, represented by Matthiessen and Teruya (2016), propose the notion of registerial hybridity, which refers to the fact that a text utilizes several text types. They (Matthiessen&Teruya, 2016) further classify registerial hybridity on the basis of the field of activity, which involves expounding, reporting, recreating, etc.

The third strand of researchers, represented by Bhatia (2010), uses the concept of interdiscursivity to analyze the similar phenomenon. Interdiscursivity, as stated by Bhatia (2010:36), refers to the appropriation of generic resources across professional genres, practices, and cultures. For instance, the corporate annual report is an archetypal combination of accounting discourse, discourse of finance, public relations discourse, and legal discourse.

Drawing on the above-mentioned notions of macrogenre, generic complexity, generic hybridity, and interdiscursivity, empirical studies are carried out for discovering this phenomenon in various discourses, such as RAs (Hood, 2010; Lai&Wang, 2018), textbooks (Zhao, 2014), bachelor's theses (Zhang&Pramoolsook, 2019), classroom discourses (Christie, 1997, 1999), health discourses (Jordens et al., 2001; Jordens&Little, 2004), football blogs (Thompson, 2016), advertising discourse on WeChat (Wu et al., 2018), corporate posts in Sina Weibo (Xu&Feng, 2020), legal discourses (Ge&Wang, 2019; Ren et al., 2020), and business discourses (Bhatia, 2010, 2017).

The re-examination of previous studies on generic complexity shows that although the phenomenon of generic complexity has caught the attention of many researchers, especially the scholars with SFL or English for Specific Purposes (henceforth abbreviated as ESP) academic background, there are still at least two points that need to be improved. Firstly, there is scarce comprehensive work depicting generic complexity, especially scant research centering on describing how elemental genres are combined into a macrogenre. Secondly, there are relatively rare studies focusing on testifying the explanatory power and feasibility of the analytical frameworks.

1.2 Why research articles?

The second driving force for conducting the current project comes from the genre-based studies on RAs.

As a type of academic discourse, RAs are major academic communication channels for disseminating research results among academic discourse communities (Pang et al., 2021:1). Therefore, RAs have aroused the interest of scholars worldwide. Genre-based studies on RAs occupy a large proportion of RA studies.

These studies can be classified into two categories depending on their research content: the exploration of RA part-genres and the study of the entire RA. Regarding the studies on the part-genres of RAs, every section of RAs has been studied, including Abstracts (Abdollahpour&Gholami, 2019), Introductions (Kashiha&Marandi, 2019), Introduction and Discussion sections (Li&Xu, 2020), Introduction and Conclusion sections (Xu&Nesi, 2019a), Theoretical framework (Tseng, 2018), Methods sections (Lim, 2019), and Results sections (Parviz et al., 2020). These studies are underpinned by four strings of theoretical thoughts. The first is based on Swales' (1990, 2004) proposition of moves, discussing the rhetorical structure of RAs (e.g., Tseng, 2018; Yang&Allison, 2003). The second is move-based analysis of the distribution of lexicogrammatical resources, such as lexical bundles (Abdollahpour&Gholami, 2019), phrase-frames (Lu et al., 2021), part-of-speech gram (Lin&Liu, 2021), and citation practice (Jalilifar et al., 2018). The third is the analysis of interpersonal resources either through utilizing Hyland's (2005) framework of metadiscourse (e.g., Hyland&Zou, 2020) or Martin and White's (2005) appraisal framework (e.g., Moyano, 2019). The fourth one is the exploration of other linguistic features, such as phrasal complexity (Parviz et al., 2020).

In addition to research on RA part-genres, complete RAs are also analyzed. These studies are usually corpus-based and attempt to identify linguistic features, including informality features (Gao, 2020), authorial references (Khedri&Kritsis, 2020), reporting practice (Marti et al., 2019), authorial stances (Qiu&Ma, 2019), definitions (Triki, 2019), and exemplifications (Su&Zhang, 2020).

From the perspective of research methods, comparison is frequently employed in the genre-based studies on RAs. The comparison can be cross-cultural. For instance, Li (2021) and Zhao et al. (2018) make a comparison between Chinese RAs and English RAs. Besides, cross-disciplinary comparisons (e.g., Ren, 2021) and the combination of cross-cultural and cross-disciplinary comparisons (e.g., Friginal&Mustafa, 2017) are also conducted. The comparison of student writers and expert writers is also found in the literature (e.g., Ansarifar et al., 2018). Other studies, such as the cross-research paradigm (Arizavi&Choubsaz, 2021) and cross-genre comparison (Shen&Tao, 2021), are also discovered.

Although there are plentiful studies on RAs, as a typical instantiation of macrogenres, the generic complexity of RAs is under-explored. There are only several studies that focus on the generic complexity of RAs (see Section 2.3.5). In light of the large number of RAs in the world, more research can be done in this aspect. Therefore, this research takes RAs as the research object, aiming for revealing the nature of RAs as macrogenres.

1.3 Why generic complexity in RAs

The third motivation for conducting this research arises from the need for analyzing generic complexity in RAs, which lie in two aspects: to provide a relatively comprehensive framework for analyzing generic complexity in RAs and to see how disciplinary features influence the characteristics of generic complexity in RAs.

Two research directions can be revealed from the brief review of the extant studies on generic complexity in ERAs.

Firstly, previous research on generic complexity all take English research articles as the research object. On the one hand, some scholars (e.g., Lai&Wang, 2018) take the whole ERA as a macrogenre, exploring the elemental genre deployments. On the other hand, a part-genre of an ERA is considered as a macrogenre (Zhang, 2015; Hood, 2010). For instance, Zhang (Zhang, 2015) analyzes the types of elemental genres and the relation between elemental genres in two abstracts of ERAs. It is noticed that these studies all concentrate on generic complexity in ERAs of linguistics. Furthermore, only Zhang's study delves into the mechanism through which the elemental genres are combined into a macrogenre. In addition, except for Lai and Wang's (2018) study, which takes 120 linguistics ERAs altogether as data source, other studies merely analyze a few examples.

Therefore, the present research establishes a relatively larger corpus for scrutinizing both the overall elemental deployments and major-generic-stage-based genre allocations of ERAs in the fields of physics, linguistics, and literary studies. Moreover, the mechanism through which the elemental genres are combined in the main generic stages of ERAs is investigated. Thus, a more comprehensive study of generic complexity in ERAs is conducted.

Secondly, since linguistics ERAs are the focus of all the previous studies, there is a lack of the profile of generic complexity in ERAs of other disciplines. Therefore, the current project takes the ERAs in physics, linguistics, and literary studies as the research object, trying to show how disciplinarity can influence the features of generic complexity. The three disciplines are chosen for the following reasons.

On the one hand, in line with Martin et al. (2010:438), physics, linguistics, and literary studies represent science, social science, and the humanities respectively in the continuum of knowledge structure, which is illustrated in Figure 1.1.

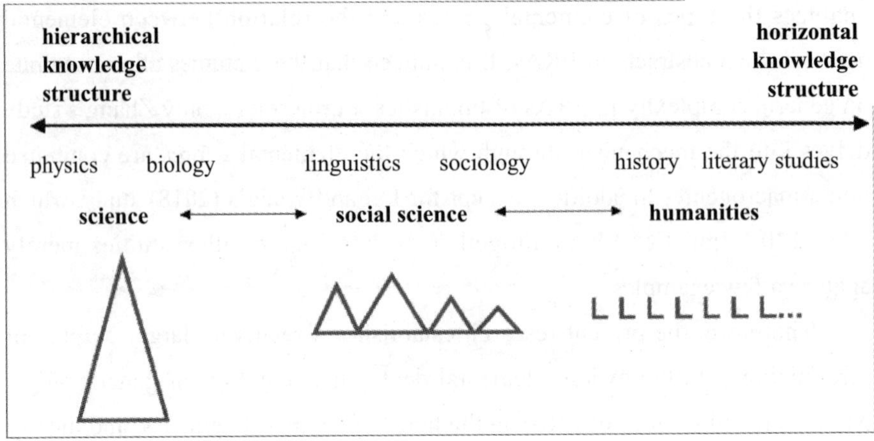

Figure 1.1 Discipline cline (Martin et al., 2010:438)

As demonstrated in Figure 1.1, physics and literary studies are located at the two poles of the continuum, representing the disciplines featured by hierarchical knowledge structure and horizontal structure respectively. Linguistics, which takes language as its research object, is a social science (Xia, 2009:1). Additionally, as reported by Ye and Xu (2010:5), linguistics is a bridge that connects natural sciences and humanities. For one thing, before linguistics became an independent discipline, language studies were part of philosophy, logic, and literature (Ye&Xu,, 2010: 5). For another, linguistics is intensively related to science given that the research orientation, methods, and interpreting approaches of science such as information sciences, cognitive sciences directly influence linguistics studies (Ye&Xu, 2010: 5).

On the other hand, the three disciplines are chosen for their own significance. Physics is considered essential in science disciplines (Young&Freedman, 2012:1). The principles of physics provide a basis for understanding other disciplines, such as chemistry, and engineering (Zhao,2012:7). Literary studies is a vital discipline in the humanities (Zhao eT al., 2019:18). Linguistics is a discipline that conducts systematic study of language, describing all aspects of language and developing theories that depict how language works (Yang, 2005:27). Therefore, the comparison in terms of generic complexity among the ERAs of the three disciplines can provide us with a deeper understanding of the impact of disciplinary characteristics on the formation of macrogenres.

Given the importance of RAs in global academic communities and scant studies on generic complexity, the present project aims to establish a framework for analyzing generic complexity in RAs. Furthermore, this framework is applied in the analysis of RAs from both cross-disciplinary and cross-cultural perspectives.

To sum up, the scrutiny of the related studies on generic complexity, RAs, and generic complexity in RAs reveals that there are three aspects that can be improved.

Firstly, although the phenomenon of generic complexity has attracted the researchers' attention, there is still a scarce theoretical framework that systematically describes it. Even fewer studies focus on the mechanism through which elemental genres are combined into macrogenres.

Secondly, in terms of verification of theoretical frameworks, though some scholars (e.g., Zhang&Guo, 2018) propose an analytical framework for discussing genre hybrid, there is a lack of studies that testify to the feasibility of this framework in certain discourse practices.

Thirdly, the extant literature sees a few studies on the generic complexity of ERAs. Furthermore, all these generic-complexity-concerned studies take ERAs in linguistics as the research object. The generic complexity in ERAs of other disciplines is still unknown.

To solve the above-mentioned problems, the current study is engaged in exploring generic complexity in RAs, based on which five research questions are presented, which are exposed in Section 1.4.

1.4 Aims of the book

The book aims to investigate generic complexity in RAs. To achieve this objective, four steps are taken. Firstly, the present project establishes a framework for analyzing generic complexity in RAs. This framework mainly scrutinizes generic complexity from two dimensions: elemental genre deployments and combining strategies. Secondly, this framework is attested by examining generic complexity in ERAs of physics, linguistics, and literary studies. Thirdly, the similarities and differences in generic complexity are discussed from the aspect of disciplinarity. Fourthly, the generic complexity features in linguistics ERAs and CRAs (Chinese research articles) are compared. The first step is accomplished in Chapter 3, where a theoretical framework for exploring generic complexity is proposed. The second and third steps are achieved through Chapters 4-6. The fourth task is fulfilled in Chapter 7.

To be specific, the present study tackles the following five research questions (henceforth abbreviated as RQs):

First, what are the macro generic structures, elemental genre deployments, and the similarities and differences in the overall genre deployments in the ERAs of physics, linguistics, and literary studies? This research question can be divided into three sub-questions: (1) What are the macro generic structures of the ERAs among the three disciplines? (2) Are there any emerging elemental genres in the three sub-corpora? (3) How are elemental genres deployed in the ERAs of the three disciplines?

Second, how do elemental genres form macrogenres in the main stages of the ERAs of the three disciplines?

Third, what are the field and discourse semantics resources used in construing distinctive elemental genres in the ERAs of the three disciplines?

Fourth, how do disciplinary features influence the elemental genre deployments and genre combining strategies in the ERAs of the three disciplines?

Fifth, what are the similarities and differences in generic complexity features between linguistics ERAs and CRAs?

The answers to these RQs are addressed in Chapters 4-7. The main generic structures, burgeoning elemental genres, and elemental genre deployments are covered in Chapter 4, which answers RQ1. The analysis of the elemental genre combining tactics in Chapter 5 responds to RQ2. The answers to RQ3 are given in Chapter 6, which draws on the field and discourse semantics resources to illustrate the elemental genres with disciplinary preference. Regarding RQ4, the influence of disciplinarity on generic complexity is demonstrated in the interpretation of research results in Chapters 4-6. Finally, the response to RQ5 is presented in Chapter 7.

Additionally, to find the answers to the above-mentioned four questions, a corpus is established. The following section will offer a brief summary of the methods and data adopted in the present project. More detailed information on the methodology is provided in Section 3.4.

1.5 Methodological preview

The book combines both quantitative and qualitative methods. Qualitatively, based on the previous studies of the classification of elemental genres and genre combining strategies, a framework for analyzing generic complexity in RAs is established, which provides guidance for screening elemental genres and combining strategies between two adjoining elemental genres. Furthermore, after the quantitative analysis of the distribution of elemental genres, those elemental genres that have distinctive disciplinary features are analyzed in terms of genre, register, and discourse semantics resources.

Quantitatively, an original corpus and a refined one are established for exploring the similarities and differences in generic complexity among the ERAs of the three disciplines. The whole analytical procedure is divided into three steps. Besides, a corpus of linguistics RAs written in Chinese is built.

1.6 Significance of the book

The study on generic complexity in ERAs boasts both theoretical and practical significance.

Theoretically, the current study can deepen understanding in the following three facets:

First, the present project can enrich the studies on RAs. Although there are profusion of research revolving around RAs, only a few of them probe into generic complexity. However, as RAs are macrogenres, RA writers must master the skills for maneuvering various elemental genres to achieve the purpose of effective communication. Therefore, a detailed description of generic complexity can enrich the understanding of RAs.

Second, the current study can broaden the explanatory scope of the SFL theory. Based on the genre theory proposed by SFL scholars, the present project builds an analytical framework for exploring generic complexity. Furthermore, the feasibility of this framework is testified by the analysis of the ERAs from the three disciplines and the comparison between ERAs and CRAs (Chinese research articles). Thus, the description, analysis, and explanation of generic complexity sharpen the SFL-inspired discourse analytical framework.

Third, this project reveals the similarities and differences in generic complexity among representative disciplines in science, social science, and the humanities. The differences in generic complexity can reflect the disciplinary features of different disciplines. Therefore, the present study can enhance the understanding of the disciplinarity of physics, linguistics and literary studies.

Fourth, this book demonstrates the common points and differences between linguistics ERAs and CRAs, providing a cross-cultural lens into examining the generic complexity features. Practically, this study contributes to the teaching of academic English in two ways:

First, the findings of the study can guide the writing of academic journal articles. This research describes delicately the overall elemental genre deployments, the elemental genre allocation in the major generic stages, and the elemental genre combining strategies in ERAs. All the detailed descriptions can help teachers and students in the course of academic writing gain a clearer picture of the generic complexity of ERAs.

Second, the present study can provide a realistic basis for the compiling of teaching materials for writing academic papers. The differences in generic complexity in ERAs of different disciplines should be taken into consideration. The findings of this project might be used as a guide when creating instructional resources for writing academic papers with distinctive characteristics of disciplines.

1.7 Organization of the book

The whole book consists of eight chapters. The first chapter introduces the research background, objectives, and research questions, as well as the methodological preview and the research significance of the current study.

Chapter 2 is the literature review of the previous studies, including the studies on genre, generic complexity, and genre-based studies on ERAs.

After the critical review in Chapter 2, the theoretical framework and methodology of this research are presented in Chapter 3. The theoretical framework is divided into theoretical motivation and a descriptive basis. To be specific, the descriptive basis contains basic notions of elemental genres, genre combining strategies, field, and discourse semantics.

Chapter 4 presents the general findings in terms of the elemental genre deployments, showing the similarities and differences in overall elemental genre distribution and elemental genre allocation in major generic stages in the ERAs of the three disciplines.

Chapter 5 turns to the other analytical dimension of the current project, i.e., the elemental genre combining strategies within the major generic stages in the ERAs. The strategies explored include extension, elaboration, enhancement, embedding, and projection.

Chapter 6 discusses the field and discourse semantics resources used for construing elemental genres with disciplinary features in each sub-corpus. Based on the statistical analysis in Chapter 4, several elemental genres with prominent distribution features in each discipline are further discussed in genre, register, and discourse semantics strata.

Chapter 7 compares the generic complexity features of linguistics ERAs and CRAs.

Chapter 8 concludes the current study by summarizing the major findings. Besides, the implications and limitations of this research are also presented in the final chapter.

Chapter 2 Genre, Generic Complexity, and Research Articles

This chapter reviews the previous studies that center around genre, generic complexity, and RAs. In the first section, different approaches to genre are sorted out from theoretical and empirical perspectives with an emphasis on the definitions of genres and the analytical frameworks. In the second section, studies on generic complexity are evaluated following the thread of theoretical underpinnings and practical applications. In the third section, research concerning RAs are classified and evaluated from the genre perspective. At the end of this chapter, some comments are made on the previous studies in these fields, and the research space left for the current study is discussed.

2.1 Studies on genre

Over the past a few decades, the study of genre has been flourishing in literary studies (Bakhtin, 1986), rhetoric studies (Bazerman, 1988; Berkenkotter&Huckin, 1993; Miller, 1984, 2014), cognitive linguistics (Bax, 2011; Paltridge, 1997), ESP (Bhatia, 1993, 2004, 2017; Swales, 1990, 2004), SFL (Halliday&Hasan, 1985; Hasan, 2014; Martin, 1992, 1994, 1999; Martin&Rose, 2008; Matthiessen, 2015, 2019), corpus-based approach (Biber, 2009, 2019), and metadiscourse-based study (Hyland, 2005).

Since the current study explores the generic features of English RAs, the literature review is conducted to evaluate the rhetoric and linguistics approaches to genre. However, the contribution of Bakhtin to genre study is included since he advocates applying genre theory to non-literary domains (Li, 2017:11). Moreover, his proposition and classification of speech genres into primary and secondary genres shed light on the studies of genre formation processes (Bakhtin, 1986).

The reviews of those approaches to genre are conducted from theoretical and empirical perspectives. Theoretically, the definition of genre and genre analytical frameworks are emphasized. Empirically, research are classified according to the objects of study.

2.1.1 Rhetoric approach

Traditionally, genre has been studied in terms of its rhetoric features in discourse. Aristotle (1920:7) proposes three identifying criteria for classifying genres, i.e., differences in means, objects, and imitation manners. Another theorization of genre comes from Plato (1961:392), who considers everything said by poets and storytellers as a narration of past, present, or future things.

As time goes by, a variety of approaches have emerged to study genre from rhetorical perspectives. The development of "rhetorical genre studies" (Bazerman et al., 2013; Miller et al., 2018) shows that these studies can be roughly divided into three types: the particular theorization of genre (Berkenkotter&Huckin, 1993; Miller, 1984, 2014; Miller et al., 2018), the application of theories to the analysis of various genres, and the studies of individuals' writing development.

In terms of theoretical exploration of genre, Miller (1984:163) characterizes genre as a typification of rhetorical action. Inspired by Miller's (1984) action-based definition of genre, Berkenkotter and Huckin (1993) consider disciplinary activities such as writing laboratory experiments, and drafting conference proposals as genres, and examine the ways through which genre knowledge is employed in those genres. The results of Berkenkotter and Huckin's (1993) study show that genres are intrinsically dynamic rhetorical structures with the features of dynamism, situatedness, form and content, the duality of structures, and community ownership.

With the development of technology and the emergence of the Internet, Miller (2014:67) expands her definition of genre to a more multidimensional one, which not only mediates the intention/exigence and the form/substance dimension but also serves as a medium linking action and construction, agent and organization, past and future. Moreover, Miller et al. (2018) summarize the 30 years' development of "genre as social action" (Miller, 1984). They (Miller et al., 2018) encapsulate the four features of genre as multimodal, multidisciplinary, multidimensional, and multimethodological.

In terms of the application of the action-based genre theory to analysis of various genres, health discourse (Berkenkotter, 2001, 2009; Berkenkotter & Hanganu-Bresch, 2011), newspaper and editorials (Huckin, 2002) are studied.

Regarding the health discourse, psychotherapy paperwork is studied by Berkenkotter (2001) for revealing four discursive practices of professional writers, namely, intertextuality, interdiscursivity, genre systems, and recontextualization. Case history narratives in psychiatry are explored by Berkenkotter (2009) for demonstrating the complexity of patients' narratives. Furthermore, by using Austin's (1962) concept of uptake, Berkenkotter and Hanganu-Bresch (2011) view case histories of patients as occult genres, which are hidden from view by all but a few physicians and medical supervisors. This study confirms the role of historical genre analysis in the rhetoric of medicine and health.

As far as newspaper articles and editorials are concerned, Huckin (2002) identifies five types of textual elision in the discourse of homelessness with the research emphasis on manipulative silences.

In terms of tracing an individual's writing development, Bazerman et al. (2013) use written samples of classroom observation and participation to discover the relationship between writing and the development of domain-specific forms of thinking. They (Bazerman et al., 2013) find that the assigned tasks' genre is directly related to the features of the thought expressed. Bazerman (2019) focuses on writing development in early schooling by exploring the relationship between writing progress, text quality, and curriculum events.

2.1.2 Cognitive linguistics approach

Scholars influenced by ideas from cognitive linguistics are also interested in analyzing genres. They try to describe the psychological mechanism that facilitates the comprehension and creation of texts (Yu, 2018:17). This approach can be divided into theoretical and applied studies.

Theoretically, discourse-modes-based framework (Bax, 2011) and cognitive-pragmatic models (Papi, 2018; Tseng, 2018) are proposed for analyzing specific genres.

From a cognitive viewpoint, Bax (2011) proposes a three-level genre analytical framework that consists of discourse modes, genre schema, and actual texts. Bax (2011:60) defines genre as mental constructs that members of a particular community share. He (Bax, 2011:63-94) uses discourse modes to indicate a more abstract level above genres and texts.

Genre is viewed as a dynamic cognitive category by Papi (2018) and Tseng (2018). Papi (2018) uses satire as an example to illustrate his view that genre is the result of a complicated interaction of heterogeneous linguistic and rhetorical factors. Tseng (2018) takes patient decision aid as the representative genre for demonstrating his cognitive-pragmatics-driven view towards the genre.

In terms of studies of the application of cognitive linguistics to the analysis of genre, there are abundant cognitive studies of various genres, which can be divided into three groups.

The first group views genre as the potential influencing factor and examines its impact on syntactic features or lexicogrammatical features, including the frequency adverbs "always" and "never" in oral and written discourse (Lindley, 2016), Spanish first-person plural subject and object in media discourse (Jose Serrano, 2017), the use of Right Dislocation in oral discourse (Lai et al., 2017), dependency distance and dependency direction (Wang&Liu, 2017), discourse connectors in academic lectures (Baicchi&Erviti, 2018), and the functions of "always progressive" (Lindley, 2020).

The second group focuses on the writing process with metacognition and genre knowledge as the major research interest (Negretti&McGrath, 2018; Tardy et al., 2020; Yeh, 2015; Wang, 2019).

Yeh (2015) explores how a metacognition-based online writing system can enable students to apply academic genre knowledge to writing, in which tasks are designed for the planning, monitoring, evaluating, and revising stages of writing to arouse students' genre knowledge. Negretti and McGrath (2018) discuss how genre knowledge and metacognition are constructed in a writing course for guiding doctoral students' writing of RAs. Tardy et al. (2020) propose a socio-cognitive framework for teaching and researching genre knowledge. In the socio-cognitive framework, genre-specific knowledge, genre awareness, metacognition, recontextualization, social context, and the relationship among them are clarified. Furthermore, the application of this framework is illustrated in pedagogical activities design and the development of multilingual genre knowledge. Wang (2019) explores the impact of metacognition on genre awareness and genre knowledge development by analyzing interviews, learning diaries, and written texts of students participating in an academic writing course.

The third group focuses on a cognitive interpretation of rhetorical devices in literary genres. By integrating the analysis of Piers and Voltaire's *Candide* with conceptual blending theory, Kasten and Gruenler (2011) argue that the cognitive affinities of allegory remain thriving.

2.1.3 ESP approach

The ESP approach to genre is represented by Swales (1990, 2004), and

Bhatia (1993, 2004, 2017).

The ESP-based genre studies can be divided into four strands. The first strand concerns the theoretical discussion of genre and genre analytical frameworks. The second strand discusses lexicogrammatical resources in academic discourses. The third strand deals with the teaching of academic writing. The fourth strand is ESP-based studies on other non-academic genres.

Regarding the first strand, Swales (1990:45-54) proposes his working definition of genre as a class of communicative events categorized by a set of shared communicative purposes, which constrains content, positioning, and form of texts. Furthermore, Swales (1990:141) puts forward the influential CARS (Create a Research Space) model, where the introduction part of RAs is divided into three moves and each move can be further demarcated with various steps. Swales (1990: 142-166) further analyzes the lexicogrammatical resources in each move and step. Later, Swales (2004) makes a synthesis of research in genre study, which furthers genre research through shifting from native speakers' usage of genre to that of non-native speakers, and from RAs to other genres.

Another representative in the first strand is Bhatia (1993, 2004, 2017), who (Bhatia, 1993:53) further explicates Swales' (1990) definition of genre by emphasizing the utilization of private intentions within boundaries of socially-recognized purposes and the cognitive aspects of genre building. Bhatia proposes a multi-perspective framework for genre analysis in 2004, and a critical genre analysis model in 2017.

In terms of genre analysis framework, Bhatia (2004:160-167) presents a multi-perspective and multidimensional framework for identifying generic integrity, where genre analysis is implemented in textual, socio-cognitive, and social spaces. In Bhatia's (2004) framework, textual space is lexicogrammar-based while the socio-cognitive space involves genre construction processes, rhetorical strategies, and appropriation of generic resources. Moreover, the social space includes socio-critical practices, wider social structures, and social changes.

In recent years, Bhatia (2017) has proposed a model of critical genre analysis (hereafter CGA), which contains three key aspects, i.e., the interdiscursive dimensions of professional genres, the discursive practices of professionals, and the methodology for exploring discursive and professional practices. This model is applied in analyzing interdiscursive features in genres of lawyers' defense opinions (Ren et al., 2020), corporate annual reports (Qian, 2020), and the discourse of judges of civil trials (Ge&Wang, 2019).

With the development of ESP-based genre analysis, the theoretical consideration of the notion of genre and genre analytical frameworks are refined by different scholars (Askehave&Swales, 2001; Moreno&Swales, 2018; Swales, 2019). For example, the problems caused by using communicative purpose as the identifying criteria of genre are discussed by Askehave and Swales (2001), who hold that communicative purpose can be considered as a viable and valuable concept in genre identification but not as the centrality for distinguishing genres. A fine-grained step-focused genre analytical method is proposed by Moreno and Swales (2018), which aims for improving the reliability and validity of move analysis. The overdone genre research are discussed by Swales (2019). In addition, Swales (2019) points out the more fruitful direction for future genre studies, which involves studies on syntactic and phraseological patterns and uses, local cohesive elements in students' texts, and genres in interdisciplinary fields.

In the second strand, the study of RAs receives the most attention. Some studies focus on a certain kind of lexicogrammatical resources across various disciplines, such as imperatives (Swales et al., 1998). Some scholars focus on different parts of the RA, such as texts that state pedagogical needs and implications (Cheng, 2019), Methods section (Cotos et al., 2017), Discussion section (Zhao et al., 2019), and Conclusion section (Loi et al., 2016).

Besides RAs, other academic discourses are also explored through the ESP approach, such as RA manuscript reviews (Samraj, 2016), master theses

(Maher&Milligan, 2019), conference discussions (Wulff et al., 2009), and conference abstracts (Yoon&Casal, 2020).

Among these studies, Wulff et al.'s study (2009) focuses on oral discourse and analyzes the phraseological differences between the presentation and discussion section, regular patterns of the chair's utterance, and different causes of laughter in the discussion sections. Samraj (2016) explores the discourse units and lexicogrammatical features of manuscript reviews of RAs, a genre that receives relatively less attention. Samraj's (2016) study shows that discourse units function differently in "major revision" and "reject" reviews. Yoon and Casal's (2020) study is distinctive for the application of Moreno and Swales' (2018) move-step analytical framework to explore conference abstracts in the discipline of applied linguistics, finding that five moves occur more frequently in the seven-move model.

In the third strand, Swales et al. (2001) discuss EAP course design and implementation for architecture graduates. Lee and Swales (2006) establish a corpus-based EAP course for doctoral students with English as a second language, who are required to build two corpora: one of their own academic writings and one of published articles of experts. The purpose of Lee and Swales' (2006) course is to enhance the students' rhetorical consciousness. Lee (2016) explores the moves and lexical phrases in 24 EAP classroom lessons. Interviews are also conducted by Lee (2016) to obtain insider views towards teachers' discursive practices. Swales and Post (2018) apply Neiderhisher et al.'s (2016) research on imperative use to designing pedagogical tasks for academic writing, ranging from activities promoting rhetorical consciousness, micro-analyses tasks to editing tasks during different stages of the class.

In the fourth strand, rhetorical organization, such as the move-step-structure in clinical case reports (Burdiles Fernandez, 2016), persuasive email requests (Du-Babcock&Feng, 2018), financial stability report of banks (Gonzalez Riquelme&Burdiles Fernandez, 2018), standard terms of limited compensation in uninsured express mails (Cheng&Pei, 2018), gravestone inscriptions (Karimnia&Jafari, 2019), and welcome address (Kithulgoda&Mendis, 2020), is the key research object. For instance, Gonzalez Riquelme and Burdiles Fernandez (2018) compare the rhetorical organization in the financial stability reports from two banks, thus identifying three macromoves in the two corpora.

2.1.4 SFL approach

The genre studies based on SFL are mainly divided into two strands. One strand devotes to the theorization of genre, represented by Halliday (1978), Halliday and Hasan (1985), Hasan (2014), Matthiessen (2015, 2019), Matthiessen and Teruya (2016), Martin (1985, 1992), and Martin and Rose (2008, 2012b). The other strand aims to apply the SFL-informed genre analytical framework to teaching studies and discourse analysis (Fenwick&Herrington, 2021; Matthiessen&Pun, 2019; Maxim, 2021; Mitchell et al., 2021).

In the first strand, there are basically two approaches to the definition of genre. On the one hand, Halliday (1978:145) shows clearly that genre is an aspect of mode. In other words, genre is just one aspect of context of situation. On the other hand, for Martin (1999), genre represents context of culture, which is realized by register, representing context of situation.

Hasan (1984, 1985, 1989) focuses on generic structural potential (henceforth abbreviated as GSP) and defines genre as "genre-specific semantic potential". Hasan (1984) applies the GSP model to analyze nursery tales, where the elements of the GSP, their semantic attributes, and the lexicogrammatical patterns realizing the semantic features are identified and summarized.

In addition, Matthiessen (2015) focuses on register, offering a typology of fields of activity. Matthiessen (2015) holds that register is a functional variety of a language and proposes a field-based topology of register with eight major types. Furthermore, he (Matthiessen, 2015) illustrates the semantic organization relations of the texts operating under those types of field activities through rhetorical relations. He (Matthiessen, 2015) also figures out the potential application of his register map in educational linguistics, health communication, and medical discourse studies.

On the basis of Maththiessen's (2015) study on register, Matthiessen and Teruya (2016) propose the concept of registerial hybridity and discuss the topology of hybridity with specific examples. Matthiessen (2019) gives a comprehensive review of register studies by revisiting the conceptualizing processes of register within SFL, relating register to the overall research purposes, and summarizing the main research methodology of SFL-based register studies.

Furthermore, Martin (1984, 1985), Martin and White (2005), and Martin and Rose (2008) contribute a lot to the study of genres. Two representative definitions of genre, a stratified model of context, and genre relation can be summarized as the major contributions of those scholars to the study of genres.

Martin (1992: 505) defines genre as "a staged, goal-oriented social process". With the development of the genre theory, genre is defined by Martin and Rose (2008:6) as "recurrent configuration of meanings for enacting the social practices of a given culture".

Besides the discussion of genre definitions, Martin and Rose (2008) further develop the theory of genre by probing into the relations between genres. They (Martin&Rose, 2008) use textbooks as examples and examine the relation among elemental genres by reference to the concept of logico-semantic relation.

Recently, the concept of field, mode, and recontextualization are discussed thoroughly by Martin (2020), Rose (2020a, 2020b), and Maton and Doran (2021). For example, Martin (2020:114-147) approaches field from three metafunctions. The metalanguage in curriculum genres is described under the guidance of Bernstein's (2000: 34-35) concept of recontextualization and Rose's (2020b:236-267) notions of mass and presence. According to Maton and Doran (2021:49-75), recontextualization is understood through constellation analysis by focusing on the schematic constellation and pedagogic constellation.

In the second strand, the appliable nature of the genre theory in SFL is found vitality in the studies of language teaching and the discourse analysis of texts instantiating various genres.

Regarding the teaching-oriented application of the genre theory, there are roughly three groups of research. The first group concerns the efforts made in developing genre-based pedagogy. The second group focuses on teacher development through utilizing genre-based pedagogy. The third group is concerned with classroom teaching.

The first group of research centers around the development of genre-based pedagogy. Some scholars focus on the classification and teaching of genres at the primary school (e.g., Rothery, 1989) while some turn their attention to the genres which students encounter at the secondary school or workplaces through analyzing linguistic resources such as classification, cause-and-effect, and evaluation (e.g., Rose, 1997; Wignell, 1994; Wignell et al., 1989). There are still others who take heed of the importance of reading in genre-based pedagogy and propose the integration of reading and writing in primary and secondary schools, involving the design of classroom interactions, and explorations of reading strategies in stories, factual texts, and arguments (e.g., Rose, 2005, 2007, 2008, 2011).

In recent years, there have been studies that focus on knowledge practice by combining SFL with Legitimation Code Theory (hereafter abbreviated as LCT). Disciplinarity becomes the keyword of studies. Studies of this type include the introduction of the DISKS (disciplinarity, knowledge, and schooling) project (Maton et al., 2016), explorations of the story genre in RAs of social sciences and humanities (Hood, 2016), students' answers to exams in thermodynamics (Georgiou, 2016), research projects written by jazz performance students (Martin, L. 2016) and so on. Hood (2021:211-235) analyzes health science lectures through context dependency and semantics. Doran and Martin (2021:105-133) explore the field system in scientific explanations from static and dynamic perspectives. Doran (2021:162-184) focuses on the use of language, mathematics, and images in knowledge building in physics textbooks.

The second group of studies examines teachers' development after receiving training in genre-based pedagogy. Generally speaking, changes in teaching methods are observed and the effect of genre-based pedagogy are evaluated through case studies. For example, Shi et al. (2019) use workshop interviews and classroom observation to explore Chinese EFL teachers' beliefs on the effectiveness of genre pedagogy. Moreover, longitudinal ethnographic case studies (Accurso, 2020; Troyan et al., 2019) are employed for evaluating the effect of SFL knowledge on teacher education. Brisk et al. (2021) use narrative analysis to investigate the changes of a third-grade teacher's instruction in teaching autobiography writing. Fenwick and Herrington (2021) focus on high-school biology teachers' pedagogical variations after receiving training in using genre pedagogy. Troyan (2021) employs the appraisal system and Christie's (2002) framework for discourse analysis to discover the ways through which a teacher contextualizes language learning with his students in three curriculum genres.

The third group concerns the design and implementation of classroom teaching approaches. Generally speaking, longitudinal case studies in writing classrooms are conducted and the research methodologies of discourse analysis and interviews are used.

Some scholars manage to find new teaching pedagogy by integrating SFL with other theories. For instance, Ramirez (2020) combines the SFL-based reading-to-learn approach with culturally relevant pedagogy and proposes the Culturally and Linguistically Relevant Pedagogy. Cavallaro&Sembiante (2021) focus on middle school intensive reading classes and propose a culturally-sustaining, SFL-informed pedagogy for promoting students' involvement in building community and sharing experiences. Ryshina-Pankova et al. (2021) propose a content-language multi-literacy framework and discuss SFL's role in this framework, illustrating that SFL-based tasks can help examine the narrative structure and patterns of language use of tales used in class, through which particular dimensions of regional culture can be constructed. By employing SFL and the argumentation theory, Han Baocheng and Wei Xing (2021) focus on instruction of argument genre and suggest specific classroom activities to facilitate students' command of argument genres.

In addition, the effectiveness of SFL-informed pedagogy is also studied in terms of students' written texts. Uzun and Zehir Topkaya (2020) testify the effectiveness of genre-based instruction and genre-focused feedback on L2 writing performance, showing that genre-based instruction can improve students' mastery of genres while the types of genre-focused feedback cannot influence the command of the literary analysis essay. Crane and Malloy (2021) investigate whether the genre-based teaching approach can improve L2 writers' written stories of travel experiences, by exploring this type of personal recount through temporal-spatial circumstantial meanings realized as adverbial and prepositional phrases. Maxim (2021) traces the effectiveness of genre-based tasks in improving the writing development of undergraduate students learning German, measuring the written texts through syntactic complexity indexes and SFL-supported variables such as transitivity, taxis, and thematization patterns.

Apart from the studies of the genre-based pedagogy on the teacher development and the students' improvement, there are studies that focus on academic-related genres, such as RAs (Benelhadj, 2019; Stosic, 2021; Zhang, 2009), historical discourse used in the classroom or written by students (Ignatieva, 2021; Kindenberg, 2021), teaching and reading materials (Ariely et al., 2019; Matthiessen&Pun, 2019; May et al., 2020; Mitchell et al., 2021; Pun, 2019) and so on.

In the studies of RAs, Zhang (2009) proposes a multi-stratal framework for exploring modality in RAs through the attitude system at the context stratum, the modal meaning system at the semantics stratum, and the modal forms at the lexicogrammar stratum. Benelhadj (2019) focuses on prepositional phrases in RAs and Ph.D. theses of medicine and sociology and explores the impact of context on the choice of prepositional phrases, finding that Ph.D. theses display more disciplinary and personal variations. With the framework of the appraisal system, Stosic (2021) explores the Introduction section of clinical psychology RAs and the use of evaluative language for expressing topic significance.

As for the study of historical genres, Kindenberg (2021) examines stages, narrative elements, and expressions of historical significance in thirteen history texts used in a lower-secondary history-instructional unit. Ignatieva (2021) focuses on ideational and interpersonal meanings of two historical genres written by students: essays and answers to questions, and compares the similarities and differences between these two genres.

The teaching materials used in the classroom are also explored. Mitchell et al. (2021) analyze the genre of case analysis used in information system programs by unpacking the linguistic features. Mitchell et al.'s (2021) study reveals that students try to make a balance between the academic and professional tension in the genre. Matthiessen and Pun (2019) analyze chemistry textbooks used in secondary schools and discuss the way knowledge is expounded at the context, semantics, and lexicogrammar strata. The occurrence of subtypes of explanations and language features in those textbooks are expounded by Pun (2019).

As far as extracurricular reading materials are concerned, May et al. (2020) focus on science trade books and propose a purpose-driven typology of those books following two main aims of introducing the lives of scientists or accepted knowledge. Ariely et al. (2019) analyze informational density, abstraction, technicality, authoritativeness, and hedging in the original versions of science books and popular science, revealing that adaptation reduces lexical complexity while retaining authenticity.

2.1.5 Other approaches to genre

In addition to the aforementioned genre studies in rhetoric and linguistics, there are other approaches to genres. In methodology, the corpus-based multidimensional approach proposed by Biber (2009, 2019) deserves attention. In terms of the research object, the metadiscourse study by Hyland (2005) inspires many scholars to engage in genre studies. Moreover, some scholars (Parodi, 2016; Vian, 2016) apply different theories of genre and use mixed approaches in their studies.

Regarding research methodology, Biber (2009, 2019) takes a multidimensional approach to genre and register varieties, involving three components: the situational context, the linguistic features, and the functional relationships between the two components. This corpus-based approach is employed in the classification of conversational discourse types (Biber et al., 2021), exploration of grammatical complexity (Biber et al. 2020), and the study of the effectiveness of EAP training (Crosthwaite, 2016).

For Hyland (2005:87), genre is a term for grouping texts together, representing how writers typically use language to respond to recurring situations. Thus, he (Hyland, 2005:88-89) views metadiscourse analysis as a key aspect of genre analysis because linguistic choices represent the different purposes of writers, the different assumptions they make about their audiences, and the different kinds of interactions they create with their readers. Hyland and his colleagues have applied the metadiscourse framework to the analysis of various genres, such as academic blogs (Hyland&Zou, 2020; Zou&Hyland, 2020a, 2020b), manuscript translation (Luo&Hyland, 2019), RAs (Hyland&Jiang, 2018), and metadiscursive nouns (Jiang&Hyland, 2017).

Besides the aforementioned studies on genre, Vian (2016) figures out the theoretical origins of Brazilian genre studies, including socio-discursive interactionism theoretical framework (Bronckart, 1999), French textual linguistic perspectives of genre proposed by Adam (2011), and complexity theory (Morin, 2011). Parodi (2016) provides us with a corpus-based genre analytical model from social, linguistic, and cognitive dimensions in assessing the academic genres that university students are required to read.

2.1.6 Summary

This section reviews studies on genre from theoretical and empirical perspectives. Theoretically, the definition of genre and genre analytical framework are given particular attention. Empirically, genre studies are classified according to the major research objects.

In terms of definitions of genres, Aristotle proposes a structure-oriented classification of genres. Bakhtin's speech genres are utterance-focused. Researchers in cognitivelinguistics consider genre as a schema or frame existing in our mind. Scholars with the rhetoric genre approach adhere to an action-based definition of the genre, while researchers in the ESP group employ communication purposes for screening genres. Besides, Biber emphasizes the structure completeness of genre whereas Hyland focuses on the interpersonal resources used for indicating genre variations. In SFL, Halliday considers genre as belonging to mode, whereas Martin holds that genre lies at the stratum above register.

In terms of the genre analytical framework, Swales' move-based analysis framework is still influential nowadays. In the domain of SFL, the multistratal model with context, semantics, and lexicogrammar provides us with a comprehensive framework for analyzing genres.

Empirically, all these genre studies approach various genres through different research emphases. Rhetorical genre studies tend to focus on health and media discourse. Cognitive-linguistics-based genre study examines metacognition and genre knowledge in the writing process. ESP approach focuses on the move-step structure of genres. While the SFL genre approach is found widespread application in pedagogy.

The review of the genre-related literature highlights the following three trends of genre analysis.

Firstly, all these approaches to genre show an increasing interest in research on writing pedagogy, which is reflected in the studies of individual writing development by Bazerman (2019), the emphasis on genre knowledge and metacognition proposed by Tardy et al. (2020), the exploration of academic writing pedagogy by ESP scholars, and the development of genre-based instruction by SFL researchers. Furthermore, a dynamic research perspective is adopted for tracing the teachers' and students' development, which are revealed in studies examining the effectiveness of genre-based pedagogy.

Secondly, these approaches show more theoretical considerations on context, which is reflected in cognitive-pragmatic approaches to genre studies proposed by cognitive linguists, in Bhatia's (2004, 2017) emphasis on text-external factors, as well as in SFL's theoretical thinking of the relationship between context, semantics, and lexicogrammar.

Thirdly, the genres explored extend from academic genres to other genres, such as translation, speeches, legal discourses, and new media discourses.

2.2 Studies on generic complexity

Compared with the abundance of genre studies, systematic research on generic complexity are relatively scant. This section reviews studies concerning generic complexity from theoretical and empirical perspectives with the purpose of clarifying the definition of generic complexity and presenting the current research on it.

2.2.1 Theoretical studies on generic complexity

Generic complexity is coined by Jordens et al. (2001) under the influence of Martin's (1996) classification of narrative genres. Focusing on spoken accounts of illness, Jordens et al. (2001) propose the notion of generic complexity for describing the number and variety of identified story genres that are employed to finish an illness narrative. In other words, generic complexity refers to the phenomenon that several elemental genres are instantiated in a text. Within SFL, the elemental genre families involve Reports, Explanations,

Arguments, Recounts, and Text responses, the elemental genres of which are detailed in Chapter 3.

Theoretically, the phenomenon of generic complexity is mainly discussed by three strands of researchers. The first strand of researchers analyzes the phenomenon by creating the notion of macrogenre, generic complexity, and generic hybridity. The second strand of scholars approaches the phenomenon by using register hybridity. The third strand of research is conducted by Bhatia (2010, 2017) in his discussion of intertextuality and interdiscursivity.

In terms of the first strand, some researchers (Martin, 1994, 1995, 2002; Jordens et al., 2001; Zhang&Guo, 2019) are dedicated to creating and proposing a theoretical framework for exploring macrogenres and generic complexity.

The concept of marcogenre and the mechanism through which elemental genres combined to form macrogenres are discussed by Martin (1994/2012). On the one hand, Martin (1994/2012:2) employs the concept of macrogenre to refer to the combinations of elemental genres. Martin (1994/2012:125) uses the method of listing for giving the instances of elemental genres, such as reports, procedures, explanations, expositions anecdotes, exemplum, recounts, and so on. On the other hand, Martin (1994/2012:78-126; 1995) explores the mechanism that elemental genres form macrogenres from three metafunctions. Martin (1994/2012) uses an analogy between clauses and texts for extending clause expansion and projection strategies to texts.

Except for the discussion of macrogenre, it deserves mentioning Martin's consideration of "mixed genre". According to Martin (2002/2012:313), "mixed genre" is a misnomer because it confuses genres with the texts that instantiate one or more genres. On the one hand, as a system-confined term, genre cannot be mixed. While textual instances can be mixed by utilizing one or more genres (Martin, 2002/2012:298). On the other hand, Martin (2002/2012:298) holds that there are varied ways by which texts can make use of genres, which include renovation, hybridization, multimodality, macrogeneric assemblages, embedding, and contextual metaphor.

In contrast to Martin's discussion of genre from a system perspective, Zhang and Guo (2019) try to clarify the notion of genre hybridity from both system and instance perspectives. From the perspective of the system, genre hybridity implies the emergence of a new genre rather than the mixing of several genres. From the instance perspective, a specific text instantiates genre hybridity. An analytic framework for describing genre hybridity is proposed by dividing genre hybrid into mixed genre and fused genre. In terms of mixed genre, genre embedding and expansion are discussed. In terms of fused genre, genre variation and genre metaphorization are explored.

In terms of the second strand, the term registerial hybridity is used for exploring the phenomenon that a text utilizes several text types (Matthiessen&Teruya, 2016). Matthiessen and Teruya (2016:205-232) provide a typology and topology-based research on registerial hybridity, offering us an operational framework for analyzing this phenomenon. On the one hand, Matthiessen and Teruya (2016) introduce register typology based on the field of activity and distinguish eight primary fields of activity, namely, expounding, reporting, recreating, sharing, doing, enabling, recommending, and exploring. On the other hand, they propose a typology of indeterminacy, namely, ambiguities, blends, overlaps, neutralizations, and complementarities. Matthiessen and Teruya (2016) make a detailed explanation of the former four types of indeterminacy with examples.

In terms of the third strand, interdiscursivity refers to the appropriation of generic resources across professional genres, practices, and cultures (Bhatia, 2010:36). Bhatia (2010:39-46, 2017:90-104) takes corporate annual reports to illustrate the phenomenon that different discourses are included in the same text. According to Bhatia (2010:39), the annual report is a typical combination of accounting discourse, discourse of finance, public relations discourse, and legal discourse.

2.2.2 Empirical studies on generic complexity

Drawing on the above-mentioned notions of macrogenre, generic complexity, generic hybridity, and interdiscursivity, empirical studies are conducted to explore this phenomenon in various discourses, including academic discourses, classroom discourses, health discourses, new media discourses, legal discourses, business discourses, literature, and so on.

In terms of academic discourses, RAs (Hood, 2010; Lai&Wang, 2018), textbooks (Zhao, 2014), and bachelor's theses (Zhang&Pramoolsook, 2019) are taken as instances of macrogenres and studied.

Regarding RAs, Hood (2010) views introductions of RAs as a macrogenre and explores evaluation resources expressed through RAI. Lai and Wang (2018) take SSCI-indexed RAs of applied linguistics as a research object for approving that RA is a macrogenre with Report elemental genres as the basis, the elemental genre of Exposition as nuclear and facilitated by Recounts and Explanations.

Regarding textbooks, Martin and Rose (2008) use science textbooks as an example to illustrate how elemental genres are combined in forming the macrogenre. Zhao (2014) analyzes genre complexing in middle school science textbooks. He (Zhao, 2014) finds that elemental genres in textbooks are elaborated through specification and reformulation, while elemental genres of reporting and explaining are extended in different ways. Moreover, the reporting elemental genre is enhanced by elemental genres of explaining or arguing.

As far as the theses are concerned, Zhang and Pramoolsook (2019) explore the generic complexity of bachelor's theses written by Chinese English majors. The variety and distribution of elemental genres in those theses are discussed. The motivation of using the elemental genres is analyzed by their rhetorical functions.

In terms of classroom discourses, Christie (1997) discusses curriculum macrogenres from the perspective of genre and register. The lexicogrammatical resources are identified through three metafunctions in different stages of a curriculum genre to explore the distribution of regulative and instructional registers. Christie (1999) views a lesson of English literature in a middle school as a macrogenre with three elemental genres, i.e., curriculum initiation, curriculum activity, and curriculum closure. Christie (1999) further details the stages in each elemental genre.

In terms of health discourses, Jordens et al. (2001) consider illness narratives as a macrogenre which is composed of sequences of the elemental genre of story, including recounts, narratives, anecdotes, exemplum, and observations. By defining generic complexity as the variety and number of elemental genres by which a marcogenre is formed, Jorden et al. (2001) discover the strong and significant relation between life disruption and generic complexity. Jordens and Little (2004) view clinicians' narrative-style interviews as a marcrogenre. They (Jordens&Little, 2004) discover a new elemental genre–policy genre. The semantic characters of this genre and its function in demonstrating ethical reasoning are discussed. Muntigl (2006) considers counseling interviews as a macrogenre. The logogenesis of two cases of counseling is explored through ideational, interpersonal, and textual metafunctions. Similar linguistic patterns are discovered in the two cases for identifying generic stages and elemental genres.

In terms of new media discourses, Thompson (2016) analyzes football blogs and newspaper blogs to reveal that blogs are hybrid genres with the mixture of casual conversation and other types of discourses. Furthermore, casual conversation serves as the basis of the hybrid, with other types of discourse grafting in the base by various methods and to different extent, which is reflected in speech functions, message units, and interactant references at semantic and lexicogrammatical strata. Wu et al. (2018) discuss genre embedding in advertising discourse on WeChat by illustrating one advertising text is composed of weather reports and a recipe. Feng (2019) analyzes universities' recruitment posts on WeChat in terms of the semantic, lexicogrammatical, and multimodal realizations of each move. He (Feng, 2019) finds this genre is a mix of policy discourse and promotional discourse. Xu and Feng (2020) apply Matthiessen's (2009) typology of register to analyze corporate posts in Sina Weibo and identify six types of register hybridity in those posts. Moreover, they (Xu&Feng, 2020) figure out hybridization is one of the features of new media business discourses. Ye (2020) focuses on the rhetorical structure of a podcast, showing that this genre is the hybridity of news reports and RA abstracts.

In terms of legal discourses, Townley and Jones (2016) explore emails and covering letters of two lawyers in a legal negotiation of a commercial contract and analyze the moves and discursive features, showing that the two text types display hybridity of technical discourse and interpersonal professional discourse. Ge and Wang (2019) examine the interdiscursive features of judges' discourse in civil trials by analyzing generic structures and kinds of professional genres and find that the discourse of judges is a hybrid of instructive, expository, interrogative, evaluative, and adjudicating discourse. Ren et al. (2020) probe into lawyers' defense opinions by summarizing their rhetorical structure and discursive hybridity. They (Ren et al., 2020) find that this genre is a hybridity of legal, moral, therapeutic, and legitimation discourse.

With regard to business discourse, Bhatia (2010, 2017) explores the organizational structure and lexicogrammatical resources in corporate annual reports to show this genre is a combination of four discourses. Bhatia (2012, 2013) focuses on the corporate social responsibility report from generic structures and communicative functions, revealing that the report is a hybrid with discourses of promotion and self-justification.

Concerning literature, Woolf's *A Room of One's Own* is analyzed by Torsello (2016:240-267) for illustrating the literature work as a hybridity of essay, lecture, and novel. Hasan's (1989:63-67) propositions on the generic structure and contextual configuration, Martin's (1985:86) structure for an essay, Young's (1990) structural observation of an academic lecture, and

Labov and Waletsky's (1967) proposal on structures of the novel are used as theoretical underpinnings of this study. The analysis is conducted by analyzing textual indications of genres, generic structures, and contextual configuration.

Finally, the elemental genres and the logico-semantic relations between those genres in the first three sections of a sermon are analyzed. The results show the sermon is a mixture of a dominant subgenre with one or more other subgenres (Cummings, 2016:273).

2.2.3 Summary

This section reviews studies on the phenomenon of generic complexity. Theoretically, this phenomenon is mainly explored by scholars within SFL. On the one hand, Matthiessen and Teruya (2016) discuss registerial hybridity at the semantics stratum with the motivation from the field of activity and explain the reasons for hybridity through indeterminacy. On the other hand, Martin's (1994, 1995) framework for analyzing macrogenre provides a delicate model for describing the methods through which elemental genres form macrogenres. Besides, one type of Bhatia's (2010, 2017) interdiscursivity is concerned with the generic complexity discussed in the current study, i.e., the employment of resources across genres within a text.

Empirically, the generic complexity in different discourses is explored. While researchers inspired by interdiscursivity prefer to analyze legal and business discourses. The SFL scholars tend to analyze generic complexity in academic and health discourse.

The SFL-based studies view RAs, textbooks, theses, and classroom discourses as macrogenres and discuss the formation mechanism and linguistic realization of the generic stages of those macrogenres.

2.3 Studies on ERAs from the genre perspective

ERAs have been the research focus that attracts the attention of scholars from all over the world. In this section, research on ERAs from the genre perspective are analyzed for revealing the necessity of the current study. These genre-focused studies are mainly oriented to the organizational structures and lexicogrammatical features of part-genres of ERAs. Furthermore, the genre studies on ERAs of physics, linguistics, and literary studies are explicated for laying the realistic motivation of the present project.

2.3.1 Studies on part-genres of ERAs

Studies be longing to this category view different sections of ERAs as their part-genres (cf. Lu et al., 2018). Every section of ERAs has been studied, including Abstracts (Abdollahpour&Gholami, 2019; Ansarifar et al., 2018; El-Dakhs, 2018; Friginal&Mustafa, 2017; Huang, 2018; Ruan, 2018), Introductions (Cortes, 2013; Jalilifar et al., 2018; Kashiha&Marandi, 2019; Kawase, 2015; Lu et al., 2018; Lu et al., 2020; Wang&Yang, 2015; Xu&Nesi, 2019b), Introduction and Discussion sections (Li&Xu, 2020), Introduction and Conclusion sections (Xu&Nesi, 2019a), Theoretical framework (Tseng, 2018), Methods sections (Lim, 2019), Results sections (Parviz et al., 2020), Results and Discussion sections (Kwan&Chan, 2014; Le&Pham, 2020), Results, Discussion and Conclusion sections (Yang&Allison, 2003), Discussions (Cheng&Unsworth, 2016; Golparvar&Barabadi, 2020; Khany&Kafshgar, 2016; Liu&Buckingham, 2018; Moyano, 2019; Peacock, 2002; Sadeghi&Alinasab, 2020; Samraj, 2013), Discussions and Conclusions (Sheldon, 2019), and Conclusions (Chen&Zhang, 2017; Loi et al., 2016; Sheldon, 2018). These studies can be divided from their research content, research methodology, and disciplines explored.

From the perspective of research content, these studies can be categorized into five strands. The first strand analyzes the rhetorical structure of each part-genre of ERAs. The second strand discusses the distribution of various resources such as lexical bundles, appraisal resources, and citations on the basis of the move segmentations of part-genres of ERAs. The third strand focuses on the interpersonal resources in the whole ERAs. The fourth strand explores lexical bundles, and phrase-frames or conducts the multi-dimensional analysis of the ERAs. The fifth strand focuses on the linguistic complexity of the sections of ERAs.

Regarding the first strand, inspired by Swales' (1990, 2004) analytical framework for exploring the move-step structure in ERA introductions, scholars investigate the rhetorical structure of various sections of ERAs from different disciplines, such as Result and Discussion sections in ERAs of mechanical engineering (Le&Pham, 2020), Result, Discussion, and Conclusion sections in ERAs of applied linguistics (Yang&Allison, 2003), Discussion and Conclusion sections in ERAs of applied linguistics (Sheldon, 2019), and the Theoretical framework section in ERAs of linguistics (Tseng, 2018). For example, Tseng (2018) tries to create a move-based model for analyzing the theoretical framework section. The model contains three moves: offering a theoretical background, compiling a theoretical framework, and emphasizing the significance of one's study.

Regarding the second strand, researchers first demarcate the move-step structure of different sections of ERAs with the guidance of Swales' (1990, 2004) move analytical model, then the distribution of various linguistic resources across moves and steps are analyzed, such as lexical bundles, appraisal resources, citations, metadiscourses, and linguistic features indicating syntactic structures. For instance, Abdollahpour and Gholami (2019) explore lexical bundles deployments in Abstracts of ERAs from medical sciences. Cortes (2013) investigates the lexical bundles distribution in Introductions of ERAs from various disciplines. He (Cortes, 2013) first extracts lists of lexical bundles from the corpus of RAI and then analyzes the distribution of those lexical bundles. The findings show that some lexical bundles are exclusive in certain moves of RAI. In addition, lexical bundles perform different functions.

Appraisal resources proposed by Martin and White (2005) are also explored across moves in sections of ERAs, such as those in Conclusions (cf. Loi et al., 2016; Sheldon, 2018). For instance, Sheldon (2018) compares engagement resources across moves in the Conclusion sections of RAs in applied linguistics written by English L1, English L2, and Spanish L1 scholars. The results show that English L1 writers negotiate a consistent space for readers to approve or disapprove of the writers' propositions. The Spanish L1 group aligns with readers, using a limited space through contracting resources. The English L2 group tends to move towards international practice but without fully abandoning their L1.

Differences in citations across moves are analyzed in various sections of ERAs, such as Introductions (Jalilifar et al., 2018), Discussions (Samraj, 2013), Results and Discussions (Kwan&Chan, 2014). For example, Kwan and Chan (2014) propose a classification of citations according to their rhetorical functions and content cited. Then this classification is applied in comparison of citation deployments in ERAs of empirical and theoretical studies. The findings demonstrate that citations occur sporadically in empirical studies. Furthermore, the distribution of citations in theoretical studies differs significantly across sections.

Besides, metadiscourse proposed by Hyland (2005) are explored across moves in different sections of ERAs, such as Introductions (Kashiha&Marandi, 2019) and Discussions (Liu&Buckingham, 2018). For instance, the frequency and functions of interactive metadiscourse are analyzed and compared in the main moves of Introductions of ERAs from chemistry and applied linguistics by Kashiha and Marandi (2019). The results reveal marked similarities and disciplinary differences in the types and functions of interactive discourse markers.

Based on move-step segmentation, the syntactic complexity of sentences forming the steps in ERAs of social sciences are examined by Lu et al. (2020). They (Lu et al., 2020) discover that sentences that performing different rhetorical functions display significant variance in syntactic complexity.

Regarding the third strand, interpersonal resources in different sections of ERAs are explored, such as hedges (Chen&Zhang, 2017), metadiscourse proposed by Hyland (2005) (Kawase, 2015), reflexive metadiscourse (Li&Xu, 2020), appraisal resources (Moyano, 2019; Xu&Nesi, 2019a), evaluative style (Xu&Nesi, 2019b), academic conflict (Cheng&Unsworth, 2016), and promotion strategies (Wang&Yang, 2015). For instance, Moyano (2019) applies appraisal framework proposed by Martin and White (2005) to reveal disciplinary differences in the employment of appraisal resources in Discussion sections of ERAs of microbiology and sociology.

Regarding the fourth strand, analytical dimensions proposed by corpus linguists are explored in part-genres of ERAs. For example, Golparvar and Barabadi (2020) extract key phrase-frames in Discussion sections in ERAs of higher education. They (Golparvar&Barabadi, 2020) find 58 four-word and 40 five-word p-frames that are significant in ERAs of this discipline. Furthermore, the syntactic features and discourse functions of those p-frames are discussed. Except for the studies of part-genres of ERAs from corpus linguistics, Biber's (1988) multidimensional analysis is also employed. For example, Friginal and Mustafa (2017) compare RA abstracts in four disciplines (agriculture, nursing, engineering, and languages) from the US and Iraq with the utilization of Biber's (1988, 1995) multi-dimensional approach and Hardy and Römer's (2013) MDA framework.

Regarding the fifth strand, linguistic complexity is explored in the part-genres of ERAs. Khany and Kafshgar (2016) analyze linguistic complexity of Discussion sections in ERAs of humanities, life sciences, and physics in terms of syntactic complexity and lexical complexity. Ansarifar et al. (2018) explore phrasal modification features in Abstracts of ERAs. Parviz et al. (2020) focus on phrasal complexity features in Results sections of ERAs from applied linguistics and physics.

From the perspective of research methods, comparison is the frequent method used in studies on ERAs. There are altogether six types of comparison.

The first group of researchers compares sections of RAs from a single discipline written by scholars with different cultural backgrounds (cf. Li&Xu, 2020; Loi et al., 2016; Ruan, 2018; Sadeghi&Alinasab, 2020). For instance, Loi et al. (2016) combine appraisal framework (Martin&Rose, 2003) and genre analysis (Swales, 1990) to analyze Discussion sections of English and Malay RAs. They (Loi et al.,2016) find that rhetorical effects are achieved by evaluative and dialogic stances.

The second group of researchers compares sections of ERAs among various disciplines (cf. Cortes, 2013; Friginal&Mustafa, 2017; Kashiha&Marandi, 2019; Khany&Kafshgar, 2016; Lu et al., 2020; Lu et al., 2018; Moyano, 2019; Parviz et al., 2020; Peacock, 2002). For instance, Lu et al. (2018) focus on the p-frames in the Introduction sections in ERAs of six social science disciplines. The structure and function of those p-frames are analyzed. Moreover, a random sample of 100 p-frames is evaluated by academic writing teachers and student writers in terms of their pedagogical usefulness.

The third group of researchers compares sections of ERAs among different sub-disciplines of a single discipline. For example, Huang (2018) analyzes the rhetorical structure and linguistic features in abstracts of ERAs of three sub-disciplines of marine engineering, i.e., automatic control, structure and dynamics, and heat and flow. The results show noticeable differences in rhetorical structures, verb tenses, and first-person pronouns between the automatic control and the other two sub-disciplines.

The fourth group of scholars compares both disciplinary differences and cultural impact on various sections of RAs. Friginal and Mustafa (2017) analyze abstracts in RAs published in the US and Iraq between four disciplines, which reveal similarities and differences in the rhetorical structures, corpus-based patterns, and discourse markers.

The fifth group of researchers compares sections of ERAs from a single discipline written by writers of different levels of professional training (cf. Ansarifar et al., 2018; El-Dankhs, 2018; Samraj, 2013). For example, El-Dankhs (2018) compares the abstracts of Ph.D. theses and RAs in applied linguistics by employing the model of rhetorical structure proposed by Hyland (2000) and the metadiscourses summarized by Hyland (2005) in terms of move subcategories and metadiscourse markers. To explain these differences, El-Dankhs draws on Kawase's (2015) arguments that the theses are educational genres, while RAs are professional genres.

The sixth group of scholars compares sections of ERAs for theoretical studies and empirical studies. For example, Kwan and Chan (2014) analyze citations in Results and Discussion sections of ERAs from theoretical information systems and empirical information management.

Among the disciplines studied, sections of ERAs from applied linguistics receive the most attention, followed by comparative genre studies of ERAs from various disciplines. Sections of ERAs from ecology (Samraj, 2013), engineering (Huang, 2018; Le&Pham, 2020), higher education (Golparvar&Barabadi, 2020), sociology (Li&Xu, 2020), and medical sciences (Abdollahpour&Gholami, 2019) are also studied.

To sum up, the mainstream studies on various sections of ERAs usually employ move analysis proposed by Swales (1990, 2004) as a basis. Based on the move demarcation, on the one hand, the distribution of interpersonal resources is analyzed and compared within moves and steps. On the other hand, the corpus-driven approach is closely related to these studies. The research focuses reflect the development of corpus linguistics itself, i.e., the extracted forms shift from lexical bundles to phrase-frames.

In the next three sub-sections, genre studies on ERAs of physics, linguistics, and literary studies are reviewed. The three disciplines are selected because they are the representatives of science, social science, and humanities (cf. Martin et al., 2010:438).

2.3.2 Genre studies on ERAs in physics

Genre studies on ERAs in physics can be divided into two strands. One strand focuses on the lexicogrammatical resources of the whole ERA. The other strand analyzes the semantic and lexicogrammatical resources of the part-genres of ERAs in physics.

Regarding the first strand, ERAs of physics are used as representatives of hard sciences, the lexicogrammatical resources of which are compared with ERAs of other disciplines. Harwood (2005a) compares the distribution of inclusive and exclusive personal pronouns *I* and *We* across ERAs from the disciplines of business and management, computing science, economics, and physics, revealing that inclusive pronouns occur least frequently in physics ERAs. Harwood (2005b) discusses the functions of personal pronouns *I* and *We* in ERAs of four disciplines for emphasizing the promotional functions of those lexicogrammatical devices even in RAs from hard sciences. Gao (2020) makes a cross-cultural and cross-disciplinary comparison between RAs in terms of informal features and discovers that more informal lexicogrammatical devices are employed in physics RAs. Besides, the lexicogrammatical features of physics RAs and textbooks are compared. Yang (2018) explores the differences and similarities in the use of evidential verbs in physics academic articles and textbooks, aiming to demonstrate how source information is introduced in different genres.

Regarding the second strand, researchers explore the semantic and lexicogrammatical resources in particular part-genres of ERAs in physics, such as Discussion sections (Khany&Kafshgar, 2016; Parkinson, 2011) and Results sections (Parviz et al., 2020). For example, Parkinson (2011) compares Discussion sections of physics ERAs and student physics laboratory reports with the guidance of SFL. His (Parkinson, 2011) research framework is two-fold. One is at the stratum of semantics, where causal, conditional, and purposive meanings at clause rank are analyzed. The other is at the lexicogrammatical stratum, where the lexicogrammatical resources used for expressing those meanings are discovered by using concordance software. Khany and Kafshgar (2016) focus on the Discussion sections of ERAs in the disciplines of humanities, life sciences, and physics. They (Khany&Kafshgar,

2016) explore linguistic complexity through two aspects. One is lexical complexity, which includes lexical diversity and lexical density. The other is syntactic complexity involving average sentence length and the ratio of subordination. The results show that except for average sentence length, all the other three factors are significantly higher in ERAs of humanities.

2.3.3 Genre studies on ERAs in linguistics

Genre studies on ERAs in linguistics can also be divided into two strands. Research in one strand focus on semantic and lexicogrammatical resources in the whole ERA, including authorial references (Khedri&Kritsis, 2020), reporting (Marti et al., 2019), use of stance features (Qiu&Ma, 2019), definition (Triki, 2019) and exemplification (Su&Zhang, 2020).

Khedri and Kritsis (2020) compare personal and impersonal authorial references in ERAs of applied linguistics, psychology, environmental engineering, and chemistry to reveal the disciplinary differences in terms of the use and functions of authorial references. They (Khedri&Kritsis, 2020) discover that exclusive first-person plural pronouns are employed in ERAs of applied linguistics to establish authorial identities. Marti et al. (2019) make a cross-cultural and cross-expertise comparison in reporting practices in RAs of applied linguistics. They (Marti et al., 2019) focus on verbs controlling that-clause to show that expertise level is an important factor in disciplinary writing. Qiu and Ma (2019) compare the use of stance features between masters' theses, doctoral dissertations, and ERAs of applied linguistics. The results show masters use more hedges, boosters, attitude markers, and fewer self-mentions than doctoral candidates and ERA writers. Moreover, the latter two types of authors utilize similar metadiscourse to express stances. Su and Zhang (2020) apply a local grammar approach to analyze exemplifications in ERAs of linguistics for revealing their discourse-semantic patterns. Triki (2019) displays the disciplinary differences in definitions in ERAs of linguistics and computing sciences in terms of building units and functions.

Research in the other strand explores rhetorical structures and lexicogrammatical resources in various part-genres of ERAs in linguistics, involving Introductions (Kashiha&Marandi, 2019; Xu&Nesi, 2019b), Results (Parviz et al., 2020), Discussions (Liu&Buckingham, 2018; Sadeghi&Alinasab, 2020), Conclusions (Chen&Zhang, 2017; Sheldon, 2018), and biodata (Mwinlaaru, 2017).

In terms of Introductions, guided by Swales' (1990) CARS model and Hyland's (2005) model of metadiscourse, Kashiha and Marandi (2019) analyze the differences in the distribution of interactive metadiscourse in the main moves of Introductions in ERAs of chemistry and applied linguistics. Xu and Nesi (2019b) investigate differences in evaluative style in introductions to ERAs written by scholars from China and Britain. The introductions are marked for rhetorical structure in terms of the three moves in the CARS model developed by Swales (2004). The frequencies of the appraisal features (Martin&White, 2005) are calculated for each move.

In terms of the Results sections, Parviz et al. (2020) compare phrasal complexity features in empirical ERAs of applied linguistics and physics. The findings reveal that pre-modifying adjectives, post-modifying prepositional phrases, and nominalization are the three major lexicogrammatical resources for displaying phrasal complexity in the Results sections of ERAs.

In terms of the Discussion sections, Liu and Buckingham (2018) combine Yang and Allison's (2003) schematic structures of ERAs and Dafouz-Milne's (2008) classification of textual and interpersonal metadiscourse, exploring the moves and metadiscourse deployments in Discussion sections of ERAs. They (Liu&Buckingham, 2018) affirm the applicability of Yang&Allison's (2003) model and discover the differences in the distribution of textual and interpersonal markers across moves. Based on Hunston's (1993) framework for academic conflict, Sadeghi and Alinasab (2020) explore the differences in the utilization of academic conflict components (proposed claims, opposed claims, conflict resolution) between English and Persian writers in Discussion sections of RAs in applied linguistics.

In terms of the Conclusion sections, following Crompton's (1997) classification of hedges, Chen and Zhang (2017) compare hedges in the Conclusion sections of ERAs in applied linguistics written by Chinese and Anglophone researchers. They (Chen&Zhang, 2017) discover that Anglophone writers use more hedges, while only one type of hedge shows a statistically significant difference between Chinese and Anglophone writers. Combining Swales' (1990, 2004) move analysis framework with engagement system in Martin and White's (2005) appraisal framework, Sheldon (2018) focuses on the Conclusion sections of RAs written by English L1, English L2, and Spanish L1 scholars.

Apart from the above-mentioned part-genres in ERAs, biodata written by applied linguistic scholars in ERAs and seminars are compared by Mwinlaaru (2017). By using Hasan's (Halliday&Hasan, 1985) GSP model, the study focuses on the field and mode parameters in analyzing the macro-organization of biodata. The biodata genre is described from above (at the context stratum) by examining the staged activities; from a roundabout perspective (at the semantic stratum) by considering the logico-semantic or rhetorical relations that exist among stages and phases; and from below (at the lexicogrammar stratum) by examining phraseological patterns that are pertinent to biodata, including appraisal resources that are deployed by writers to present credible academic identity.

2.3.4 Genre studies on ERAs in literary studies

Compared with the abundance of research on ERAs of linguistics and physics from the genre perspective, genre studies on ERAs of literary studies are relatively scarce. Generally speaking, those studies focus the organizational structures of part-genres of literature ERAs (cf. Tanko, 2017; Zhao et al., 2019) on the one hand, and the lexicogrammatical resources across various part-genres of ERAs of literary studies (cf. Afros&Schryer, 2009) on the other.

In terms of the analysis of the rhetorical structures of literature ERAs, Tanko (2017) focuses on the abstracts of literature research articles (hereafter LRA) by exploring the move organization, functions of identified moves, and linguistic features of those moves. The results show that LRA abstracts have a non-hierarchical eight-move structure with four stable moves. Furthermore, the study reveals LRA abstracts are a mix of descriptive and informative abstracts and structurally overlap with the rhetorical organization of RA introductions. Zhao et al. (2019) follow Tanko's (2017) study by analyzing LRA abstracts at the step level. Moreover, they (Zhao et al., 2019) find that the most frequent move sequence in abstracts of LRA is Purpose ^ Conclusion.

In terms of the exploration of lexicogrammatical features in part-genres of ERAs of literary studies, Afros and Schryer (2009) compare the distribution of lexicogrammatical resources reflecting evaluation across part-genres between ERAs of literary studies and linguistics. Those part-genres include abstracts, Introductions, Discussions, Conclusions, and Footnotes. The results show authors in both ERAs positively evaluate their own studies while negatively evaluating opposing views. However, writers employ different lexicogrammatical resources for achieving evaluation in the same part-genres of ERAs.

2.3.5 Studies on generic complexity of ERAs

The generic complexity of ERAs is studied by several scholars (Hood, 2010; Lai&Wang, 2018; Zhang, 2015). On the one hand, the whole ERA is taken as a macrogenre. The elemental genre deployments in each part-genre of ERAs are identified. A case in point is conducted by Lai and Wang (2018), who analyze the ERAs of linguistics and discover that the dominant elemental genre is descriptive report followed by exposition.

On the other hand, the part-genres of ERAs are also viewed as a macrogenre. Zhang (2015) views abstracts of ERAs as a macrogenre and illustrates this view with three abstracts in ERAs of linguistics. One illustration is an instance of genre embedding in which the Method stage of a procedural recount is replaced by two procedural recounts. The other two abstracts are genre complexes with a descriptive report and a procedural recount.

Besides, Hood (2010:6) takes both the whole ERA and some part-genres of ERAs as macrogenres. She (Hood, 2010:69) summarizes the elemental genres in RA introductions as a descriptive report of the study object, a descriptive report of other research and knowledge in the field, and a description of the writer's own study.

2.3.6 Summary

The survey on previous genre studies of ERAs can be summarized in terms of research content, theoretical underpinnings, and research methodology.

Thematically, on the one hand, the lexicogrammatical resources of the whole ERA are analyzed. However, the research of physics ERAs emphasize linguistic complexity, whereas the studies on ERAs of linguistics tend to explore interpersonal resources such as metadiscourse and appraisal resources. However, scarce studies take ERAs of literary studies as the research object. On the other hand, many researchers view each section as part-genres of ERAs and explore the move structure, lexicogrammatical and semantic resources across moves in those part-genres.

Theoretically, Swales' (1990,2004) move analysis, Hyland's (2005) metadiscourse model, corpus linguistics, and Martin and White's (2005) appraisal system are the mainstream underpinnings for the genre studies of ERAs. Based on the segmentations of moves and steps within part-genres of ERAs, the distribution of metadiscourse, lexical bundles, and appraisal resources are explored. However, few studies employ the SFL-based multi-stratal model to explore the generic resources in ERAs. Moreover, scant research take ERAs as macrogenres and analyze the elemental genre distributions within them. Furthermore, less discussion is conducted to analyze the way through which the elemental genres are linked into ERAs.

Methodologically, the comparative approach permeates through those studies, either through comparison between disciplines, between speakers with various native languages, or both. The quantitative approach advocated by corpus linguists is also gaining popularity with the emergence of studies on p-frames. However, few studies make a comparison between ERAs of literary studies and ERAs of other disciplines.

2.4 Comments

This chapter reviews previous studies on genre analysis, generic complexity, and ERAs, and offers a basis for explaining the necessity and feasibility of the current study.

In terms of necessity, firstly, among the studies of genre analysis and generic complexity, the SFL framework is usually employed for analyzing lexicogrammatical resources. However, as a comprehensive multi-stratal model, SFL's focuses lie not only in lexicogrammatical features, but also in genre, register, and semantics strata. Therefore, it is necessary to sharpen the multi-stratal framework for analyzing generic complexity in SFL.

Secondly, though there is a huge number of research on ERAs, ERAs of literary studies seem to gain relatively little attention. Furthermore, the comparison between ERAs of physics, linguistics, and literary studies can be strengthened for exploring the characteristics of the three representative disciplines.

Thirdly, there are scant studies on ERAs in the aspect of genre combining. However, in reality, writers often combine various elemental genres to construct a macrogenre. Martin (2008) uses science textbooks as illustrations to explain the genre forming mechanism. Therefore, it is necessary to examine the generic complexity in ERAs, which is another important resource for transmitting disciplinary knowledge.

In terms of feasibility, the previous studies on generic complexity, especially those studies conducted by Martin and his colleagues, have already established operational models for exploring genre relations in textbooks, which guides the framework construction of the current study.

To sum up, the examination of studies on genres, generic complexity, and genre-based research on ERAs reveals that there are three problems that can be addressed.

Firstly, although generic complexity has attracted the attention of several scholars, there is a lack of a comprehensive framework for exploring generic complexity in ERAs. In particular, the mechanism through which elemental genres in ERAs combine to form macrogenres is still under-explored. Secondly, there are scarce studies that demonstrate the viability of theoretical frameworks in analyzing certain genres. Thirdly, the existing studies on generic complexity of ERAs have mostly focused on the complexity features in the linguistics ERAs, with less attention being paid to other disciplines.

In view of this, the current study aims to solve the above-mentioned problems through three steps. First, a framework for exploring generic complexity in ERAs is established. Then, this framework is applied to the analysis of generic complexity in ERAs from the disciplines of physics, linguistics, and literary studies. Finally, the influence of disciplinary features on the generic complexity of ERAs from the three disciplines is discussed. In the next chapter, the framework for analyzing generic complexity is presented with the elucidation of its theoretical motivation and descriptive basis. Meanwhile, data and methodology are also discussed.

Chapter 3 Theoretical Framework and Methodology

As stated in the previous chapter, there are still some issues that need to be addressed in terms of genre studies. Theoretically, although generic complexity has aroused the research interest of scholars from SFL and ESP, scant studies focus on systematic descriptions of its mechanism for forming macrogenres[①] in ERAs. In this context, a framework for analyzing generic complexity which can be used to explore the generic complexity in ERAs is in need of development. Practically, first, the existing studies on ERAs mainly focus on interpersonal resources such as metadiscourse. However, the generic complexity in ERAs is largely left unnoticed. Second, although some attention has been paid to the configuration of elemental genres in ERAs, the semogenetic strategies through which elemental genres combine are understudied. Third, from the aspect of genre, there are few cross-disciplinary studies, especially the comparison between literary studies and other disciplines.

Taking these into consideration, this chapter presents the framework for studying generic complexity in ERAs. As mentioned in Chapter 1, the current study aims to address the following RQs.

First, what are the macro generic structures, elemental genre deployments, and the similarities and differences in the overall genre deployments in the

① Macrogenre was first used by Martin (1994:29) with a hyphen between macro and genre. In this book, the author adheres to the opinion of Szenes (2017:73), considering it as a term in SFL. Thus, the hyphen is omitted.

ERAs of physics, linguistics and literary studies?

Second, how do elemental genres form macrogenres in the main stages of the ERAs of the three disciplines?

Third, what are the field and discourse semantics resources used in construing distinctive elemental genres in the ERAs of the three disciplines?

Fourth, how do disciplinary features influence the elemental genre deployments and genre combining strategies in the ERAs of the three disciplines?

Fifth, how do cultural differences affect the elemental genre deployments in linguistics ERAs and CRAs?

To answer the research questions, the present project proposes a framework for analyzing the generic complexity of RAs, followed by the elaboration on the theoretical motivation that involves SFL's conception of context, genre, and logico-semantic relation. Then, the chapter describes in detail each dimension in the analytical model, including elemental genre, genre expansion and projection, genre embedding, field, discourse semantics, and disciplinarity. At the end of the chapter, the data and methodology used in this study are introduced.

3.1 The framework for analyzing generic complexity

Before elaborating the framework, the working definitions of genre, macrogenre, and generic complexity are presented.

The concept of genre refers to "staged, goal-oriented social processes" (Martin, 1992; Martin&Rose, 2008), which is the working definition adopted in this study. According to Rose (2012:209), genres are staged because more than one step is taken to achieve the goal, and they are social and goal-oriented because texts are interactive events and unfold according to the interactants' purposes. Furthermore, genres involve the recurrent configuration of meanings which serve to establish the social practice and are realized and instantiated at the stratum of discourse semantics (cf. Zhao, 2014:60). In this book, this definition of genre is presented for identifying elemental genres in terms of their purposes and stages. Thus, it can provide the rationale for exploring the semogenetic strategies in the formation of macrogenres.

Macrogenre is a large-scale text that instantiates more than one elemental genre to achieve complicated purposes (Martin, 1994, 2002; Martin&Rose, 2008; Zhang&Pramoolsook, 2019). In this sense, the research article, as seen by Hood (2010:6), is by nature a macrogenre, as it contains a series of linked segments and each segment has its own generic structure.

For Jordens et al. (2001), the variety and number of elemental genres instantiated by texts can be referred to as generic complexity. The current study explores generic complexity in disciplinary discourse and the semogenetic strategies that function to combine elemental genres. Therefore, this study approaches generic complexity in terms of the axial relation. Paradigmatically, the selection of elemental genres from a genre family can be described. Syntagmatically, genre complexing and genre embedding can be explored as strategies to form elemental genre sequences.

This study focuses on generic complexity across three disciplines in natural sciences, social sciences, and the humanities, i.e., physics, linguistics, and literary studies. The phenomenon of generic complexity is approached through the framework proposed in Figure 3.1.

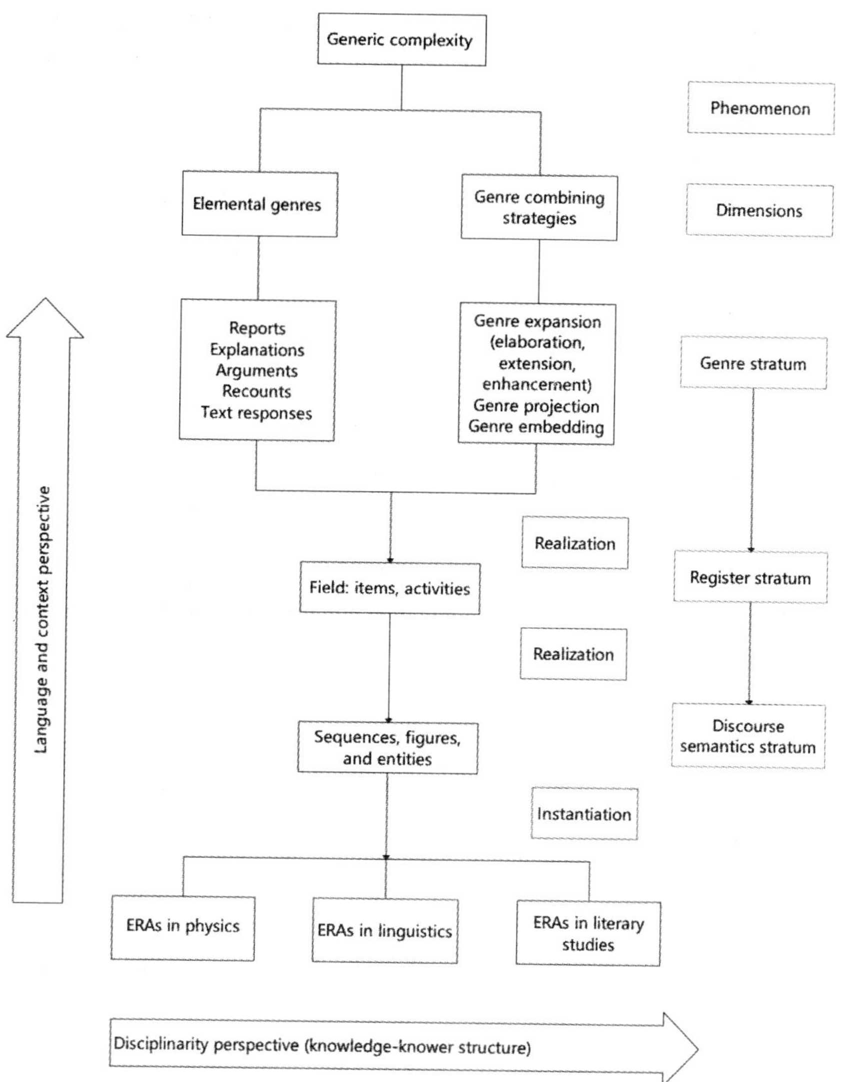

Figure 3.1 Theoretical framework for studying generic complexity in RAs

Figure 3.1 indicates that the present study analyzes generic complexity from two perspectives. One is from the perspective of language and context, aiming at describing the deployments of elemental genres and genre linking strategies in ERAs of the three disciplines. The other is from the perspective of disciplinarity, which can explain the similarities and differences in generic complexity in terms of disciplinary variations (see the two arrows on the left side and at the bottom of Figure 3.1).

The linguistic-contextual perspective is chosen for addressing research questions 1-3, i.e., to describe generic complexity within the framework of SFL, including the description of elemental genre deployments and genre combining strategies. Additionally, the field and discourse semantics resources of discipline-sensitive elemental genres are analyzed. In other words, this perspective is employed to settle the "what" aspect of this research.

The perspective of disciplinarity is emphasized in response to research question 4, where disciplinarity is taken as one possible reason that leads to the similarities and differences concerning generic complexity. It is worthy of mentioning that, to some extent, disciplinarity, which is mainly realized as knowledge and knower structures in the present study is included in the domain of context. However, the perspective is extracted from context and given a foregrounding position as it serves for the "why" aspect of this project, namely, it can provide us with potential explanations for the common points and variations in generic complexity among ERAs of the three disciplines.

From the perspective of language and context, a tri-stratal analytical framework is proposed, and generic complexity in ERAs is explored from two aspects: elemental genres and genre combining strategies. There are three strata in this framework: genre, register, and discourse semantics, as shown on the right side of Figure 3.1.

At the genre stratum, elemental genres and genre combining strategies in the main stages of ERAs are identified. In this framework, elemental genres are classified on the basis of typical purpose, phase allocation, and thematic shift according to systemicists' (e.g., Hao, 2020; Martin&Rose, 2008; Rose, 2012; Rose&Martin, 2012; Veel, 1997) theories on genre. As far as genre combining strategies are concerned, the mechanism through which elemental genres are linked into the main stages of ERAs is explored through the logico-semantic relations of expansion and projection, particularly the transphenomenal strategies proposed by Halliday (1994), i.e., elaboration, extension, and enhancement. Besides, genre embedding, which refers to the phenomenon in which one stage of an elemental genre is replaced by another elemental genre, is also taken as one kind of elemental genre combining strategies.

At the register stratum, static items and dynamic activities are studied as they realize resources at the genre stratum. For instance, implication activities can construct scientific explanations (cf. Doran&Martin, 2021: 111).

At the discourse semantics stratum, sequences, figures, and entities are coded as they realize items and activities at the register stratum. For example, thing entities and activity entities can be identified as realizations of items and itemized activity (cf. Hao, 2021:144). Based on this tri-stratal framework, generic complexity in ERAs of the three disciplines is explored.

From the perspective of disciplinarity, the differences and similarities in the deployment of elemental genres and the genre combining strategies within the ERAs of the three disciplines are discussed in terms of the theory of knowledge and knower structure developed by Maton (2014). This perspective is chosen for two reasons. First, since the data of this project are ERAs from the three disciplines, it is assumed that disciplinary differences can be reflected in the variations in the elemental genre deployments and elemental genre combining strategies. Second, Maton's (2014) knowledge and knower structure can be a guide for the research of the nature of disciplines, which lays the foundation for studying discipline characteristics based on the elemental genre deployments and genre combining strategies.

The following sections address the framework from three aspects. First, the theoretical motivation that weaves the descriptive dimensions together is explained. Second, the key notions involved in the description of generic complexity across the three disciplines are discussed. Third, the data and methodology of the present study is explicated.

3.2 Theoretical motivation

After the brief introduction to the theoretical framework of the current study, this section focuses on the theoretical motivation that supports the study and weaves the research dimensions of the study together. This theoretical framework can serve as the guideline for the analytical work in this study. Generally speaking, the analytical dimensions of the present research are driven by such basic and essential concepts as context, genre, logico-semantic relation, stratification, realization, and instantiation, which are to be elucidated in the following sub-sections.

3.2.1 Context

Context is the key notion that lays the basis of the current study. This is because within the theoretical framework of SFL, the theory of genre is developing accompanying the discussion of context. Although there are two strands of thought for the theorization of context within SFL, both of them emphasize the activation-construal dialectic between context and language. Context activates the choices of language while the choices of language construe context. It is this dialectic relation that makes it possible to examine generic complexity in texts that realize and instantiate the phenomenon.

Seen from a functional perspective, context consists of context of culture and context of situation (Halliday, 1978:109). However, there are two strands of thought about context. One is represented by Halliday, Hasan, and others (cf. Halliday, 1978; Halliday&Matthiessen, 2014; Hasan, 2009; Matthiessen, 2015, 2019); while the other is represented by Martin (cf. Martin, 1992; Martin&Rose, 2008).

The first strand views context with an instantiation and realization-driven model (cf. Hasan, 2009:169). From the perspective of instantiation, context of culture and context of situation are situated at the two poles of the instance-potential continuum (Hasan, 2009:168-169; Halliday&Matthiessen, 2014:32).

The former refers to the contextual potential of a community and sits at the potential pole of the cline of instantiation while the latter refers to a specific cultural domain and is located at the instance pole (Halliday&Matthiessen, 2014:32-33).

From the perspective of realization, contextual choices activate semantic choices that activate the lexicogrammatical ones, and at the same time, lexicogrammatical choices construe semantic choices that construe contextual ones (Hasan, 2009:170). Scholars (e.g., Halliday, 1978:109-110; Halliday&Hasan, 1985; Halliday&Matthiessen, 2014:33; Matthiessen, 2015, 2019) in this strand of thought approach the potential pole by analyzing situation types, which are featured by field, tenor, and mode. Moreover, register is viewed as a semantic phenomenon (cf. Matthiessen, 2019). For instance, Matthiessen (2019:15) views register variation as a semantic variation which occurs in the region between the meaning potential of language and text instances.

The other strand describes context through a stratification-driven model (cf. Martin, 1992; Martin&Rose, 2008). From the perspective of stratification, context is divided into genre and register (Martin, 1992, 1999; Martin&Rose, 2008). For Martin (1999/2012:225-227), genre and register belong to the connotative semiotic systems whose expression plane is language. In this stratified model of context, genre realizes ideology and is realized by register, which is formed by the contextual variables of field, tenor, and mode (Martin, 1992:496; Matthiessen et al., 2016:120).

The studies above show that genre is an important part of context. Thus, the study of genre and especially generic complexity should take context into consideration and therefore the concept of context constitutes one of the major theoretical bases of the framework in this book.

3.2.2 Genre

Genre is the concept that directly motivates the framework of the current study. Previous studies on the schematic structure and lexicogrammatical resources of educational genres offer references for the model of elemental genre classification of the present study.

Regarding the theorization of genre, similar to that of context, there are two different groups about the concept of genre within SFL. One group considers genre as a feature of mode, which is a variable of context of situation (e.g., Halliday, 1978:62,145). Hasan (Halliday&Hasan, 1985:108) defines genre as genre-specific semantic potential, which is the verbal expression of contextual configuration. In other words, genre is the realization of context. Besides, the notion of GSP is proposed for depicting the potential structure of texts (Halliday&Hasan, 1985: 63-65). While the other group (e.g., Martin&Rose, 2008:16) views genre as a configuration of tenor, field, and mode variables, namely, register① realizes genre.

However, according to Martin (1992: 505), the differences between seeing genre as a realization of context of situation and seeing register as a realization of genre are not crucial to the actual analysis of texts in terms of their structure. Furthermore, in this book, a macro generic structure is used for describing the schematic structure of ERAs instead of GSP for the following reasons. First, the theoretical basis of this study is the genre theory proposed by Martin (cf. Martin, 1992; Martin&Rose, 2008). Therefore, the term GSP is not employed so that terminological confusion can be avoided. Second, according to Martin (1999/2012:235), GSP concentrates on the differences among text types which share obligatory structural components. Yet, this monograph explores relationships among genres with distinctive compulsory elements.

To facilitate analyses, this book takes genre as goal-oriented social

① Here register refers to a semiotic system formed by contextual variables of field, tenor, and mode (Martin, 1992:502), i.e., context of situation. It is different from Halliday and Hasan's (1985:38) use of register, which is a semantic concept referring to a configuration of meanings related to the situational configuration of field, mode, and tenor.

processes which are realized and instantiated at the discourse semantics stratum as the configuration of meanings (cf. Martin&Rose, 2008).

The common points of the two groups in analyzing techniques will be utilized to reveal the elements of structure in the ERAs and to characterize their disciplinary differences and similarities. Except for the theorization of genre, the investigation of schematic structure in various educational genres offers analytical guidance for building an elemental genre identification model in this study.

The previous studies which focus on school science (Veel, 1997) and various educational genres (Martin&Rose, 2008; Rose&Martin, 2012) provide a detailed description of elemental genres with their typical stages and phases, thus shedding light on the establishment of elemental genre classification model for ERAs.

Regarding the third aspect of the theoretical motivation of genre, based on Martin's (1996) classification of story-type genres, Jordens et al. (2001) propose the notion of generic complexity for the exploration of patients' narratives[①]. The concept of generic complexity is the key aspect which the analytical framework revolves around.

3.2.3 Logico-semantic relation

The concept of logico-semantic relation motivates the exploration of the strategies employed in the formation of macrogenres in ERAs. This sub-section introduces the definition of logico-semantic relation and teases out the development of this term within SFL, aiming to explain why logico-semantic relation can be applied in genre analysis.

---

① Jordens et al. (2001:1228) take narratives (plural form) as a macrogenre which are combined by various story-type genres, including the elemental genre "narrative" (singular form). In the current study, to avoid terminological confusion, the narrative is a type of elemental genre belonging to the genre family of Recounts.

Logico-semantic relation is the defining feature of the system of logico-semantic type, which consists of expansion and projection (Halliday&Matthiessen, 2014; Matthiessen et al., 2016). It can establish the logical relations in clause complexes, group and phrase complexes, and all kinds of text (Matthiessen et al., 2016:150). In other words, the strategies for generating complex structures operate across different strata, as well as across various ranks at the same stratum, including the lexicogrammar stratum, the semantics stratum, and the genre stratum.

In the studies of the logico-semantic relation at the lexicogrammar stratum, the system of clause complexing receives the most attention. According to Halliday&Matthiessen (2014:436-440), clause complexing involves two aspects. One is taxis, known as the degree of interdependency between two clauses, which are either of equal status (parataxis) or unequal status (hypotaxis). The other is the logico-semantic type, which consists of two types, i.e., expansion and projection. The former relates phenomena as being of the same order of experience, while the latter relates phenomena of one order of experience to phenomena of a higher order. As for expansion, there are three types: elaborating, extending, and enhancing, each of which is further divided into several subtypes (Halliday&Matthiessen, 2004:395-422).

The theoretical motivation of clause complexing can be summarized through stratification, metafunction, and rank.

In terms of stratification, the natural relation between semantics and lexicogrammar is apparently highlighted. Sequences of figures at the semantics stratum are thought to be realized by clause complexes at the lexicogrammatical stratum (Halliday&Matthiessen, 2014:429).

In terms of metafunction, according to Halliday and Matthiessen (2014:433), the choice to expand a clause is determined metafunctionally. As mentioned by Halliday and Matthiessen (2014:435), a clause complex is arranged by the logical metafunction with univariate structure. Moreover, circumstantial augmentation of the clause is organized by experiential metafunction with multivariate structure, whereas cohesive sequences are combined by textual metafunction (Halliday&Matthiessen, 2014:432).

In terms of rank, the clause complex is located at the clause rank in the lexicogrammatical stratum.

At the genre stratum, Martin (1994, 1995) uses the analogy between clauses and texts as the basis for applying clause-complexing strategies to text enlargement. Therefore, the semogenesis strategies of expansion and projection can be utilized for analyzing genre combining strategies.

The notions of context, genre, and logico-semantic relation provide direct motivation for exploring elemental genres and genre combining strategies in the present research. However, the framework for exploring generic complexity is organized through three basic principles, i.e., stratification, realization, and instantiation.

3.2.4 Stratification

Stratification is a major driving force that enables this book to operate at the strata of context and language. As a matter of fact, this study focuses on generic complexity at the genre stratum, the register stratum, and the discourse semantics stratum. It is through stratification that a tri-stratal framework for analyzing generic complexity becomes possible and the concept of genre becomes observable in texts through the register stratum and the discourse semantics stratum.

According to Matthiessen et al. (2016:231), stratification can organize language in context into subsystems regarding the degree of symbolic abstraction. As proposed by Martin (1999/2012:233-235), the strata in the organization of language are discourse semantics, lexicogrammar, and phonology/graphology, and context involves both genre and register. For Martin (1992, 1999/2012), Martin and Rose (2007), and Doran (2018:9), discourse semantics refers to meanings made through entire texts while lexicogrammar involves meanings within clauses, groups or phrases, words, and morphemes, which are further realized in phonology for spoken language and graphology for written language.

According to Martin (1999/2012:226), genre and register are connotative semiotics, which use language as their expression plane. In Martin's model (1999/2012), choices in language are determined by register and genre. As the highest stratum of context, genre depicts the purposes of texts, spreads through recognizable stages, and controls the meanings at the stratum below, i.e., register (Martin, 1992; Rose&Martin, 2012).

Register is related to the three contextual variables of field, tenor, and mode (Martin,1992). Through stratification, genre is realized at the register stratum, and at the same time, the genre-related resources at the register stratum are realized at the discourse semantics stratum. Driven by the concept of stratification, this study can examine genre complexity by identifying resources at the register stratum with an emphasis on field, and at the discourse semantics stratum with a focus on sequences, figures, and entities, which indicate distinctive genre-specific characters.

3.2.5 Realization

Realization is a theoretical concept that facilitates the examination of generic complexity through various strata and makes the abstract resources at the genre stratum observable at the discourse semantics and the lexicogrammar strata.

Realization can be found in the inter-stratal realization and the intra-stratal realization (Matthiessen et al., 2016).

Inter-stratal realization refers to the relationship between semantics and lexicogrammar, between lexicogrammar and phonology, and between phonology and phonetics (Halliday, 1992a/2002:352; Matthiessen et al.,2016:194). This point is closely related to the current theoretical framework because the realization of genre lies in the register stratum, where the resources are realized by discourse semantics and further realized by lexicogrammatical resources.

Intra-stratal realization, as viewed by Matthiessen et al. (2016:194), refers to the relationship between ranks at a given stratum, or the relationship between paradigmatic and syntagmatic axis in a given rank. This point also supports the two major research dimensions of this study: the examination of elemental genres from the genre family and the syntagmatic manifestation of the elemental genre sequence through genre complexing and embedding.

3.2.6 Instantiation

Instantiation is another significant concept that offers the theoretical motivation for this project. The relationship between language as meaning-making potential (i.e., system) and as actual usage in a text (i.e., instance) is referred to as instantiation by Halliday and Matthiessen (2014:27). As far as the present research is concerned, guided by the system of elemental genres, the instances of elemental genres can be identified in ERA texts. At the same time, based on the observation and analysis of texts, new elemental genres can be discovered.

Following Matthiessen et al. (2016:136), the cline of instantiation, the spectrum of metafunction, and the hierarchy of stratification constitute the global dimensions in the organization of language in context. The cline of instantiation offers methodological and theoretical guidance for discourse analysis. On the one hand, the potential pole can be approached by observing, sampling, and analyzing texts (Matthiessen et al., 2016:138). On the other hand, instances can be identified in terms of systemic potential (Hao, 2020:19).

These basic principles about language and context serve as the theoretical thread that intertwines the descriptive dimensions for exploring generic complexity. In the following section, the descriptive basis of the present research will be presented, including elemental genre, genre combining strategies, field, discourse semantics, and disciplinarity.

3.3 Descriptive basis

As mentioned above, this book proposes a tri-stratal framework for studying generic complexity. Based on the theoretical motivation of stratification, realization, and instantiation, this study explores elemental genres and genre combining strategies at the genre stratum. The stages of ERAs are identified and the elemental genres in each stage of ERAs are recognized. Moreover, the elemental genre combining strategies within each stage of ERAs are analyzed, because elemental genre deployments and combining strategies constitute the major analytical dimensions of the current study. However, as the concept of the highest abstractness proposed by Martin (1992, 1999/2012), genre is to be approached through the strata below it, i.e., the register stratum and the discourse semantics stratum. Therefore, this study is engaged in several tasks. At the genre stratum, elemental genre deployments and genre combining strategies are discussed. At the register stratum, field is an important index for classifying stages, and activities and items of the characteristic elemental genres of the ERAs are analyzed. At the discourse semantics stratum, ideational meanings of sequences, figures, and entities of distinctive elemental genres in ERAs of the three disciplines are explored.

3.3.1 Elemental genres

This sub-section is devoted to the analysis of elemental genres. First, schematic structures, stages, and phases are introduced, as they form the basis for segmenting ERAs and distinguishing various elemental genres in each stage of ERAs. Then, the genre families and the classification of elemental genres proposed by different scholars are evaluated before a modified classification of elemental genres can be proposed for ERA analysis. Furthermore, the classification of elemental genres is summarized on the basis of their social purpose and typical stages.

It is worth mentioning that the modified classification of elemental genres in this study is based upon previous studies of elemental genres and used as a guideline for identifying elemental genres in ERAs. In the real application of this model, there is the possibility that elemental genres which are not included in the framework can be encountered.

Martin and Rose (2008:6) label recurrent local patterns within genres as schematic structures and take the schematic structure of an experiment report in school science as a typical example, which includes such stages as Aim, Equipment, Steps, Results, and Conclusion.

A stage in a genre constitutes one or more phases. For example, in the generic stages of a story, there are phases such as setting, description, and events with various functions for engaging listeners (Martin&Rose, 2008:82). For Martin and Rose (2008:82), stages of a genre are relatively stable components, whereas phases within each stage are much more variable and may be unique to a particular text.

Besides, many scholars (e.g., Hao, 2020; Martin&Rose, 2008; Rose, 2012; Rose&Martin, 2012; Veel, 1997; Zhang&Pramoolsook, 2019) have conducted research on the typology of genre families and elemental genres. Among these studies, Martin and Rose (2008) present an overall classification of genres, which can be applied in the analysis of genres ranging from school disciplines to workplace discourse. Some scholars (e.g., Rose, 2012; Rose&Martin, 2012) summarize the genres in schools and some (e.g., Hao, 2020; Martin&Rose, 2008; Veel, 1997) focus on genres in science.

In terms of a comprehensive account of genre families and elemental genres, Martin and Rose (2008) summarize and analyze the elemental genres in histories, reports, and explanations in geography and science, and the procedural and associated genres in the workplace. However, this kind of classification can cause overlapping and confusion in identifying elemental genres. For example, according to Martin and Rose (2008), response genres are used in evaluating stories, and expositions, discussions and challenges are included in the history genre family. Yet, in real operation, these elemental genres are not confined to story or history genre families exclusively.

As for the studies of genres in the education domain, Rose and Martin (2012:128-130) offer a model of genres in secondary school, in which seven genre families with twenty-two elemental genres are identified, showing that the genre family of stories is used for engaging; chronicles[①], explanations, reports, and procedures are functioning for informing; and arguments and text responses are utilized for evaluating.

In another study, Rose (2012) summarizes the common educational genres into eight genre families and twenty-eight elemental genres. Unlike Rose and Martin (2012), Rose (2012:212) adds recounting genre family in the framework and divides the genre family of text responses into literary and academic text responses.

The reasons for the differences may lie in the application domain of the two models. Rose and Martin's (2012) typology of genres is a summary of genres in the secondary school, whereas Rose's (2012) framework is a synthesis of genres in the whole educational domain.

Furthermore, Veel (1997), Martin and Rose (2008), and Hao (2020) have been devoted to summarizing the various types of elemental genres in science.

Veel (1997:170-172) studies the elemental genres in written texts in school science and focuses on the factual genres by categorizing them into four groups (i.e., enabling, explaining, documenting, and persuading), with each group being divided into several elemental genres. As shown in Figure 3.2, there are altogether twelve types of elemental genres in Veel's (1997) discussion of factual genres. Among these types, theoretical explanation and exploration are worthy of mentioning since they do not exist in Martin and Rose's (2008) classification of genres in science. Theoretical explanation serves to introduce and illustrate a theoretical principle, whereas exploration describes events for which there are two or more viable explanations (Veel, 1997:172).

① Rose and Martin (2012:130) use histories to refer to this type of genre family.

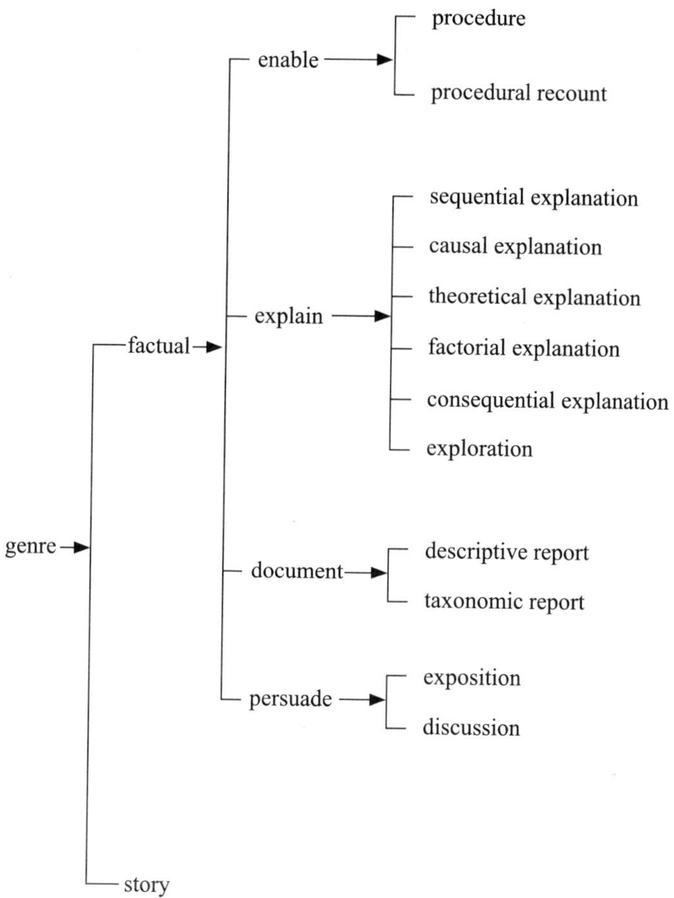

Figure 3.2 Genres in secondary school science (Veel, 1997:171)

Apart from Veel's (1997) summary of genres in school science, Martin and Rose (2008:167) propose a typology of elemental genres in science. In this model, descriptive reports, taxonomic reports, and compositional reports fall into the genre family of Reports (Martin&Rose, 2008:142-147). Sequential, factorial, consequential, and conditional explanations are included in the genre family of Explanations (Martin&Rose, 2008:150) and procedures and procedural recounts are considered as families of genres (Martin&Rose, 2008:141).

However, in Rose and Martin's (2012:130) classifications, procedures and procedural recounts are considered as elemental genres in the genre family of Procedures while Lai and Wang (2018) classify procedural recounts as elemental genres in the Recount genre family. Though there are differences in deciding whether procedures and procedural recounts are genre families or elemental genres, the existence of procedures and procedural recounts in the genres of school science is acknowledged.

Hao (2020:26-27) combines Veel's (1997) and Martin and Rose's (2008) typology of genres in science. Theoretical explanation and exploration are added to the genre family of Explanations but historical recount is removed in Hao's (2020:27) model.

When analyzing elemental genres in bachelor's theses, Zhang and Pramoolsook (2019) establish their analytical framework in reference to Rose's (2012) model. In Zhang and Pramoolsook's (2019:307) framework, there are twenty-seven types of elemental genres in seven genre families, involving stories, chronicles, explanations, reports, procedural genres, arguments, and text responses. This research is of particular importance to the current study because it explores bachelor's theses on literary studies. Their (Zhang&Pramoolsook, 2019:313) findings indicate that the genre family of Text responses occurs exclusively in literature theses.

In terms of the elemental genres deployment in ERAs of linguistics, Lai and Wang (2018) propose a network of elemental genres with four genre families, i.e., Reports, Expositions, Recounts, and Explanations, and the genre family of Recounts is mentioned for subsuming historical recount and procedural recount as its elemental genres.

Taking all the studies on the typology of elemental genres into consideration, this book proposes a modified typology for exploring elemental genres in ERAs, which is presented in Table 3.1. The framework contains five genre families: Reports, Explanations, Arguments, Recounts, and Text responses. The reasons for the modification are as follows.

First of all, the research object of the present project is ERAs in the disciplines of physics, linguistics, and literary studies. Although there is no research on the elemental genres in ERAs of physics, scholars (e.g., Hao, 2020; Martin&Rose, 2008; Veel, 1997) have already conducted surveys on elemental genres in science, which can shed light on the studies of generic complexity in ERAs of physics. Detailed scrutiny of these studies shows that Reports, Explanations, Arguments, Procedures, and Procedural recounts are genre families in science discourse.

Second, as far as the elemental genres in ERAs of literary studies are concerned, though there are no studies on the elemental genre deployments in literature ERAs, Zhang and Pramoolsook (2019) provide guidance for the classification of elemental genres of the present research since they explore bachelors' theses on literature. According to Zhang and Pramoolsook's (2019) study, the genre family of Text responses can occur in literature theses.

Third, regarding the elemental genres in ERAs of linguistics, Lai and Wang's (2018) study is of direct relation to the study of generic complexity. That is to say, the genre family of Reports, Explanations, Arguments, and Recounts can be included in the framework for exploring generic complexity in RAs.

Fourth, although a relatively comprehensive elemental genre classification is proposed by Martin and Rose (2008), Rose (2012), and Rose and Martin (2012), these classifications are made from the perspective of disciplines or education. Therefore, the genre family of stories and histories may cause overlap with elemental genres in other genre families. In the current study, the genre family of Recounts is proposed for encapsulating all the elemental genres related to depicting, including all the elemental genres in "stories", biographical recounts and historical recounts in "histories", procedural recounts, and procedures.

To avoid confusion in the analysis and after summarizing the major elemental genres in the studies mentioned above, this study presents a list of twenty-four types of elemental genres in ERAs with five genre families. The social purposes and typical stages of these elemental genres are illustrated in the Table. 3.1. This list paves the way for the analysis of genres but is subject to adaptation in real operation. In other words, new elemental genres which are not included in the list can be discovered in ERAs.

Table 3.1 Summary of Elemental genres in ERAs

Genre family	Elemental genres	Social purpose	Stages
Reports	Descriptive report	to classify a phenomenon and then describe its attributes or properties	Classification ^Description
	Classifying report	to classify and describe types of phenomena	Classification system ^Types
	Compositional report	to describe the parts of an entity	Classification of entity^ Components
Explanations	Sequential explanation	to explain causes and effect in sequences	Phenomenon identification^ Explanation sequence
	Factorial explanation	to explain numerous causes	Phenomenon identification^ Factor [1-n]
	Consequential explanation	to explain numerous effects	Phenomenon identification^ Effects [1-n]
	Conditional explanation	to explain the effects by various conditions	Phenomenon identification^ Explanation sequence
	Theoretical explanation	to explain theoretical principles/or counterintuitive events	Phenomenon identification/ statement of theory^ Elaboration [1-n]
	Exploration	to account for events with two or more viable explanations	Issue^Explanation1^Explanation [2-n]
Arguments	Exposition	to persuade the reader to accept a point of view	Thesis^ Arguments 1-n ^ Reinforcement of thesis
	Discussion	to discuss two or more points of view, among which, one particular point of view is accepted	Issue^ Sides^ Resolution
	Challenge	to demolish an established position	Issue ^ Rebuttal

(continued)

Genre family	Elemental genres	Social purpose	Stages
Recounts	Personal Recount	to record a series of events within a single episode of one's life	Orientation^ Record ^ Reorientation
	Anecdote	to share an emotional reaction	Orientation^ Remarkable Event^ Reaction
	Exemplum	to share a moral judgment	Orientation^ Incident ^Interpretation
	Observation	to share a personal response to things or events	Event Description ^ Comment
	Narrative	to narrate how the protagonists resolve a complication in their lives	Complication^ Evaluation ^ Resolution
	Autobiographical recount	to account for events in a life	Orientation^ Record
	Biographical recount	to account for stages in a life	Orientation ^ Record
	Historical recount	to account for stages in episode time	Background ^ Record
	Procedural recount (including experiment reports and research articles)	to recount in order and with accuracy the aim, steps, results, and conclusion of scientific activity	Introduction ^Method ^Result/ Investigation ^Discussion/ conclusion
Text responses	Review	to describe and evaluate products	Context ^Description^ Evaluation
	Interpretation	to describe and evaluate the message of the text	Evaluation (of the text and its message) ^Synopsis (that selects certain elements of the text to illustrate the message) ^Reaffirmation (of the evaluation)
	Critical response	to challenge the message of a text	Evaluation^Deconstruction ^Challenge

Note: This table is based on the previous studies on the classification of elemental genres (Hao, 2020; Martin&Rose 2008; Rose 2012; Rose&Martin, 2012; Veel, 1997; Zhang&Pramoolsook, 2019; Lai&Wang, 2018)

This table shows that twenty-four elemental genres are grouped into five genre families, which are illustrated in the left column of the table. Furthermore, each elemental genre is explicated by social purposes and main stages, which are shown in the third and fourth columns of the table.

According to Martin and Rose (2008:141), two complementary sets of linguistic resources are employed by Reports and Explanations for construing entities in terms of their description, classification, and composition on the one hand, and hand activities in terms of a sequence of cause and effect on the other.

As can be seen in Table 3.1, the genre family of Reports can be divided into three elemental genres—descriptive reports, classifying reports, and compositional reports (Martin&Rose, 2008). The genre family of Explanations functions to explain how processes happen. Combining Martin and Rose's (2008:150-163) and Veel's (1997:171) classification of Explanations, the present study includes six elemental genres of Explanations: sequential explanations, factorial explanations, consequential explanations, conditional explanations, theoretical explanations, and explorations.

According to Veel (1997), Martin and Rose (2008), Rose (2012:212), and Rose and Martin (2012:130), the Arguments genre family of the current project includes expositions, discussions, and challenges. Expositions are designed to persuade the reader to accept a point of view (Rose&Martin, 2012:130), and the arguments are organized around a single position. Discussions state more than one position explicitly and challenges are used to demolish an established point of view (Martin&Rose, 2008:122).

In addition, the genre family of Recounts in the current study includes personal recounts, anecdotes, exemplum, observations, narratives, biographical recounts, historical recounts, and procedural recounts. These subtypes are characterized by their own special schematic structures, as shown in Table 3.1.

In the present project, the research article is considered as a macrogenre, and therefore it will not be annotated as a procedural recount. The schematic structure is used as a macro segmentation, i.e., Introduction, Literature Review, Methods, Results, Discussion, and Conclusion are used as the guidance of global stages of ERAs. With the guidance of titles and content, these stages are segmented firstly in the ERAs of physics, linguistics, and literary studies. Then, the elemental genres in each global stage of ERAs are identified.

Furthermore, the genre family of Text responses includes reviews, interpretations, and critical responses (Martin&Rose, 2008; Rose, 2012). Reviews are used for describing and evaluating products (Rose, 2012:220), but interpretations are used for responding to the cultural values in the text (Rothery, 1994:156). Critical responses are employed to challenge the message of a text (Rose, 2012:221).

3.3.2 Around genre: genre combining strategies

Besides the identification of elemental genres and the description of the elemental genre deployments within each stage of ERAs, the genre combining strategy is another important dimension of analysis in this book. Briefly speaking, genre combining strategies include genre expansion, genre projection, and genre embedding.

Martin (1994, 1995) proposes a framework for analyzing genre expansion and projection. As far as genre expansion is concerned, elaboration means that the text which instantiates one elemental genre re-interprets the texts before it (Martin, 1994/2012:94) while in extension, one text which instantiates one elemental genre is extended through addition or alternation (Martin, 1995:34). Enhancement means that texts which instantiate one elemental genre embellish another text by instantiating the same or another elemental genre with circumstantial features of time, place, cause, or condition (Martin, 1994/2012:98).

Projection of locution indicates that one text that instantiates an elemental genre is quoted by another text but projection of ideas means that the text which instantiates an elemental genre projects a diagram in the same text (Martin, 1994/2012:91-92).

For Martin (1994/2012:99), the texts involved in projected locutions, elaboration, and extension are of relatively equal relationship with the text initiating them, whereas texts in projected ideas and enhancements are more dependent on the text that leads them.

Besides genre expansion and genre projection, genre embedding is also a strategy that is utilized in the formation of macrogenres. Genre embedding refers to the fact that one multivariate stage of an elemental genre is replaced by another elemental genre (Martin, 1994/2012:102). For example, the stage deployment of the genre of solicitation is Involvement ^ Product ^ Appeal. When the stage of Involvement is replaced by [[news story]], with the schematic structure of Lead ^ Background, then a news story is embedded in the solicitation (Martin,1995:25).

3.3.3 Underlying genre: field

The previous two sections focus on the two major analytical dimensions of the current study—elemental genres and genre combining strategies. In the identification of these elemental genres and semogenetic strategies, a perspective from below is adopted. Through realization and instantiation, genre is realized at the register stratum, then at the discourse semantics stratum, and further down at the lexicogrammar stratum, making themselves instantiated in texts. This section will focus on one of the register variables–field. This variable is chosen because field plays an important role in the identification of stages of genres or shifts from one sub-genre to the next in the macrogenre (Hood, 2010:119). Moreover, a recent systemic framework for analyzing field proposed by Doran and Martin (2021) offers some evidence that some fields features are generic indexes.

In this book, the field perspective is taken as the focus point for revealing the connection between field resources and genre. According to Halliday and Hasan (1985:12), the field of discourse is a feature of context of situation and denotes what is happening. Martin (1992:536-537) defines field as a series of activity sequences focusing on some global institutional purposes and adopts Barthes's (1977:101) definition of sequence, which is a logical succession of nuclei bound by a relation of solidarity. For Martin (1992:540), the participants involved in sequences are arranged into taxonomies of composition and superordination.

Doran and Martin (2021) regard field as a resource not just for constructing items①, activities, and properties, but also a resource for reconstruing meanings and thus develop a network of fields based on interdependency, field perspective, and property. The field perspective is divided into dynamic and static aspects, which is shown in Figure 3.3.

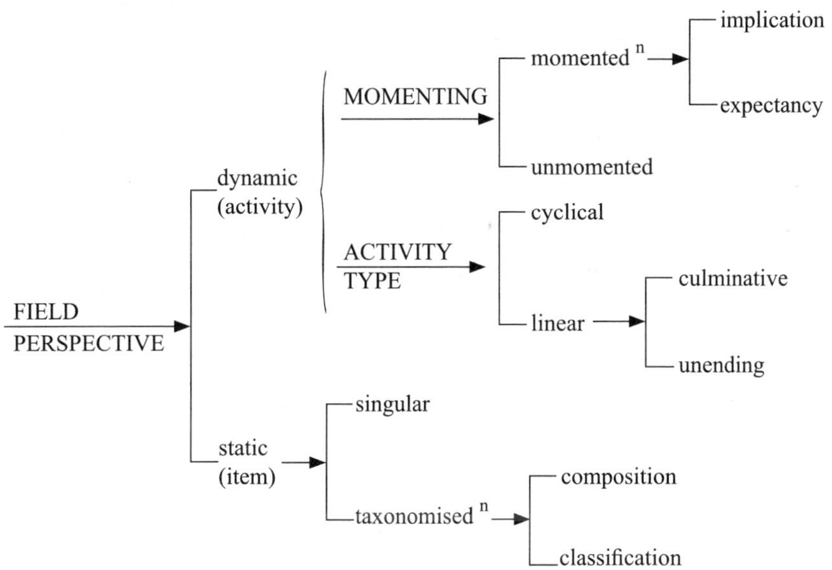

Figure 3.3 Dynamic and static perspectives on field (Doran&Martin, 2021:115)

As illustrated by Figure 3.3, field is basically viewed from static and dynamic perspectives. The static orientation views phenomena as a single item or items organized into particular taxonomies, which can be further divided into classification and composition. Classification views relations between items in

① For avoiding terminological confusion, items are used for indicating resources at the register stratum, whereas entity is a term for indicating resources at the discourse semantics stratum.

terms of types and sub-types and composition interprets part-whole relations among items (Doran&Martin, 2021:108).

Dynamically, field identifies phenomena in terms of activities, which involve change that is oriented to some purposes (Doran&Martin, 2021:109). As shown in Figure 3.3, activities in a field can be divided into momented or unmomented, depending on whether activities unfold with a series of activities, and there are two types of momented activities: implication and expectancy. Implication activities are a set of activities where one activity necessitates another (Doran&Martin, 2021:110). Expectancy activities imply that the series of activities can be interrupted or go against what is expected (Doran&Martin, 2021:113).

As for genre identification, according to Doran and Martin (2021:111-112), implication activities are found in scientific explanations where events tend to be described in terms of causal or conditional relations. However, activities with expectancy relations tend to be found in texts instantiated experimental procedures, procedural recounts or protocols, or stories of scientific discoveries (cf. Hood, 2010; Hao, 2015, 2020). Besides, story genres also employ momented activities with expectancy relations for establishing the main complication of the story (cf. Martin&Rose, 2008).

3.3.4 Below genre: discourse semantics

As seen from the discussion above, items and activities are of particular importance in identifying elemental genres. Following the principle of realization, activities, and items are realized by sequences, figures, and entities at the discourse semantics stratum. Hao (2021:143) summarizes the choices across genre, field, discourse semantics, and lexicogrammar and points out that items at the field stratum are realized by entities at the discourse semantics stratum, which are realized by nominal groups at the lexicogrammar stratum.

Considering the genre of Reports, items of composition and classification are realized by thing entities at the discourse semantics stratum. Implication activities that are typical in scientific explanations are realized by implication sequences, where figures form sequential cause-and-effect relations (Wignell et al., 1992:157, cited in Rose, 1997:48).

In short, for exploring elemental genre deployments and the genre combining strategies, schematic structures and resources across strata of language are analyzed.

3.3.5 Disciplinarity

The present project takes the perspectives of language and context, and disciplinarity in exploring the generic complexity in ERAs of physics, linguistics, and literary studies.

To deal with the fourth research question presented at the beginning of this chapter, the notion of disciplinarity is discussed and then followed by an elaboration of disciplinarity in terms of knowledge and knower structure proposed by Maton (2007, 2009, 2014).

Disciplinarity can either refer to the nature of a discipline (Muller, 2011:13) or signify interdisciplinarity (Chandler, 2009:738). However, Christie and Maton (2011:7) hold that disciplinarity and interdisciplinarity are two sides of the same coin, two dimensions of knowledge formations.

Following Christie and Maton (2011:2-4), the present study approaches disciplinarity as a phenomenon with two characteristics: the organization of knowledge and the organization of intellectual and educational practices for knowledge creation, teaching, and learning.

In terms of the organization of knowledge, Bernstein (1996,1999) makes a distinction between horizontal and vertical discourses, and within vertical discourse, there are hierarchical and horizontal knowledge structures. For Bernstein (1999:157-162), a horizontal discourse tends to be oral, local, context-dependent and specific, while a vertical discourse is a hierarchically-organized and systematically-principled structure. Science discourses are typical examples of vertical discourses with hierarchical structures (Bernstein,

1999:161-162). Bernstein (1999:157, 162) adds that a vertical discourse can also take the form of "a horizontal knowledge structure", which can be found in social sciences and the humanities.

Maton (2000, 2007, 2009, 2014) takes the concept of knowledge structures a step further by focusing on knower structure. According to Maton (2007:91), the humanities demonstrate a hierarchical knower structure where knowers are integrated hierarchically in the construction of an ideal knower and knowledge claims are predicated on attributes of knowers. Nevertheless, science is characterized as a horizontal knower structure, in which the social characters of the scientist are considered irrelevant to their scientific outlooks (Maton, 2007:92).

Maton (2000, 2009, 2014) uses the concept of specialization codes to refer to these principles for describing knowledge-knower structures. In Maton's (2000:154, 2014:69-75) model, specialization codes are approached through the epistemic relation and the social relation. The former is the relation between educational knowledge and its proclaimed object of study, whereas the latter is the relation between educational knowledge and its author or subject. According to Hood (2011:108), disciplines can be differentiated in terms of the relative strength or weakness of their epistemic relation and their social relation.

All things considered, the aim of this monograph is to examine the differences and similarities in elemental genre deployments and genre combining strategies in ERAs of physics, linguistics, and literary studies through the above-mentioned knowledge-knower structure and basic components of disciplinarity.

3.4 Data and methodology

On account of the theoretical and analytical framework for exploring the generic complexity of ERAs, this book adopts a textual analysis approach. First, a corpus of randomly-selected ERAs is established, with 50 ERAs from each discipline. Then, a macro generic stage identification is conducted to obtain the refined corpus of ERAs. This refined corpus is further coded by the macro generic stage, elemental genre deployments, and genre combining strategies.

This section elaborates on the data and methodology from three aspects: data collection, data coding, and data analysis.

3.4.1 Data collection

The corpus of the present study is constructed in three steps, including selection of disciplines, choices of journals, and macro generic stage segmenting.

As mentioned above, the current study focuses on the disciplines of physics, linguistics, and literary studies. The reasons for the selection of the disciplines are presented as follows.

First, based on Bernstein's (1996, 1999) and Martin et al.'s (2011) ideas of knowledge structure, which have been mentioned in Chapter 1, the three disciplines lie at different positions of the discipline continuum, with physics and literary study at the two poles and linguistics in the middle. Second, physics is considered fundamental in science disciplines (Young&Freedman, 2012:1). The principles of physics lay the basis for understanding other disciplines, such as chemistry, and engineering (Zhao, 2012:7). Third, linguistics is a discipline that makes systematic exploration on languages, describing and formulating the working mechanism of languages (Yang, 2005:27). In addition, based on the survey of related studies on ERAs, it is noticed that linguistic studies on ERAs in the field of literature are relatively scarce. However, literary studies is an important discipline in the humanities (Zhao et al., 2019:18). Therefore, it is necessary to conduct comparative research between ERAs of literary studies and the other two disciplines.

In terms of the selection of academic journals, for the ERAs in physics and linguistics, ten top-tier SCI or SSCI-indexed journals are selected. For the ERAs in the domain of literary studies, combining the studies of Tanko (2017), Zhao et al. (2019), and the journal list of ERAs indexed by A&HCI with the title of literary theory and criticism, the ten renowned journals of literary studies are chosen. The list of journals for this study is shown in Table 3.2.

Table 3.2 List of journals for the current study

	Physics	Linguistics	Literary Studies
1	*Applied Physics Reviews*	*Applied Linguistics*	*PMLA*
2	*Physical Review X*	*Journal of Memory and Language*	*Narrative*
3	*Physical Review D*	*Language Teaching*	*Neohelicon*
4	*Physical Review Applied*	*Modern Language Journal*	*American Literatrue*
5	*New Journal of Physics*	*Language Learning*	*New Literary History*
6	*Physics of Fluids*	*Journal of Second Language Writing*	*Modern Fiction Studies*
7	*Soft Matter*	*English for Specific Purposes*	*Cambridge Journal of Postcolonial Literary Inquiry*
8	*Physical Review C*	*TESOL Quarterly*	*Ariel: A Review of International Literary Inquiry*
9	*Chaos*	*System*	*Shakespeare Quarterly*
10	*Physical Review A*	*Journal of English for Academic Purposes*	*Style*

As far as corpora are concerned, three sub-corpora are built by choosing one article from each journal published every year from 2016 to 2020. To be more specific, one article from the issue published in December is randomly chosen. Therefore, each sub-corpus contains 50 ERAs. The texts are numbered by "DisciplineYearNo." for further analysis and reference, e.g., Lin201901, Phys202001, and Lite201801.①

According to the section titles and content, the macro generic stages of these ERAs are identified and segmented. 35 ERAs are retained after excluding review articles or ERAs with macro generic stage embedding in the corpus of linguistics ERAs. 40 ERAs are retained after excluding review articles

① Lin is the abbreviation of linguistics. Phys is the abbreviation of physics. Lite is the abbreviation of literature.

or articles without section titles in the corpus of literature ERAs. To maintain the balance of the number of ERAs, 35 ERAs are chosen in each of the sub-corpora, thus, a refined corpus used for the analysis of elemental genres and genre combining strategies is established. UAM CorpusTool Version 6.2e (O'Donnell, 2022) is used for counting the total tokens and words of each sub-corpus.

Table 3.3 The overall tokens and words of the three sub-corpora

Discipline	Tokens	Words
Linguistics	44819 5	37071 2
Physics	29339 3	24354 2
Literary studies	38378 0	32900 2
Total	112536 8	94325 6

As shown in Table 3.3, the sub-corpus of linguistics ERAs contains 448195 tokens. While the sub-corpus of ERAs in literary studies is composed of 383780 tokens. The sub-corpus of ERAs in physics consists of 293393 tokens. The total capacity of the corpus amounts to 1 million tokens, which is suitable for carrying out the research (Xu, 2019:48). As for CRAs, 35 empirical studies published in 2023 are selected from three linguistics journals (Modern Foreign Languages, Foreign Languages in China, Foreign Languages Teaching and Research).

These RAs are converted from PDF. to text forms with the UTF-8 format tool. Tables and figures are removed. Formulas are replaced with the label "Formula". Then, the RAs are imported to UAM CorpusTool (Version 3.3w) (O'Donnell, 2021) for further annotating.

3.4.2 Data coding

The data coding process of this study proceeds in three steps.

Firstly, a pilot annotating study is conducted. Three ERAs in each sub-corpus are chosen as samples. The macro generic structure, elemental genre deployments, and elemental genre combining strategies are identified by two coders independently. The inter-rater reliability is calculated. In terms of the coding of macro generic stage, the two coders in linguistics, physics, and literature

ERAs achieve 88.24%, 100%, and 85.71% agreement respectively. Regarding the annotating of elemental genres, the agreement between the two coders in the above-mentioned three disciplines reaches 86.76%, 86.67%, and 91.67% respectively. Concerning elemental genre combining strategies, the percentages of the agreement in the three sub-corpora are 84.44%, 93.94%, and 92.21%. The disagreements are settled down through discussion until a consensus is reached.

Secondly, based on the pilot study, UAM CorpusTool is used for annotating macro generic structures and elemental genre deployments. As for the elemental genre combining strategies, the annotation is marked on the paper copy of the ERAs with the results being recorded by Excel.

Regarding the macro generic structure, the annotating scheme is shown in Figure 3.4. The majority of the macro generic stage types are named following the ERA section titles except for "argumentation", which is one of the macro generic stages of literature ERAs. This term is adopted for describing the macro generic structure of literature ERAs as "Introduction-Argumentation-Conclusion".

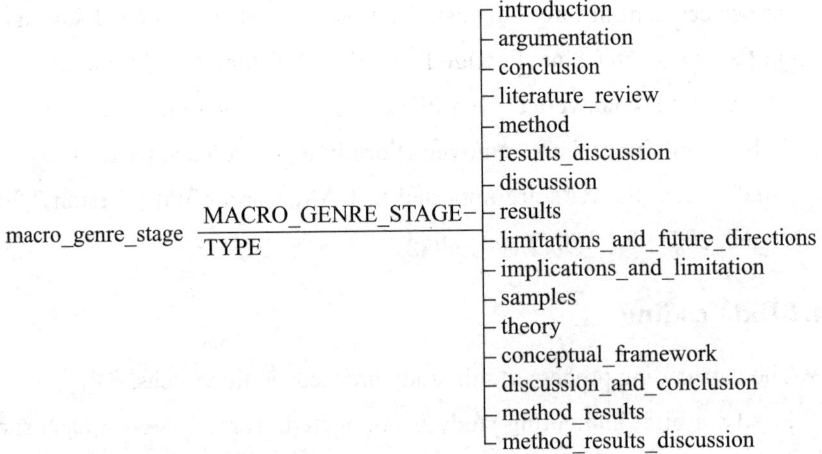

Figure 3.4 Annotating scheme of macro generic stage

As for the elemental genre deployments, the coding scheme is illustrated in Figure 3.5. Six new elemental genres (elucidations, exposition reviews, figure expositions, direct formula recounts, conditional formula recounts, and sequential formula recounts) are summarized through the observation of data. Besides, many embedding elemental genres are coded with dashes before and after the names of elemental genres.

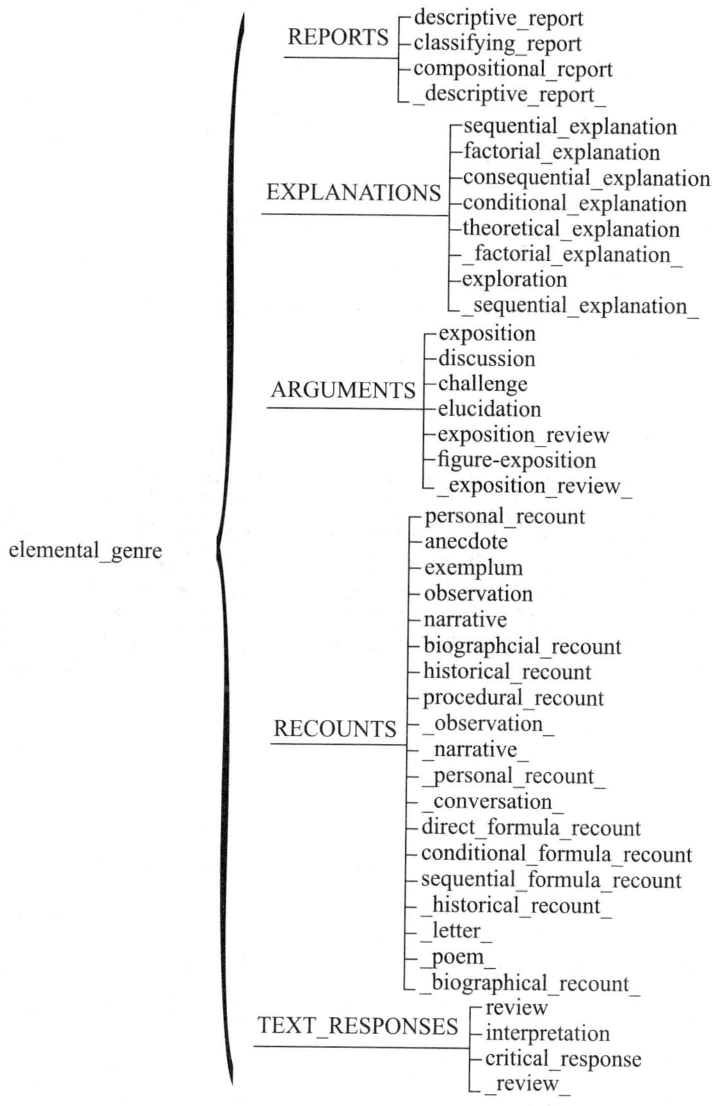

Figure 3.5 Annotating scheme of elemental genre deployments

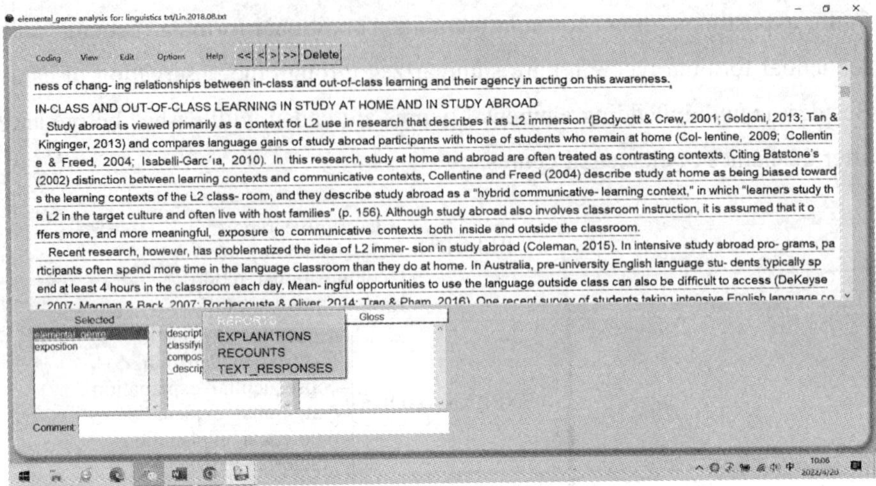

Figure 3.6 Sample of elemental genre coding operated by UAM CorpusTool: step 1

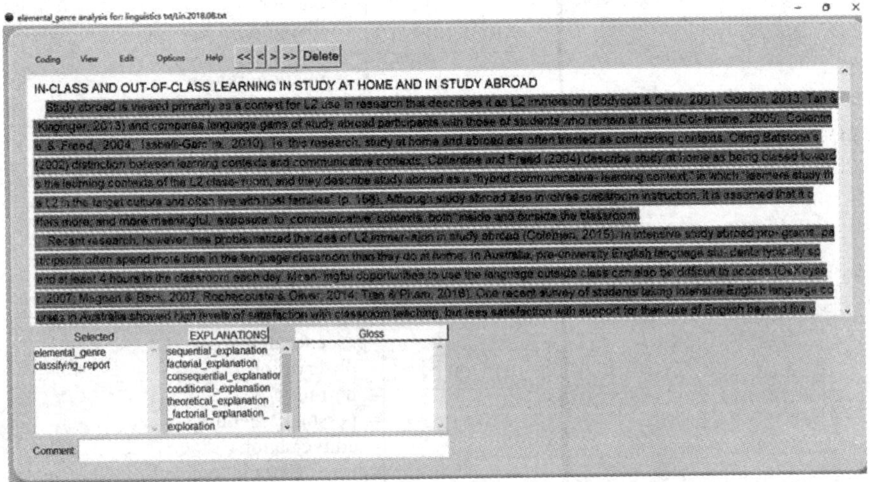

Figure 3.7 Sample of elemental genre coding operated by UAM CorpusTool: step 2

Figure 3.6 and Figure 3.7 illustrate the elemental genre annotation process. The text clips are selected and coded following the order of choosing the elemental genre family, which is shown in Figure 3.6, and selecting the elemental genre, which is illustrated in Figure 3.7.

Regarding the elemental genre combining strategies, the logico-semantic relation between two adjacent elemental genres in the same macro generic stage is marked as extension (+), elaboration (=), and enhancement (×).

3.4.3 Data analysis

Based on the data coding of the present study, the data analytical process unfolds in the following steps.

Firstly, the "statistics" function of UAM CorpusTool is utilized for calculating the overall elemental genre deployments in the sub-corpora of the ERAs of the three disciplines, the deployment of elemental genres across macro generic stages, and elemental genre deployments in each macro generic stage of ERAs. A series of one-way ANOVAs operated by IBM-SPSS (version 25.0) are operated for comparing the disciplinary impact on the normalized frequencies (per 1,000 tokens) of the various elemental genres in the ERAs of the three disciplines.

Secondly, based on the marking results of elemental genre combining strategies in Excel, the major elemental genre linking methods are discussed.

Thirdly, based on the results of elemental genre deployments, the field and discourse semantics resources of the distinctive elemental genre (i.e., the elemental genre which is significantly more frequently distributed in ERAs of one discipline than that in the other two disciplines) are analyzed. The field resources include activities and items. The discourse semantics resources involve sequences, figures, and entities.

3.5 Chapter summary

This chapter proposes a theoretical framework for analyzing generic complexity in RAs of physics, linguistics, and literary studies.

The theoretical framework unfolds with a reasonable theoretical motivation and a descriptive basis. This book is motivated by the essential concepts and principles such as context, genre, logico-semantic relation, stratification, realization, and instantiation, all of which constitute the rationale for the main descriptive dimensions of the present project.

In terms of the descriptive foundation, this study approaches generic complexity in ERAs mainly by exploring elemental genres and semogenetic strategies. The identification of elemental genres is completed through a multi-stratal framework by examining resources at the register and discourse semantics strata. Furthermore, the disciplinary features of the similarities and differences in elemental genre deployments and genre combining strategies are discussed.

Therefore, in Chapters 4 to 7, the theoretical framework is applied to the analysis of generic complexity in ERAs in physics, linguistics, and literary studies. Chapter 4 focuses on depicting the elemental genre deployments in each stage of these ERAs and Chapter 5 centers on the investigation of genre combining strategies. Chapter 6 describes the field and discourse semantics resources of characteristic elemental genres in the ERAs. Chapter 7 compares the similarities and differences in elemental genre deployments between linguistics ERAs and CRAs.

Chapter 4 Elemental Genre Deployments

In order to tackle the first and the second research questions, this chapter is devoted to analyzing the macro generic structures and elemental genre deployments of ERAs in the three sub-corpora. Section 4.1 focuses on demarcating the macro generic structures of ERAs, which paves the way for the detailed identification of elemental genres in each macro generic stage. Macro generic structure is referred to in this study as the generic stages (Martin&Rose, 2008) or generic structures (Hasan, 1985) in ERAs, such as Introduction, Literature review, Methods, Results, Discussion, and Conclusion. Section 4.2 analyzes the overall genre deployments of ERAs in the three disciplines. Section 4.3 compares genre deployments in the same generic stage across ERAs of the three disciplines. Section 4.4 summarizes the main findings of the current chapter.

4.1 Macro generic stages of ERAs

Before analyzing the elemental genre deployments in ERAs, it is necessary to demarcate the ERAs in terms of macro generic stages. In this subsection, some conceptual preliminaries for scrutinizing major ERA types are first explicated, followed by the identification of major ERA types, the macro generic structures, and the major generic stages of ERAs.

4.1.1 Conceptual preliminaries

Based on the journal lists mentioned in Chapter 3, altogether 150 ERAs are randomly collected from these SSCI, SCI, or A&HCI indexed journals. The following introduces article classification, identifying criteria for analyzing the macro generic structures, and variants of each macro generic stage for eliminating unqualified ERAs in the three sub-corpora, thus obtaining refined sub-corpora for in-depth analysis of elemental genre deployments.

First of all, there are two ways to classify research articles. Weissberg and Bucker (1990) classify ERAs into empirical, theoretical, and review ERAs. For Weissberg and Bucker (1990), empirical ERAs record the results of experiments or observations and for Lester&Lester (2006), theoretical ERAs trace the progress of theories. Review ERAs focus on a review of literature related to a topic or a literary work (cf. Lin&Evans, 2012). Another classification is proposed by Yang and Allison (2004), who divide ERAs into primary and secondary ERAs. According to Yang and Allison (2004), primary ERAs deal with original data from experiments, case studies, surveys, and other forms of descriptive and qualitative research, while secondary ERAs review and summarize research trends. Synthesizing Lin and Evans' (2012) and Yang and Allison's (2004) studies, this monograph subsumes empirical ERAs into primary ERAs, and considers theoretical and review ERAs as secondary ones.

The second conceptual preliminary of the current study is the main criteria for identifying macro generic structures of ERAs, which can be divided into two types. The first criterion is related to the section headings of the ERAs, which, according to Yang and Allison (2004), are categorized into conventional section headings, varied section headings, and content section headings. Among these categories of headings, conventional section headings are of direct importance for macro generic stage demarcation since they demonstrate Introduction, Literature review, Methods, Results, Discussion, and Conclusion directly through the lexicogrammar of section headings. Varied section headings are variants of conventional section headings. Following Swales (2004) and Lin and Evans (2012), *The Study* and *Research Questions* are variants of the section headings in the generic stage of Methods. When conventional section headings and variant section headings are absent, it is through content headings that the macro generic stage is classified, which often happens in the analysis of ERAs of literary studies.

In addition to demarcating macro generic stages through headings, previous studies on generic patterns can also offer guidance for the current study. For instance, Lin and Evans (2012) find that the most frequent generic stage structure of empirical ERAs is ILM[RD]C[①]. Yang and Allison (2004) summarize the generic structure of secondary ERAs as Introduction-Argumentation-Conclusion, which can become a direct reference for stage demarcation of ERAs in literary studies.

The third conceptual preliminary for macro generic stage identification is the variants of the generic stage. In real operation, besides Introduction, Literature Review, Methods, Results, Discussion, and Conclusion, there are also conventional section headings such as *Theoretical Framework.* Moreover, under the section Methods, there are other variants such as *Experiment, Experimental setup, Numerical simulation*, etc.

After the three conceptual preliminaries of the current study are introduced, every ERA in the three sub-corpora is identified in terms of macro generic structures. Firstly, the ERAs are demarcated according to obvious section headings and variants of section titles. If these section headings are not found in the ERAs, then the segmentation of macro generic stages is decided by the content of the ERAs. The following three parts present the results of the analysis in the three sub-corpora, with the linguistics ERAs being first presented, followed by the physics ERAs, which share many similarities with the empirical ERAs in linguistics. Finally, the macro generic stages of the literature ERAs are summarized.

① I=Introduction; L=Literature review; M=Methods; [RD]=merged section of Results and Discussion; C=Conclusion

4.1.2 Major ERA types

Regarding the ERA types in linguistics sub-corpus, although empirical ERAs are predominant in the selected journals, a close analysis of these ERAs leads to the classification of ERAs in linguistics corpus into two categories.

The first category is empirical ERAs, which can be characterized by explicit conventional headings, such as Introduction, Methods, Results, Discussion, and Conclusion. The second category is review ERAs, which shows a distinctive journal character. Four out of the five review ERAs are from the journal *Language Teaching*, and follow the generic structure of Introduction-Argumentation-Conclusion.

Another feature of the ERAs is the generic structure embedding, which refers to other generic stages embedded in one generic stage. There are nine ERAs in the corpus that use generic structure embedding and five of them are from the *Journal of Memory and Language*. For instance, the generic structure of Lin 201802 is I E<M R D> E<M R D> E < M R D> D C[①]. In this ERA, Methods, Results and Discussion are embedded in the Experiment section. Thus, the whole ERA resembles a report of three experiments.

In terms of the ERA types in the physics corpus, according to Lin and Evans (2012), the explicit way for categorizing ERAs into empirical ERAs is the section of Methods, which is illustrated by the section titles such as *Experiment*, *The current study*, *Data*, and *Research design*. Following this criterion, the majority of ERAs in physics belong to empirical ERAs. However, two ERAs in the physics corpus do not contain Methods. Therefore, they are excluded from further analysis of elemental genre deployments.

Among the 50 articles in the corpus of literary studies, one article (Lite 202008) is a report on an interview and another (Lite 201807) is an introduction to a special issue. The remaining ERAs neither unfold as empirical ERAs, with

① I=Introduction; E=Experiment; M=Methods, R=Results; D=Discussion; C=Conclusion; < >=Genre embedding an overt Methods section as the screening character (cf. Lin&Evans, 2012) nor review the development process of theories as the review ERA does (cf. Lester&Lester, 2006).

Based on their content, literature ERAs are basically an "opinion-stating" type of ERA, which takes the generic pattern proposed by Yang and Allison (2004) in their discussion for review ERAs, viz. Introduction-Argumentation-Conclusion. The next sub-section further explicates the variants based on this IAC pattern.

4.1.3 Macro generic structures of ERAs

This sub-section summarizes the sequences of the macro generic stage of ERAs in the three disciplines. Table 4.1 encapsulates the macro generic structures of each ERA in the three sub-corpora with numbers and percentages.

Table 4.1 Macro generic structures in ERAs of the three disciplines

Linguistics ERAs	N	P	Physics ERAs	N	P	Literature ERAs	N	P
ILMRDC	16	32%	IM[RD]C	14	28%	(I)A	25	50%
Generic structure embedding	9	18%	IMRDC	7	14%	NONE	10	20%
IADC	5	10%	IMRC	5	10%	IAC	4	8%
ILM[RD]C	5	10%	ILMC	3	6%	(I)AC	3	6%
IMRDC	5	10%	IRCM	3	6%	IA	3	6%
IMR[DC]	3	6%	ITMRC	3	6%	A	2	4%
IM[RD]C	2	4%	IMDC	2	4%	(I)Ca<ET>Ca<D>	1	2%
ILTf Ap	1	2%	ITDC	2	4%	(I)C	1	2%
ILM[RDC]	1	2%	ILMRC	1	2%	AC	1	2%
ILMRD	1	2%	ILMRD	1	2%			
ILMD	1	2%	ILMRDC	1	2%			
IMRC	1	2%	ITM[RD]C	1	2%			
			I[MR][DC]	1	2%			
			I[MRD]C	1	2%			
			IMTC	1	2%			
			I[RD]CM	1	2%			
			ITMC	1	2%			
			I[TM]C	1	2%			
			ITD	1	2%			

Note: I=Introduction; A=Argumentation; D=Discussion; C=Conclusion; L=Literature review; M=Methods; [DC]=merged section of Discussion and Conclusion; [RD]=merged section of Results and Discussion; Tf=Theoretical framework; Ap=Application; [RDC]=merged section of Results, Discussion, and Conclusion; T=Theory; [MR]=merged section of Methods and Results; [MRD]=merged section of Methods, Results, and Discussion; [TM]=merged section of Theory and Methods; (I)= Introduction inferred from content; Ca=Case studies; E=Experiment; NONE=No section headings; N=number; P=percentage

In terms of the linguistics ERAs, there are three points worthy of noting. First, the most frequent sequence of the macro generic stages is ILMRDC (32%), followed by generic structure embedding (18%), which shows distinctive journal characters. The other three generic configurations possess similar percentages, viz., IADC[①], ILM[RD]C, and IMRDC, with each taking up 10% of the whole corpus respectively. IMR[DC] takes 6%, and IM[RD]C takes 4%. Other generic patterns occur only once in the corpus.

These findings correspond to the results of Yang and Allison's (2004) exploration of generic patterns of ERAs of applied linguistics, who discover that Swales' (1990) IMRD framework cannot be applied to ERAs of applied linguistics. Furthermore, these findings differ from Lin and Evans' (2012) study on the generic structure of empirical ERAs, which find that the most frequent generic structure is ILM[RD]C in empirical ERAs.

Second, the exploration of the macro generic stage of ERAs shows that L, R, D, C are important independent sections in contemporary ERAs in linguistics. However, as reviewed in Chapter 2, Literature review parts are seldom explored. The distinctive characteristics of citations and reporting verbs are discussed in the section Introduction, rather than in an independent section of Literature review (Lin&Evans, 2012).

Third, ILMRDC seems to possess a larger proportion in the current corpus. However, the remaining types of generic patterns take on similar distribution, which suggests the multiple choices ERA writers employ to organize their articles within the basic framework of IMRD.

As for the generic patterns of the ERAs in physics, three key points deserve noting. Firstly, the most frequent macro generic structure is IM[RD]C (14 cases), followed by IMRDC (7 cases). IMRC appears five times. ILMC and IRCM occur three times respectively. ITMRC, and IMDC, ITDC each appears twice. The remaining generic patterns such as ILMRC, ILMRD, ILMRDC,

① A=Argumentation

ITM[RD]C, I[MR][DC], I[MRD]C, IMTC, I[RD]CM, ITMC, ITMC, I[TM]C, ITD occur only once in the corpus.

Secondly, T, which represents the theoretical model, shows the characteristics of the physics corpus. T is abbreviated from the conventional section headings. In other words, the writers of physics ERAs emphasize the theoretical basis of their studies.

Thirdly, there are altogether 19 types of macro generic patterns in the ERAs of physics, which show a larger diversity compared with the ERAs of linguistics. Furthermore, the position of M can appear at the end of ERA, which supports Cargill and O'Connor's (2009) findings that the IRDM pattern is employed in ERAs for highlighting the new contributions while downgrading the significance of M.

Regarding the macro generic stages of the literature ERAs, it can be divided into two major types. One type of ERA in literary studies does not contain any section headings. Ten ERAs in the literature corpus belong to this type. The authors of the other type of the literature ERAs divide the article with at least one content heading. 40 cases of literature ERAs display content headings. The macro generic patterns of those ERAs are depicted as follows.

(I)A is the most frequent generic pattern in the ERAs of literary studies. 25 (50%) ERAs employ this kind of macro generic structure. (I) indicates that no explicit conventional heading stands at the beginning of the ERAs. However, inferring from the content between the beginning of the articles and the first content headings, it is discovered that this part serves the function of the Introduction. A is the abbreviation of Argumentation, which is not directly realized with the section headings but inferred from the content of the ERAs.

IAC occurs four times (8%) in the corpus with clearly-illustrated titles of introduction and conclusion. (I)AC, which is demonstrated by a clear conventional heading of conclusion, appears three times (6%). IA, which shows the ERA does not have distinctive headings of conclusion occurs three times

(6%). A, which means the whole ERA only has content headings showing the argumentation part, appears twice (4%). (I)C and AC occur only once (2%) in the corpus. It is worth noting that Lite 201910 uses a generic pattern like (I) Ca<E T> Ca<D>[1], which resembles the schematic structure of linguistics ERAs. The whole ERA is unfolded by the reporting of two case studies. In one case study, *Experiment* (E) and *Theoretical perspective* (T) are embedded.

Comparing the generic structure of the ERAs of the three disciplines, there are several similarities and differences which are worthy of mentioning.

Regarding similarities, the physics ERAs and the linguistics ERAs share six types of macro generic structure, such as ILMRDC, IM[RD]C, IMRDC, IMRC, ILMRD, and ILMRDC.

As for differences, the ERAs of the three disciplines differ in their most frequent macro generic structure. The linguistics ERAs favor the macro generic structure of ILMRDC. The physics ERAs prefer IM[RD]C and the literature ERAs tend to use the macro generic pattern of (I)A.

Furthermore, the linguistics ERAs show a diversity of variants in the macro generic stage of Conclusion, with section titles being *Implication* or *Limitation*. The physics ERAs possess many variants in Methods, with the section titles of *Experiment*, *Numerical Simulation,* and so on. Besides, Theoretical models are frequently highlighted in the physics ERAs.

4.1.4 Major generic stages of ERAs

After identifying the ERA types and macro generic structure of ERAs of the three disciplines, this sub-section focuses on individual generic stages in the ERAs of each discipline. Table 4.2 shows the number and percentage of each generic stage in the three sub-corpora of ERAs. For instance, 50 articles in the original sub-corpus of linguistics contain an Introduction section. Thus, N in Table 4.2 of the Linguistics ERAs is 50 while P is 100% (50/50).

---

[1] Ca=case study

Table 4.2 Individual macro generic stages in ERAs of the three disciplines

Linguistics ERAs	N	P	Physics ERAs	N	P	Literature ERAs	N	P
I	50	100%	I	50	100%	I	7	14%
D	33	66%	M	48	96%	(I)	30	60%
C	27	54%	C	47	94%	A	39	78%
M	26	52%	R	21	42%	C	9	18%
L	25	50%	[RD]	17	34%			
R	20	40%	D	15	30%			
			T	10	20%			
			L	6	12%			

Note: I=Introduction; D=Discussion; C=Conclusion; M=Methods; L=Literature review; R=Results; [RD]=merged section of Results and Discussion; T=Theory; (I)=Introduction inferred from content; N=Number; P=Percentage

With the guidance of the conventional section headings and the content of ERAs, the major generic stages of ERAs in linguistics are identified. As illustrated in the first three columns in Table 4.2, I (100%) is the most frequent individual macro generic stage of linguistics ERAs, followed by D (66%). C, M, and L occur in 54%, 52%, and 50% of the corpus. R (40%) is the least frequent section in the corpus.

Introduction occurs in every ERA in the linguistics corpus. However, a sizable number (11, 22%) of ERAs in linguistics do not have conventional section headings. Inferring from the content headings, those unlabelled ERA openings are identified as I. Yang and Allison (2004) attribute the omission of conventional section headings to the specific structural requirement of the APA style.

Discussion occurs in 66% of the linguistics ERAs. It is worth noting that D takes on few variants, with only D, [D<C>], and [DC] being found in the corpus. The majority of ERA writers employ D (29 cases). [DC] indicates the merging of Discussion and Conclusion in the same section of ERAs. There are only three cases of [DC] in the corpus. [D<C>] refers to the Conclusion embedded in the Discussion section. This type of discussion appears only once in the ERAs.

Conclusion is the section of linguistics ERAs which presents many variants, including [CImF] (1), [CF] (1), [FC] (1), [LimF]+C (2), [LimFIm]+C (1), [LimImC] (1), C (12), C+LimF (1), IM+Fr (1), Im+C (1), [LimF]+[CIm] (1), [LimF]+C (2), Lim (1), and Recall+C (1)①. The findings in the ERAs indicate that the generic stage of conclusion takes on various variants and is usually divided into two sections. Furthermore, the conclusion part often includes limitations, implications, and future directions.

The generic stage of Methods occurs in 52% (26) of the linguistics ERAs in different variants. Adhering to the proposition raised by Swales (2004:219), *The current study* belongs to the Methods section. Therefore, the conventional titles include S (the current study), M (methods), Da (data analysis), Rc (research context), Rq (research question), and Sd (the study design). The findings in the corpus are presented as follows: [DaM] (1), [SM] (1), M (7), Rq+M (3), S (8), [SMDa] (1), Sd (1), and M-embedding (4). It is found that the traditional conventional M or S still accounts for the majority of the Methods section, with the two amounting to 57% of the Methods.

Literature review appears in 50% of the ERAs in the corpus, with the form of B (5), (L) (10), L (8), TpL (1), and Cf (1)②.

The Results section occurs in 40% (20) of the corpus, with the variants of R(results), F(findings), [FA] (findings and analysis), [FD] (findings and discussion), and [RD] (results and discussion). Among these variants, R or F appears 13 times, followed by [RD] with 4 times. [FA] and [FD] occur twice and once respectively.

An exploration of the physics sub-corpus reveals that I (50, 100%) appears

① C=Conclusion; F=Future direction; Lim=Limitation; Im=Implication; Fr=Future research

② B=Background; TpL= Theoretical perspective and literature review; Cf=Conceptual framework in every ERA, followed by M (48, 96%). C (47, 94%), R (21, 42%), [RD] (17, 34%), D (15, 30%), T (10, 20%), and L (6, 12%) are other macro generic stages found in the physics ERAs.

Similar to the situation of the ERAs in linguistics, all ERAs of physics contain the Introduction part. Furthermore, 49 cases in the corpus demonstrate an introduction with obvious conventional section headings. One case (Phys 201910) uses content section headings at the beginning of the ERAs.

Closely following I, M is used in 96% of the physics ERAs. The distribution and placement of M are summarized into three aspects. Firstly, as regards the deployment of M, nine ERAs in the corpus employ more than one individual section for illustrating methodology, such as M+E (experiment), M+SE (simulated events), NM (numerical method) +EM (experimental method), EM+[PfNm] (problem definition and numerical methodology) +An (data analysis), ST (setups)+monitoring, E+DA (data analysis), M+Si (simulation)+An, PS (problem statement) +M, and S (samples)+E. Moreover, four ERAs place M at the end of the article, adjoining C. Three of the four ERAs are from *Applied Physics Reviews*, which reflects the specific requirements of a particular journal.

Secondly, the section headings of M are dominated by E (experiment) or M (method). 13 cases use E (5) or the variants of E, such as EM (experimental methodology) (3), ES (experimental setup) (3), ED (experimental demonstration) (1), and EO (experimental outlook) (1). 11 instances of the ERAs employ M, including M (9), computational method (1), [MRD] (1) and [MR] (1)[①].

Thirdly, there are cases of other variants of Method parts, which can be summarized into four types, including *problem formulation*, *data analysis*, *numerical simulation*, and *model*. Two cases in the corpus belong to *problem*

① [MRD]=merged section of Methods, Results, and Discussion; [MR]=merged section of Methods and Results *formulation*. Three cases use An (analysis), Cal (calculation), and Da (data analysis) as the section headings for methodology. One case in the corpus employs *numerical simulation* as the illustration of methodology. One case uses the section heading *model and preliminaries* as the demonstration of methods.

C exits in 94% of the ERAs of physics. Different from the situation of ERAs in linguistics, which displays C in more than one individual section, the writers of the ERAs of physics usually conclude the paper in a single section. As is revealed in the corpus, 39 ERAs use *conclusion* as the section titles and four cases use *summary* as section headings. The remaining four ERAs employ merged types of conclusions, such as [CF] (conclusion and future works), [CO] (conclusion and outlook), [SuC] (summary and conclusion), and [SuD] (summary and discussion).

R occupies 42% of the ERAs in physics. Two cases in the corpus present numerical results and experimental results respectively.

It is worth noting that [RD] is a distinctive feature of the generic structure of the physics ERAs, where 34% of the sub-corpus contain this merged section of Results and Discussion. However, in the corpus of linguistics ERAs, only four (8%) of the ERAs use this type of generic stage. This finding indicates the tendency in the physics ERAs for combining Results and Discussion.

D occurs in 30% of the physics ERAs, with eight cases using *Discussion* as the section heading directly and three cases employing other content headings. Besides, one case employs *application* as the title of the Discussion section. Another case (Phys 201809) employs the content heading *influence of parameter mismatch* following [RD] as part of the Discussion section.

As mentioned in the discussion of the generic pattern of the physics ERAs, T is another distinctive character of the physics corpus. T is the part between I and M, which is illustrated by the section title as *Theoretical model* or *Theoretical framework*. In the current study, T is marked as an independent part, not included in the Literature review part or Methods part because L is usually demonstrated in the section title such as *Related works*. However, T usually presents the theoretical model upon which the research is unfolded.

L occurs least frequently in the physics ERAs. Only six cases (12%) contain a Literature review part. Compared with the finding in the linguistics corpus, which contains 25 cases of L, physics ERAs deemphasize L as an independent part of ERAs.

Compared with the complexity of generic stage variants in ERAs of linguistics and physics, the major generic stages of ERAs in literary studies are relatively simple. I, A, and C constitute the major generic stages of literature ERAs.

As for I, 37 (74%) ERAs have an introduction. Among them, 30 cases do not use the explicit conventional section heading Introduction. The remaining seven instances demonstrate the introduction part clearly with titles. As for A, 39 (78%) ERAs possess Argumentation, which is realized by sub-section headings. The number of arguments ranges from two to ten. Regarding C, only nine (18%) ERAs display a distinct Conclusion section at the end of the article.

4.1.5 General features of the three disciplines

To sum up, this section analyzes the ERAs in linguistics, physics, and literary studies in terms of ERA types, macro generic stage sequence, and individual macro generic stage.

As far as ERA types are concerned, empirical ERAs and review ERAs are found in both the linguistics corpus and the physics corpus. In the corpus of literature ERAs, review ERAs and ERAs for stating opinions are found.

As for the macro generic stage sequence, ILMRDC occurs most frequently in the linguistics ERAs while IM[RD]C is the primary schematic pattern in the physics ERAs. (I)A appears relatively more in the literature ERAs.

Regarding the independent macro generic stage, it is discovered that I, L, M, R, D, and C appear in the linguistics ERAs. The stages of I, L, T, M, R, [RD], D, and C occur in the physics ERAs, and those of I, A, and C are displayed in the literature ERAs. Among these generic stages, I, D, and C are the three generic stages that occupy more proportion in the linguistics ERAs. I, M, and C stand as the top three generic stages which occur more frequently in the physics ERAs. Besides, the merged section of Results and Discussion ([RD]) appears in 34% of the physics ERAs. I and A are the major generic stages in the literature ERAs.

Based on the demarcation of these macro generic stages, the original corpus with 50 articles in each sub-corpus is refined to three sub-corpora with each containing 35 articles. The selection criteria are twofold. One is the elimination of review articles in the corpus. The other is the eradication of articles that include generic structure embedding in the corpus. Then the refined corpus is further analyzed in the aspect of overall elemental genre deployments and distribution of elemental genres in each macro generic stage. The results are presented in Sections 4.2 and 4.3.

4.2 Overall genre deployments of ERAs in the three disciplines

In this section, the emerging elemental genres in the ERAs are summarized. Then, the overall elemental genre deployments in the ERAs of each discipline are explored. Finally, the similarities and differences in the overall elemental genre deployments are discussed.

4.2.1 Particular elemental genres in the corpus

As discussed in Chapter 3, the framework for elemental genre identification is derived from the previous studies on elemental genre deployments in primary and secondary school textbooks. In the current study, new elemental genres which are not included in the framework may be discovered. After analyzing elemental genre deployments in the ERAs of the three disciplines, it is discovered six particular elemental genres are emerging. These elemental genres are exposition reviews, elucidations, figure expositions, direct formula recounts, conditional formula recounts, and sequential formula recounts. The former three elemental genres belong to the genre family of

Arguments while the latter three are subsumed into the genre family of Recounts.

The following parts elaborate on the general purpose, schematic structure, and instances of these elemental genres in the corpus.

An exposition review is a new type of Arguments, with the major purpose of supporting the writer's position. The schematic structure of an exposition review is Thesis ^ Evidence ^ Evaluation, which outlines the writer's opinion and is followed by supporting examples or evidence. Finally, comments or evaluations of the opinions of the author serve as the last generic stage of this elemental genre.

Example 4.1

Thesis	Interpolated in italics throughout the description of the performance are the lines that would have been spoken by the actors who are instead reduced to silence or shrieking-lines that Eun-sook alone knows because she has memorized them in the course of editing the manuscript:
Evidence	...① (Excerpts from the manuscripts)
Evaluation	Eun-sook provides the words that enable the readers to see how the affects of rage and grief, discernible in the shrieking and silence of the performers on stage ··· She provides with us ..., words that give voice not only to grief but also to the inability to grieve.

(Lite 202005) (Kim, 2020: 391-392)

In Example 4.1, the exposition review begins with the thesis statement that the additional words are inserted into the manuscripts, and then it reveals these lines with the excerpts from the manuscripts. The last phase analyzes and evaluates the functions of these words.

Regarding the distribution of exposition reviews, 59 instances (6.3%, 59/938, see Table 4.3) appear in the linguistics ERAs, 138 instances (12.7%, 138/1084, see Table 4.3) in the literature ones, and one instance in the physics papers. In the linguistics ERAs, exposition reviews mainly scatter in the macro generic stage of Results. In the ERAs of literary studies, exposition reviews are predominantly located in the Argumentation section. In the physics ERAs, one

① Omission is used here to save space. This use is applied to the whole book.

instance of exposition review emerges in the R&D section.

In addition to an exposition review, an elucidation is another emerging elemental genre in the corpus. Its main purpose is also to negotiate the ERA writers' point of view. The schematic structure is Thesis ^ Example (Evidence).

Example 4.2

Thesis	Finally, the analysis of the identified bundles in Move 5 (Conclusion) showed that certain bundles exclusive to this move were found only in one discipline (i.e., Marketing). Exclusive bundles, such as *the authors discuss the implications of findings* and *the authors conclude with a discussion of* were only used by authors in the Marketing discipline. ...As illustrated in the following examples, writers of abstracts in the Marketing discipline use these bundles to briefly outline the structure of the accompanying article.
Example	...

(Lin 201810) (Omidian et al., 2018:10)

In Example 4.2, the elemental genre of elucidation is unfolded through the thesis stage which illustrates the writer's purpose for demonstrating that certain lexical bundles are exclusive to the marketing discipline, followed by the evidence stage which is an example from the corpus that supports the author's position.

Elucidations can be found in all the three sub-corpora, including eight cases (0.9%, 8/938, see Table 4.3) in the linguistics sub-corpus, 12 instances (1.6%, 12/762, see Table 4.3) in the physics one, and 45 cases in literary studies (4.2%, 45/1084, see Table 4.3). In the linguistics ERAs, elucidations usually occur in the macro generic stage of Results. In the physics ERAs, elucidations scatter sporadically in the Introduction, Literature review, Methods, Discussion, and R&D sections. In the literature ERAs, elucidations occur mainly in the macro generic stage of Argumentation.

The third emerging elemental genre in the Arguments genre family is figure exposition with the schematic structure of Figure presentation ^ Description ^ (Evaluation). It serves for describing and evaluating figures in the ERAs.

However, it should be noted that, in the corpus, not all the figure exposition abides by the three-stage schematic structure strictly. Sometimes, figure presentation and figure description can be merged into one stage.

Furthermore, the evaluation phase is implicit in the figure description. Besides, in the physics ERAs, writers use a series of figures to illustrate the results of experiments, thus, the elemental genre of figure exposition will include the elaboration of several figures. For example, in the R&D section of Phys 201909, the content under the title *Effective Multiterminal Geometry* is subsumed into one figure exposition, which includes the illustration of several figures.

As regards the distribution of figure expositions, in the current study, they appear in all three sub-corpora. In the linguistics ERAs, 31 cases (3.3%, 31/938, see Table 4.3) appear. In the physics ERAs, 95 instances (12.5%, 95/762, see Table 4.3) of figure expositions are discovered. In the ERAs of literary studies, ten cases (0.9%, 10/1084, see Table 4.3) emerge.

In the linguistics ERAs, figure expositions occur with a higher frequency in the R&D and Results sections. The same distribution pattern is seen in the physics ERAs. In the literature ERAs, figure expositions are found in the Argumentation section.

The above-mentioned three new elemental genres belong to the genre family of Arguments. The following three burgeoning elemental genres are included in the genre family of Recounts. Moreover, they are all related to formulas and occur exclusively in the physics ERAs. They are direct formula recounts, conditional formula recounts, and sequential formula recounts.

Direct formula recounts are used for describing a single formula with the schematic structure of Formula presentation ^ Description.

Example 4.3

Formula presentation	We now turn to Brownian-dynamics (BD) simulations of a system that closely resembles the one sued in the DSA calculations… Formula (16)
Description	with a timestep…Opting for the constant-velocity scenario with a deterministically driven probe allows us to explicitly prescribe the probe velocity Vp and thus the Peclet number Pe of individual simulation runs, which simplifies the direct comparison of the results to DSA calculations in order to: …

(Phys 201707) (Wulfert et al., 2017:9098-9099)

In Example 4.3, the elemental genre of direct formula recounts focuses on the description of a single formula with the phase of formula presentation serving for introducing the formula, followed by a detailed description of the parameters of the formula.

A direct formula recount appears in Literature review, Methods, Results, R&D, Discussion, and M&R&D sections in physics ERAs. Among these macro generic stages, M is the stage where more direct formula recounts are located, with 14 ERAs containing this type of elemental genre in their Methods sections.

Apart from direct formula recounts, conditional formula recounts can also be found in the physics ERAs. This type of elemental genre spreads firstly with the phase of a condition statement, which is featured by the typical lexicogrammatical resource "if", then followed by the formula description phase which states the details of the parameters of the formula.

In terms of the distribution of conditional formula recounts, this type of elemental genre appears in the Methods section or the Literature review section.

The third type of emerging elemental genre is sequential formula recount, which is instantiated by a string of mutually-related formulas. The schematic structure of this type of elemental genre is Formula presentation ^ Formula Description [1-n].

As for the distribution of sequential formula recounts, they scatter in different macro generic stages of the physics ERAs, including Literature review, Methods, Results, and R&D, with a higher frequency in the Methods section, i.e., 13 physics ERAs contain sequential formula recount in the Methods section.

This sub-section summarizes the purpose, schematic structure, and major locating macro generic stages of new elemental genres in the ERAs. The distribution of these six types of elemental genres shows distinctive disciplinary characteristics. Exposition reviews and elucidations mainly scatter in the Argumentation stage of the literature ERAs and the remaining four elemental genres occur frequently in the physics ERAs, with figure expositions being located in the R&D section and the three types of formula recounts mainly being in the Methods sections.

The next three sub-sections elaborate on the overall elemental genre deployments in the ERAs of linguistics, physics, and literary studies.

4.2.2 Overall genre deployments of ERAs in linguistics

Based on the coding scheme listed in Chapter 3 and the schematic structure of emerging elemental genres mentioned in the previous sub-section, the elemental genres in the ERAs of the three disciplines are identified and annotated. The overall results of elemental genres across three sub-corpora are presented in Table 4.3.

Table 4.3 Overall elemental genre deployments in the linguistics, physics, and literary Studies ERAs (1)

REPORTS	**Linguistics**			**Physics**			**Literary studies**		
	N	**F**	**P**	**N**	**F**	**P**	**N**	**F**	**P**
Descriptive report	312	0.7	33.3	245	0.8	32.2	242	0.6	22.3
Classifying report	114	0.3	12.2	36	0.1	4.7	28	0.1	2.6
Compositional report	12	0	1.3	16	0.1	2.1	6	0	0.6
Descriptive report	0	0	0	0	0	0	6	0	0.6
Sub-total:	**438**	**1**	**46.7**	**297**	**1**	**39.0**	**282**	**0.7**	**26.0**
EXPLANATIONS	**Linguistics**			**Physics**			**Literary studies**		
	N	**F**	**P**	**N**	**F**	**P**	**N**	**F**	**P**
Sequential explanation	40	0.1	4.3	77	0.3	10.1	90	0.2	8.3
Factorial explanation	80	0.2	8.5	62	0.2	8.1	70	0.2	6.5
Consequential explanation	1	0	0.1	4	0	0.5	6	0	0.6
Conditional explanation	2	0	0.2	0	0	0	5	0	0.5
Theoretical explanation	0	0	0	0	0	0	0	0	0
Factorial explanation	0	0	0	0	0	0	1	0	0.1
Exploration	1	0	0.1	1	0	0.1	0	0	0
Sequential explanation	0	0	0	0	0	0	3	0	0.3
Sub-total:	**124**	**0.3**	**13.2**	**144**	**0.5**	**18.9**	**175**	**0.5**	**16.1**
ARGUMENTS	**Linguistics**			**Physics**			**Literary studies**		
	N	**F**	**P**	**N**	**F**	**P**	**N**	**F**	**P**
Exposition	127	0.3	13.5	42	0.1	5.5	186	0.5	17.2
Discussion	7	0	0.7	1	0	0.1	20	0.1	1.8
Challenge	3	0	0.3	1	0	0.1	26	0.1	2.4
Elucidation	8	0	0.9	12	0	1.6	45	0.1	4.2
Exposition review	59	0.1	6.3	1	0	0.1	138	0.4	12.7
Figure exposition	31	0.1	3.3	95	0.3	12.5	10	0	0.9
Exposition review	0	0	0	0	0	0	1	0	0.1
Sub-total:	**235**	**0.5**	**25.1**	**152**	**0.5**	**19.9**	**426**	**1.1**	**39.3**

Note: N=number of elemental genres; F=frequency per 1,000 tokens; P=percentage (%) of the total elemental genre deployments; Sub-total=the total number, frequency, and percentage of elemental genres in each elemental genre family

Table 4.4 Overall elemental genre deployments in the linguistics, physics, and literary studies ERAs (2)

RECOUNTS	**Linguistics**			**Physics**			**Literary studies**		
	N	**F**	**P**	**N**	**F**	**P**	**N**	**F**	**P**
Personal recount	0	0	0	0	0	0	10	0	0.9
Anecdote	1	0	0.1	0	0	0	0	0	0
Exemplum	0	0	0	0	0	0	0	0	0
Observation	1	0	0.1	0	0	0	11	0	1
Narrative	5	0	0.5	0	0	0	23	0.1	2.1
Biographical recount	3	0	0.3	0	0	0	9	0	0.8
Historical recount	14	0	1.5	2	0	0.3	36	0.1	3.3
Procedural recount	46	0.1	4.9	34	0.1	4.5	3	0	0.3
Observation	10	0	1.1	0	0	0	3	0	0.3
Narrative	1	0	0.1	0	0	0	8	0	0.7
Personal recount	0	0	0	0	0	0	2	0	0.2
Conversation	0	0	0	0	0	0	1	0	0.1
Direct formula recount	0	0	0	50	0.2	6.6	0	0	0
Conditional formula recount	0	0	0	11	0	1.4	0	0	0
Sequential formula recount	0	0	0	43	0.1	5.6	0	0	0
Historical recount	0	0	0	0	0	0	1	0	0.1
Letter	0	0	0	0	0	0	1	0	0.1
Poem	0	0	0	0	0	0	1	0	0.1
Biographical recount	0	0	0	0	0	0	2	0	0.2
Sub-total:	**81**	**0.2**	**8.60**	**140**	**0.5**	**18.4**	**111**	**0.3**	**10.2**
TEXT_RESPONSES	**Linguistics**			**Physics**			**Literary studies**		
	N	**F**	**P**	**N**	**F**	**P**	**N**	**F**	**P**
Review	60	0.1	6.4	29	0.1	3.8	89	0.2	8.2
Interpretation	0	0	0	0	0	0	0	0	0
Critical response	0	0	0	0	0	0	0	0	0
Review	0	0	0	0	0	0	1	0	0.1
Sub-total:	**60**	**0.1**	**6.40**	**29**	**0.1**	**3.8**	**90**	**0.2**	**8.3**
Total	**938**	**2.1**	**100**	**762**	**2.6**	**100**	**1084**	**2.8**	**100**

Note: N=number of elemental genres; F=frequency per 1,000 tokens; P=percentage (%) of the total elemental genre deployments; Sub-total=the total number, frequency, and percentage of elemental genres in each elemental genre family; Total=the total number, frequency, and percentage of the elemental genres in each sub-corpus

Table 4.3 and Table 4.4 present the overall elemental genre deployments in the ERAs of the three disciplines. The dash before and after the name of the elemental genre means it belongs to genre embedding, i.e., the elemental genre is embedded in another elemental genre. Besides, N means the number of elemental genres. F indicates the frequency of elemental genres, i.e., the occurrences of a given elemental genre per 1,000 tokens. P is the percentage of a certain elemental genre in the overall genre deployments. For example, there are 312 cases of descriptive reports in the linguistics sub-corpus, with a frequency of 0.7 cases per 1,000 tokens and taking up 33.3% (312/938, see Table 4.3).

There are similarities and differences in overall elemental genre deployments among the ERAs of the three disciplines. For similarities, two points are in need of emphasis.

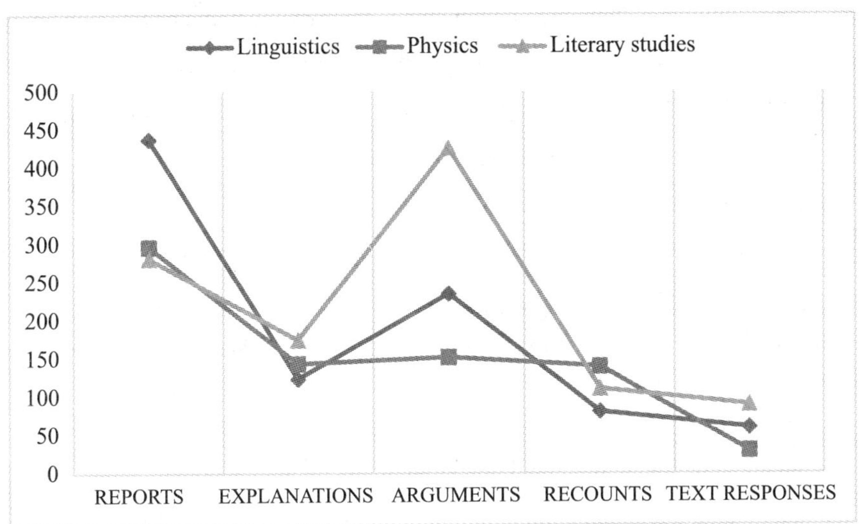

Figure 4.1 Distribution of elemental genre families among the three disciplines

Firstly, from the perspective of elemental genre families, the ERAs of the three disciplines display similar tendencies. Specifically, as illustrated in Figure 4.1, the elemental genre families scattering in the linguistics ERAs and the physics ERAs follow the same descending order, i.e., Reports > Arguments > Explanations > Recounts > Text responses. Furthermore, the elemental genre families in the literature ERAs are listed in descending order as Arguments > Reports > Explanations > Recounts > Text responses.

Secondly, from the perspective of specific elemental genres, the ERAs of the three disciplines share some elemental genres which possess higher frequency. In the genre family of Reports, the writers of the ERAs prefer to use descriptive reports and classifying reports. In the genre family of Explanations, sequential explanations and factorial explanations demonstrate more frequent occurrences in the three sub-corpora. In the genre family of Text responses, the authors of the ERAs tend to employ reviews.

In connection with the differences among the three sub-corpora in elemental genre deployments, one-way ANOVA or nonparametric tests are employed to reveal statistically significant differences in terms of the frequency (per 1,000 tokens) of elemental genre families. The results are demonstrated in Table 4.5.

Table 4.5 Statistical comparisons of elemental genre families

Type of elemental genre families	Cross-disciplinary difference	
Reports	Y(p=.006)	Phys>Lite
Arguments	Y(p=.000)	Lite>Lin; Lite>Phys
Explanations	Y(p=.002)	Phys>Lin; Lite>Lin
Recounts	Y(p=.000)	Phys>Lin; Phys>Lite
Text responses	Y(p=.001)	Lite>Phys

Note: Y=Yes; Lin=Linguistics; Phys=Physics; Lite=Literary studies

As Table 4.5 indicates, there are statistically significant differences in the use of all the five elemental genre families across the three disciplines. There are at least two points worthy of mentioning.

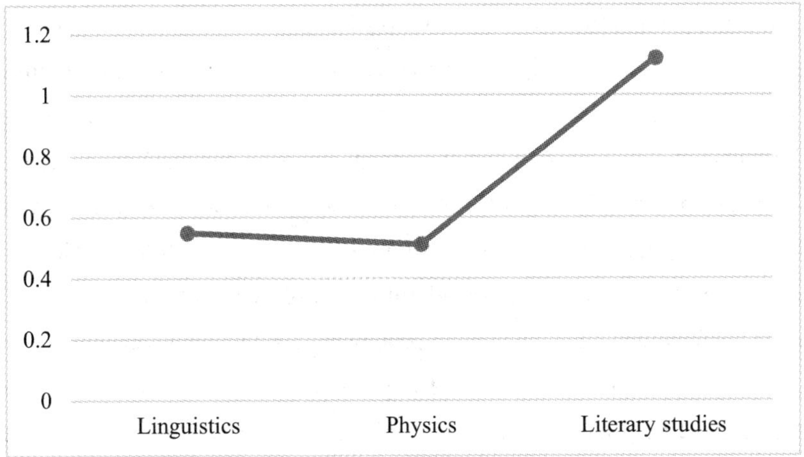

Figure 4.2 Frequency of Arguments among the three disciplines

First, as shown in Figure 4.2, the frequency of Arguments among the three disciplines is presented. It is noticed that the literature papers (1.12 per 1,000 tokens) boast nearly twice the Arguments as the linguistics (0.549 per 1,000 tokens) and the physics (0.511 per 1,000 tokens). Additionally, the ANOVA run on Arguments finds a significant effect of discipline, F (2, 102) =44.680, p=.000. Post hoc Bonferroni tests reveal that the literature ERAs (M=1.120, SD=.3324) use markedly more elemental genres in the Arguments genre family (p=.000 in both cases) than in the linguistics ERAs (M=.549, SD=.3257) and the physics ERAs (M=.511, SD=.2386). The latter two sub-corpora of ERAs do not differ significantly (p=1.000). This finding suggests the knower code orientation of literary studies, in which the knowledge is likely to be legitimated by resorting to the knowers' personal voice, expertise, experience, and authority (Hu&Cao, 2015). The authors of the literature ERAs rely heavily on elemental genres in the arguments genre family to convince the reader of their opinions towards literary works.

Second, nonparametric tests[①] run on Recounts yield a distinctive effect of discipline (p=.000). Kruskal-Wallis H pairwise tests indicate that the physics ERAs use significantly more elemental genres in the Recounts genre family than the linguistics ERAs (p=.000) and the literature ERAs (p=.003). The latter two sub-corpora do not differ (p=.493). A close observation of the elemental genres in this genre family shows that the authors of the physics ERAs employ three types of formula recounts and procedural recounts frequently in describing the meaning of formulas and experiment processes. This finding can be explained by the knowledge code orientation of physics, where procedural adequacy and methodological rigor alone could be epistemically persuasive and legitimate new knowledge claims without authorial intervention (Hu&Cao, 2015).

In the following subsections, elemental genres with statistically significant occurrences in each elemental genre family are discussed. Moreover, the similarities and differences in terms of overall elemental genre deployments among the three sub-corpora are discussed with statistical evidence in Section 4.2.5.

As Table 4.3 and Table 4.4 indicate, in the linguistics ERAs, there are altogether 938 text clips that instantiate different elemental genres.

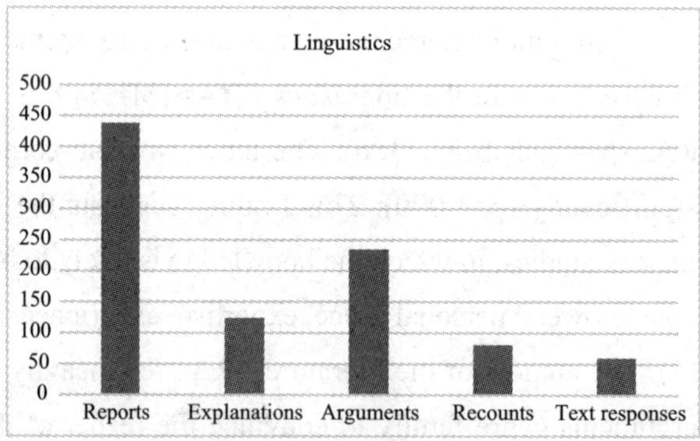

Figure 4.3 Distribution of elemental genre families in the linguistics ERAs

① Since the homogeneity of variance tests show the three sub-corpora of ERAs demonstrate uneven variance in the deployments of Recounts, nonparametric tests are employed to reveal significant differences.

From a quantitative perspective, as demonstrated in Figure 4.3, 46.7% (see Table 4.3) of elemental genres in the linguistics ERAs belong to the Reports genre family, followed by 25.1% (see Table 4.3) of the total instances from the Arguments genre family. 13.2% (see Table 4.3) of the cases are from the Explanations genre family. It is also found that 8.6% (see Table 4.4) of the instances come from the genre family of Recounts, and 6.4% (see Table 4.4) of the text clips instantiate elemental genres in the genre family of Text responses.

There are significant influences of discipline (p=.000) identified by nonparametric tests in the distribution of classifying reports. According to Kruskal-Wallis H paired tests, linguists use evidently more classifying reports than physicists (p=.000) and literary critics (p=.000). Classifying reports are used to classify a phenomenon based on different standards (Martin&Rose, 2008:144).

It should be noted that classifying reports are the only elemental genre in the linguistics ERAs that possess statistical preference over the other two sub-corpora. It could be explained by the purpose of classifying reports and the characters of the linguistics ERAs. The general purpose of classifying reports is to classify a phenomenon. 72% of classifying reports appear in the Introduction, Literature review, and Methods sections of the linguistics ERAs. They are used for classifying related studies in the Introduction and Literature review sections. Moreover, the participants, and instruments of methods employed by ERAs are elaborated on through classifying reports.

Furthermore, based on Section 4.1, the frequent macro generic stage sequence of the linguistics ERAs is ILMRDC, which possesses a distinctive independent macro generic stage of Literature review. Combining the two factors together, it is possible that the linguistics ERAs use more classifying reports than the ERAs of the other two disciplines.

With regard to the genre family of Explanations, a factorial explanation is the elemental genre that favors the most frequent occurrences (80 cases, 0.2 per 1,000 tokens, see Table 4.3). A nonsignificant effect of discipline is located in factorial explanations, where F (2,102) =.512 and P=.601, showing that factorial explanations occur equally frequently in the linguistics (M=.177, SD=.1285), the physics (M=.214, SD=.2002), and the literature (M=.180, SD=.1726) ERAs.

Factorial explanations explain several factors that lead to phenomena with the schematic structure of Phenomenon identification ^ Factors (Veel, 1997:180-181).

For example, in Lin 201910, which is part of the Methods section of one linguistics ERA (Pun, 2019), factorial explanations elucidate why chemistry textbooks are chosen as the research object with the Phenomenon identification stage illustrating the research purpose and the Factors stage demonstrating two factors leading to the choice of chemistry textbooks.

The equal distribution of factorial explanations across the three sub-corpora suggests that all the ERAs of the three disciplines use similar strategies for interpreting several reasons attributing to one phenomenon.

As regards the genre family of Arguments, 127 (13.5%, see Table 4.3) cases instantiate expositions. 59 (6.3%, see Table 4.3) incidences belong to exposition reviews, and 31 (3.3%, see Table 4.3) instances are in the elemental genre of figure expositions.

An Exposition, which is the most frequent elemental genre of the Arguments genre family, is used for organizing arguments around a single point of view with the schematic structure of Thesis ^ Arguments ^ Reiteration (Rose, 2012:219).

As for the distribution of expositions, nonparametric tests identify a weighty effect of discipline (p=.000), with the linguistics ERAs deploying this elemental genre more frequently than the physics ERAs (p=.010). The linguistics and literature ERAs, however, do not differ (p=.079). The results reflect that the linguistics ERAs share some common points with the literature ERAs, which are oriented by the knower code. The establishment of knowledge claims is constructed by legitimating the "unique insight of the knower", which necessitates a language that persuades by stressing the knower's individual authority and expertise (Hu&Liu, 2018).

In the genre family of Recounts, procedural recounts are used for depicting the purpose, steps, results, and conclusion of a scientific activity with the schematic structure of Aim ^ Record of events ^ Conclusion (Veel, 1997:172). The procedural recount (46 cases, 4.9%, see Table 4.4) is the most frequently-used elemental genre in the linguistics ERAs.

There is a noteworthy impact of discipline found by nonparametric tests on procedural recounts (p=.000), with a higher incidence of this elemental genre in the linguistics ERAs (p=.000) and the physics ERAs (p=.000) than in the literature ERAs. The former two sub-corpora do not differ significantly (p=1.000). This finding illustrates that the linguistics ERAs, like the physics EARs, highlight the procedural adequacy of legitimate new knowledge claims.

With regard to the genre family of Text responses, since the writers of the ERAs only comment on the messages, this study merges reviews and interpretations into one elemental genre: reviews, which usually follow the schematic structure like Context ^ Description ^ Evaluation. 60 instances (6.4%, see Table 4.4) belong to this type of elemental genre.

Example 4.4

Context	A number of studies have found links between receptive lexical knowledge and writing proficiency scores in independent (Koda, 1993; Schoonen et al., 2011) and source-based tasks (e.g., Baba, 2009).
Description	Koda (1993), for example, found a strong positive relationship ... In addition, Schoonen et al. (2011) used scores ... Baba (2009) also found moderate, positive relationships between ...
Evaluation	Together, these findings suggest that receptive lexical knowledge ...

(Lin 201606) (Kyle&Crossley, 2016:13)

Example 4.4 is selected from the Introduction section of one linguistics ERA. This elemental genre is usually employed for conducting literature review. Example 4.4 first summarizes the topics of research in the Context stage, then provides detailed information on these studies in the Description stage, and finally comments on research in the Evaluation stage.

Nonparametric tests produce a prominent effect of discipline (p=.001). Pairwise comparisons present the fact that reviews occur equally frequently in the linguistics ERAs and the physics ERAs (p=.212). Furthermore, the linguistics ERAs and the literature ERAs show no substantial difference (p=.170).

4.2.3 Overall genre deployments of ERAs in physics

As is shown in Table 4.3 and Table 4.4, there are altogether 762 text clips instantiating various elemental genres. The elemental genres in the genre family of Reports are most frequently used and Text responses occur least frequently in the sub-corpus. The elemental genres in the remaining genre families take similar overall distribution in the physics ERAs, i.e., Explanations take up 18.9% (see Table 4.3), Arguments 19.9% (see Table 4.3), and Recounts 18.4% (see Table 4.4) in the general elemental genre deployments. The distribution of the elemental genre families in physics is demonstrated in Figure 4.4.

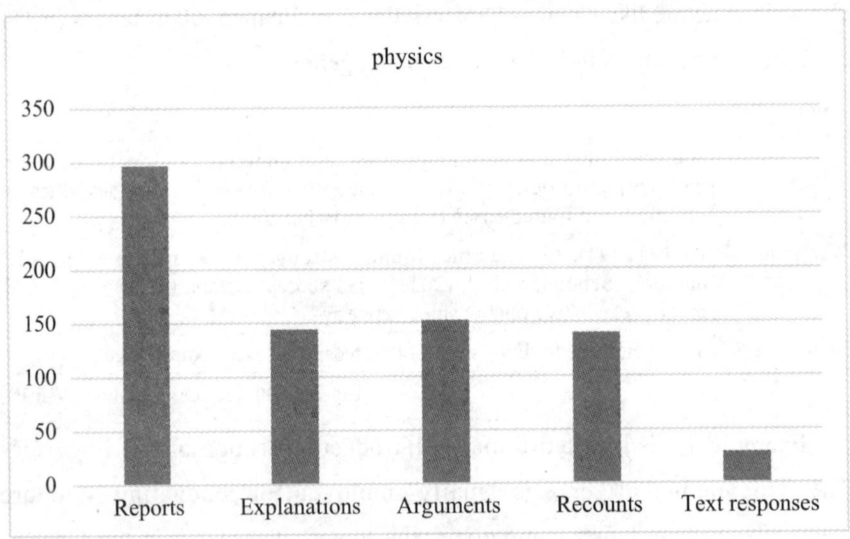

Figure 4.4 Distribution of elemental genre families in the physics ERAs

In the genre family of Reports, descriptive reports, which are used for describing a phenomenon with the schematic structure of Classification ^ Description (Martin&Rose, 2008:143), take the predominant percentage in the physics ERAs. In real operations, the Classification stages are usually omitted. 245 (32.2%, see Table 4.3) cases are instances of descriptive reports.

The ANOVA on descriptive reports detects a meaningful effect of discipline, i.e., F (2,102) =3.802, p=.026. Post hoc comparisons reveal a significant difference (p=.026) between the physics sub-corpus (M=.863, SD=.3647) and the literature one (M=.629, SD=.3816), though neither differs sharply (p=.172 for the former; p=1.000 for the latter) from the linguistics sub-corpus (M=.629, SD=.3816). This outcome suggests that the physics ERAs tend to use more descriptive reports for presenting disciplinary knowledge than the literature ERAs.

As for the genre family of Explanations, 77 instances (10.1%, see Table 4.3) belong to sequential explanations and 62 cases (8.1%, see Table 4.3) instantiate factorial explanations. A sequential explanation, which explains the cause-and-effect relation between a series of events (Rose&Martin, 2008:150), is the most frequent elemental genre in the Explanation genre family of physics ERAs.

Discipline has a significant (p=.000) influence on the distribution of sequential explanations, with the physics ERAs using more sequential explanations than the linguistics ERAs (p=.000). The physics sub-corpus and the literature one, however, do not differ to a great extent (p=1.000). This finding can be plausibly explained by further examination of the location of sequential explanations. In the physics ERAs, 70% of sequential explanations occur in the Methods, R&D, and Theory sections. The sequential explanations in M and T follow a typical cause-and-effect sequence, for instance, sequential explanations in the physics ERAs are usually used as the explanation for the taking of some methodological process. Contrary to the situation in the physics ERAs, sequential explanations in the literature ERAs usually occur in the Argumentation section as the explanation for one argument of the ERA writer.

This finding also indicates the knowledge-code and knower-code orientations of physics and literary studies respectively.

With regard to the genre family of Arguments, the physics ERAs take on their own distinctive disciplinary features. Figure expositions, which serve to describe, analyze, and evaluate figures, occur more frequently (95 cases, 12.5%, see Table 4.3).

As detected by nonparametric tests, there is a more frequent use of figure expositions in the physics ERAs than in the linguistics ERAs (p=.001) and in the literature ERAs (p=.000). This finding can possibly be attributed to the knowledge code orientation of physics, where knowledge claims are established through empirical authority that results from applying universally accepted principles of inquiry and methods of validation (Hu&Cao, 2015).

In the genre family of Recounts, the physics ERAs demonstrate the exclusive elemental genres of direct, sequential, and conditional formula recounts in the three sub-corpora. There are 50 cases (6.6%, see Table 4.4) of direct formula recounts and 43 instances (5.6%, see Table 4.4) of sequential formula recounts. The recounting of formulas also echoes the fact that physics emphasizes the precise and accurate comprehension of the physical world (Doran, 2018:33).

In connection with the genre family of Text responses, 29 cases (3.8%, see Table 4.4) belong to the elemental genre of reviews, which possess less percentage in the whole sub-corpus by comparing with the linguistics ERAs (6.4%, see Table 4.4) and the literature ERAs (8.3%, see Table 4.4).

4.2.4 Overall genre deployments of ERAs in literary studies

As is shown in the last three columns of Table 4.3 and Table 4.4, 1084 instances of elemental genres are found in ERAs of literary studies. Different from the results in the physics and the linguistics ERAs, as demonstrated in Figure 4.5, Arguments in literary studies are the genre family that occurs with a relatively higher frequency, with 39.3% (see Table 4.3) of the text clips in this corpus being in this type of elemental genre family. 26.0% (see Table 4.3) of the texts instantiate elemental genres in the genre family of Reports. 16.1% (see Table 4.3) of the texts are instances of Explanations, and 10.2% (see Table 4.4) are cases of Recounts. Text responses also have the least portion, with 8.3% of the whole texts coming from this kind of genre family.

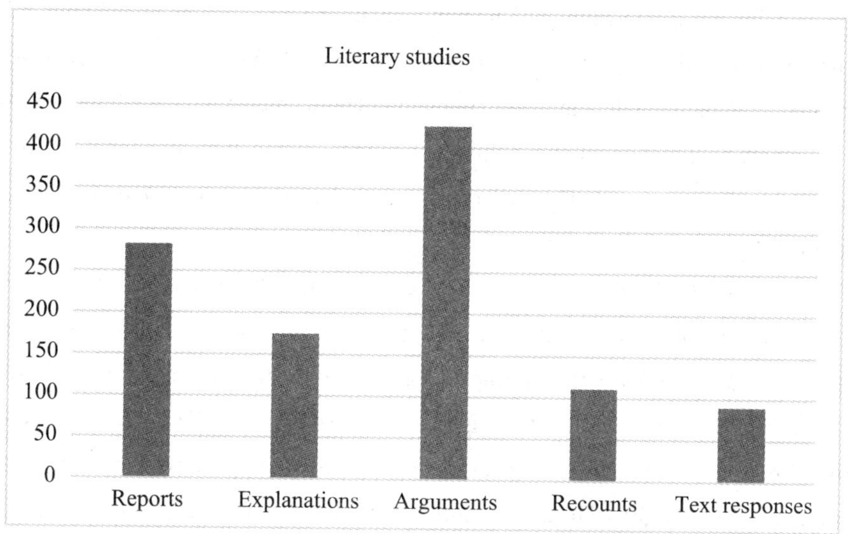

Figure 4.5 Distribution of elemental genre families in the literature ERAs

In the genre family of Arguments, 186 (17.2%, see Table 4.3) cases are instances of expositions and 138 (12.7%, see Table 4.3) instances belong to exposition reviews. Nonparametric tests show that the literature ERAs use more expositions than the physics ERAs (p=.000). The literature ERAs and the linguistics ERAs, however, do not differ (p=.079).

An exposition review is the elemental genre that represents the character of the literature ERAs. A significant effect of discipline on the deployment of this elemental genre is detected by nonparametric tests (p=.000). Kruskal-Wallis H pairwise comparisons bring out the fact that the literature ERAs utilize more exposition reviews than the linguistics ERAs (p=.000) and the physics ERAs (p=.000).

The abundance of expositions and exposition reviews in the literature ERAs may be attributed to the knower's code orientation of literary studies. The writers of literature ERAs persuade the readers to accept their individual tastes and judgement in literary works through expositions and exposition reviews.

As for the genre family of Reports, there are 242 (22.3%, see Table 4.3) cases of descriptive reports and 28 (2.6%, see Table 4.3) text clips of classifying reports. Compared with the other two sub-corpora, the literature ERAs deploy the lowest percentage of the elemental genres in the Reports genre family. However, this genre family still ranks second in the overall distribution of elemental genre families.

As regards the genre family of Explanations, 90 (8.3%, see Table 4.3) cases are instantiations of sequential explanations. A significant disciplinary effect is also found for this elemental genre, with higher occurrences in the literature ERAs than in the linguistics ERAs (p=.001). The literature ERAs and the physics ERAs, however, use sequential explanations in similar frequencies (p=1.000). These sequential explanations intensively appear in the Argumentation section of the literature ERAs, which suggests their function for establishing arguments in this discipline.

In the genre family of Recounts, historical recounts record public or personal events according to episodic time (Martin&Rose, 2008:105) with the schematic structure of Background ^ Record of stages (Rose&Martin, 2012:130). Historical recounts (36 cases, 3.3%, see Table 4.4) occur most frequently in the literature ERAs.

Nonparametric tests on historical recounts identify a significant effect of discipline (p=.000). Pairwise comparisons indicate that the literature ERAs use more historical recounts than the physics ERAs (p=.000). Yet, there is no significant difference between the linguistics and the physics sub-corpora (p=.057) and between the linguistics and the literature ERAs (p=.234).

4.2.5 Similarities and differences in overall elemental genre deployments

The previous three sub-sections describe the overall elemental genre deployments respectively. In this sub-section, the similarities and differences in overall elemental genre deployments among the ERAs of the three disciplines are summarized.

As to the similarities, the current study encapsulates the common trends in elemental genre deployments from the perspective of the overall trend and each genre family.

First, the linguistics ERAs and the physics ERAs are roughly similar in the general distribution of the elemental genres. In other words, the occurrences of elemental genre families show the string: Reports > Arguments > Explanations > Recounts > Text responses. However, the genre family distributions in the literature ERAs are Arguments > Reports > Explanations > Recounts > Text responses. Thus, the frequency of the occurrences of the latter three elemental genres takes on the same trend across the ERAs of the three disciplines.

Second, in the distribution of the elemental genres in Reports, all the ERAs in the three disciplines display the same trend. Specifically, the occurrences of Reports demonstrate the tendency: descriptive reports > classifying reports > compositional reports.

Third, among the spreading of the elemental genres in Arguments, an exposition is the elemental genre that occurs more frequently in the ERAs of the three disciplines.

Fourth, in the distribution of elemental genres in Text responses, reviews are the elemental genres that occur most recurrently in the ERAs of the three disciplines.

In terms of the differences, IBM SPSS (version 25) is employed for comparing the normalized frequency (the number of elemental genres per 1,000 tokens) of major elemental genres between the three datasets. The statistical results are discussed sporadically in Sections 4.2.1–4.2.4. This section summarizes the results in Table 4.6.

Table 4.6 Summary of statistically significant comparisons in terms of major elemental genres

Type of elemental genres	Cross-disciplinary difference	
Descriptive report	Y(p=.026)	Phys>Lite
Classifying report	Y(p=.000)	Lin>Phys; Lin>Lite
Sequential explanation	Y(p=.000)	Phys>Lin; Lite>Lin
Factorial explanation	N(p=.601)	
Exposition	Y(p=.000)	Lin>Phys; Lite>Phys
Exposition review	Y(p=.000)	Lite>Phys; Lite>Lin; Lin>Phys
Figure exposition	Y(p=.000)	Phys>Lin; Phys>Lite; Lin>Lite
Historical recount	Y(p=.000)	Lite>Phys
Procedural recount	Y(p=.000)	Lin>Lite; Phys>Lite
Review	Y(p=.000)	Lite>Phys
Direct formula recount	occur exclusively in Phys	
Conditional formula recount	occur exclusively in Phys	
Sequential formula	occur exclusively in Phys	

Note: N=No; Y=Yes; Lin=Linguistics; Phys=Physics; Lite=Literature

As illustrated by Table 4.6, the distribution of major elemental genres in the three sub-corpora indicate disciplinary similarities and differences.

About the similarities, the use of factorial explanations shows no difference among the ERAs of the three disciplines, which suggests that the writers of the ERAs of the three disciplines use similar strategies when they need to explain several factors that cause certain phenomena.

The results also display some differences between the physics, which is knowledge-code-oriented, and the literary studies, which is knower-code-focused. In addition, the results reflect the mixture of knowledge and knower code of the linguistics.

In terms of the physics ERAs, three types of formula recounts occur exclusively, providing the precise description of physical phenomena with formula recounts. Moreover, figure expositions, which serve as the direct presentation, analysis, and evaluation of the experiment results, are used more frequently than those in the other two sub-corpora, which indicates the authors of the physics papers try to legitimatize their knowledge through the analysis of figures. Furthermore, the physics ERAs use more descriptive reports and procedural recounts than the literature ERAs. Descriptive reports are used for reporting physical phenomena, while procedural recounts are utilized for depicting the procedures of experiments. The elemental genres of statistical significance reflect the knowledge-orientation of physics, where knowledge claims are legitimatized through the accurate recounting of physical phenomena, the refined description of experiment procedures, and the precise analysis or evaluation of the experiment results.

In the literature ERAs, exposition reviews are employed more frequently than those in the other two sub-corpora. In addition, historical recounts, expositions, and reviews occur more regularly in the literature ERAs than in the physics ERAs. This finding also supports the knower-orientation of literary studies, where the individual taste and judgement are emphasized (Doran, 2018:33). The authors' opinions towards literary works are expressed and conveyed more commonly through elemental genres in the genre family of Arguments.

As for the linguistics ERAs, classifying reports are the only elemental genre that is markedly more frequently used than that in the other two disciplines. Classifying reports are mainly used in the Literature review and Methods sections, serving the purpose of classifying related studies and reporting the preparation of experiments respectively. The emphasis on an independent part of the Literature review may be one possible reason for the higher occurrence of classifying reports in the linguistics ERAs.

Besides the classifying reports, the elemental genres of statistical importance in the linguistics ERAs reflect its mixture of both knowledge and knower code. On the one hand, the linguistics ERAs employ more procedural recounts and figure expositions than the literature ERAs. This finding may be explained by the emphasis on procedural adequacy and objective analysis of figures by disciplines of knowledge-code. On the other hand, the linguistics ERAs use more expositions and exposition reviews than the physics ERAs. This finding reflects that, compared with the physics ERAs, the linguistics ERAs tend to support the authors' points of view by employing arguments, which is the strategy often used in knower-code-focused disciplines.

In a nutshell, the overall elemental genre deployments suggest the disciplinary characters of the three disciplines. The physics ERAs, with their emphasis on knowledge claims, prefer to use formula recounts, figure expositions, and procedural recounts. The literature ERAs, with their focus on persuading the reader to accept the individual taste or judgement of literary works, tend to employ expositions and exposition reviews. The linguistics ERAs, which are located at the middle of the knowledge structure cline (Martin et al., 2010:438), display a mixture of knowledge and knower code.

The next section zooms into each macro generic stage of the ERAs, aiming at revealing more delicate similarities and differences in elemental genre deployments among the three sub-corpora.

4.3 Elemental genre deployments in each macro generic stage of ERAs

In this section, the variety and frequency of elemental genres in each macro generic stage of ERAs are calculated and compared. The top five elemental genres in each major macro generic stage of the three sub-corpora are presented. At the end of this section, the similarities and differences in elemental genre deployments in each macro generic stage are discussed with arithmetical evidence.

4.3.1 Elemental genre deployments in each macro generic stage of ERAs in linguistics

To obtain the number and percentage of elemental genres in each macro generic stage of ERAs, the "statistics" function of UAMCT 6.2e (O' Donnell, 2022) is employed. As is shown in Figure 4.6, the results of elemental genre deployments are displayed by the software after setting the conditions at the type of study, unit of interest, and the three sets.

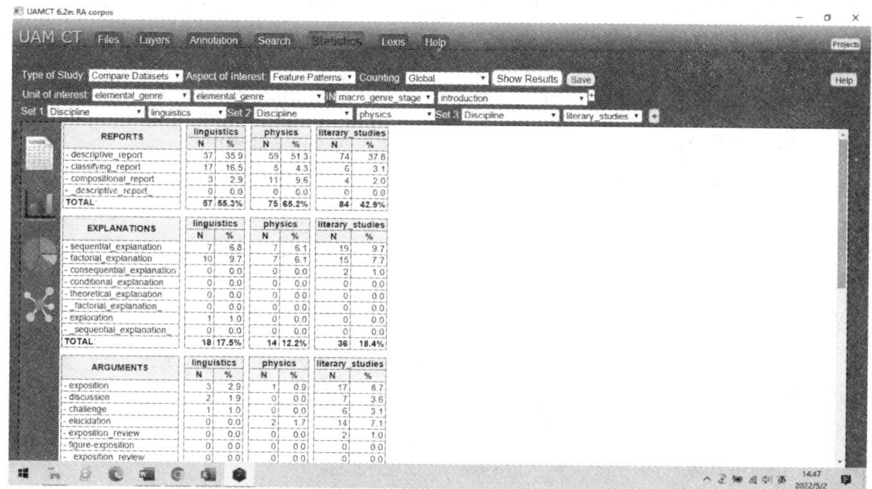

REPORTS	linguistics		physics		literary_studies	
	N	%	N	%	N	%
- descriptive_report	37	35.9	59	51.3	74	37.8
- classifying_report	17	16.5	5	4.3	6	3.1
- compositional_report	3	2.9	11	9.6	4	2.0
- _descriptive_report_	0	0.0	0	0.0	0	0.0
TOTAL	57	55.3%	75	65.2%	84	42.9%

EXPLANATIONS	linguistics		physics		literary_studies	
	N	%	N	%	N	%
- sequential_explanation	7	6.8	7	6.1	19	9.7
- factorial_explanation	10	9.7	7	6.1	15	7.7
- consequential_explanation	0	0.0	0	0.0	2	1.0
- conditional_explanation	0	0.0	0	0.0	0	0.0
- theoretical_explanation	0	0.0	0	0.0	0	0.0
- _factorial_explanation_	0	0.0	0	0.0	0	0.0
- exploration	1	1.0	0	0.0	0	0.0
- _sequential_explanation_	0	0.0	0	0.0	0	0.0
TOTAL	18	17.5%	14	12.2%	36	18.4%

ARGUMENTS	linguistics		physics		literary_studies	
	N	%	N	%	N	%
- exposition	3	2.9	1	0.9	17	8.7
- discussion	2	1.9	0	0.0	7	3.6
- challenge	1	1.0	0	0.0	6	3.1
- elucidation	0	0.0	2	1.7	14	7.1
- exposition_review	0	0.0	0	0.0	2	1.0
- figure-exposition	0	0.0	0	0.0	0	0.0
- _exposition_review_	0	0.0	0	0.0	0	0.0

Figure 4.6 Sample of elemental genre deployments in Introduction

Table 4.7 Summary of major elemental genres in each macro generic stage of the linguistics ERAs

	Elemental genres	N	P		Elemental genres	N	P
I	Descriptive report	37	35.9	L	Descriptive report	41	30.4
103 cases	Review	20	19.4	133 cases	Classifying report	31	23
	Classifying report	17	16.5		Review	22	16.3
	Factorial explanation	10	9.7		Sequential explanation	12	8.9
	Sequential explanation	7	6.8		Factorial explanation	10	7.4
M	Descriptive report	106	46.7	R	Descriptive report	46	24.5
227 cases	Classifying report	34	15	187 cases	Exposition review	44	23.4
	Procedural recount	30	13.2		Exposition	18	9.6
	Factorial explanation	22	9.7		Figure exposition	18	9.6
	Sequential explanation	10	4.4		Review	12	6.4
D	Exposition	56	40.9	R&D	Exposition	21	37.5
137 cases	Descriptive report	25	18.2	56 cases	Exposition review	12	21.4
	Factorial explanation	25	18.2		Descriptive report	7	12.5
	<observation>	10	7.3		Figure exposition	3	5.4
	Classifying report	5	3.6		Review	3	5.4
C	Descriptive report	31	57.4				
54 cases	Classifying report	9	16.7				
	Exposition	7	13				
	Factorial explanation	3	5.6				
	Compositional report	1	1.9				

Note: I=Introduction; L=Literature review; M=Methods; R=Results; D=Discussion; R&D=Results&Discussion; C=Conclusion; N=number; P=percentage

Table 4.7 demonstrates the top five elemental genres according to their counts in the linguistics sub-corpus. The total number of elemental genres in each macro generic stage is recorded under the abbreviation of the macro generic stage. For example, there are altogether 103 instances of elemental genres in the Introduction section. Besides, N represents the number of a certain elemental genre in each section of ERAs while P denotes the share of a certain elemental genre in a macro generic stage. For instance, descriptive reports occur 37 times in the Introduction section of linguistics academic papers, accounting for 35.9% (37/103). Generally speaking, descriptive reports and classifying reports occur in large quantities in the whole linguistics sub-corpus. Furthermore, the elemental genre deployments also mirror the purpose of each macro generic stage of the linguistics ERAs.

First, in the Introduction and Literature review sections, reviews take second and third place respectively. This finding can be attributed to the fact that related literature is summarized and evaluated in the two sections. Since the purpose of reviews is also to comment on and evaluate messages, reviews occur more intensively in these two sections.

Second, in the Methods sections, procedural recounts rank the third place, following descriptive reports and classifying reports. This finding can also be ascribed to the function of the Methods stage, where the research designs are presented and the description of experiment steps or observation processes is required. This aim coincides with the purpose of procedural recounts.

Third, in the Results section, figure expositions rank as one of the top five elemental genres. This can be attributable to the intensive occurrences of figures in the Results sections of the ERAs. As an elemental genre that describes and evaluates figures, figure expositions occur more frequently in this macro generic stage.

Fourth, in the Results&Discussion, and Discussion stages, the most frequently-used elemental genres are expositions and exposition reviews. This finding can be explainable by the fact that the authors' opinions should be interpreted in the Discussion sections (Swales, 2004:236).

The following elaborates on the major elemental genres in each macro generic stage. The top five elemental genres in terms of occurrences in each stage are listed in Table 4.7.

In the macro generic stage of Introduction, descriptive reports take the leading role in quantity, accounting for 35.9% of the whole elemental genres.

Following descriptive reports, reviews occupy 19.4% of the overall distribution. Classifying reports, factorial explanations, and sequential explanations rank third, fourth, and fifth, with percentages of 16.5%, 9.7%, and 6.8% respectively.

In the Literature review, descriptive reports play a predominant role in the elemental genre distribution, holding 30.4% of the overall quantity. They are followed by classifying reports, which take up 23% of the whole elemental genre. Reviews take 16.3% of the whole share. Sequential explanations and factorial explanations account for 8.9% and 7.4%.

In the Methods, descriptive reports also demonstrate their importance among elemental genres, occupying 46.7% of the whole distribution. Classifying reports and procedural recounts take the second and third position, with 15% and 13.2% of the quotient respectively. Factorial explanations and sequential explanations take up 9.7% and 4.4% correspondingly.

In the Results, descriptive reports and exposition reviews occupy 24.5% and 23.4% of the whole share. Furthermore, expositions and figure expositions have the same percentage of occurrence, each accounting for 9.6% of the overall distribution. Reviews take up 6.4% of the total.

In the Discussion, expositions rank first, accounting for 40.9% of the total share. Descriptive reports and factorial explanations each take up 18.2% of the overall distribution. It is also found that the embedded genre <observations> occupies 7.3% of the general dispersion.

In the stage of Results&Discussion, expositions take up 37.5% of the whole, and exposition reviews occupy 21.4%. Descriptive reports show a percentage of 12.5%. Figure expositions and reviews each possess 5.4% of the general distribution.

In the macro generic stage of Conclusion, descriptive reports have a share of 57.4% while classifying reports take 16.7% of the total share. Expositions take third place, accounting for 13% of the distribution.

4.3.2 Elemental genre deployments in each macro generic stage of ERAs in physics

The physics ERAs are also characterized by elemental genre deployments which are similar to and different from those of the linguistics ERAs. The distribution of the elemental genres in physics ERAs is shown in Table 4.8.

Table 4.8 Summary of major elemental genres in each macro generic stage of the physics ERAs

	Elemental genres	N	P		Elemental genres	N	P
I	Descriptive report	59	51.3	L	Descriptive report	6	40
115 cases	review	19	16.5	15 cases	Sequential explanation	3	20
	Compositional report	11	9.6		Direct formula recount	2	13.3
	Sequential explanation	7	6.1		Review	2	13.3
	Factorial explanation	7	6.1		Classifying report	1	6.7
M	Descriptive report	77	32.8	R	Figure exposition	22	32.8
235 cases	Sequential explanation	29	12.3	67 cases	Descriptive report	16	23.9
	Sequential formula recount	28	11.9		Factorial explanation	10	14.9
	Direct formula recount	23	9.8		Sequential explanation	6	9
	Procedural recount	21	8.9		Direct formula recount	4	6
D	Exposition	12	38.7	R&D	Figure exposition	48	30.2
31 cases	Figure exposition	6	19.4	159 cases	Descriptive report	30	18.9
	Sequential explanation	5	16.1		Factorial explanation	18	11.3
	Descriptive report	2	6.5		Sequential explanation	15	9.4
	Classifying report	1	3.2		Exposition	12	7.5
C	Descriptive report	30	73.2				
41 cases	Factorial explanation	5	12.2				
	Classifying report	2	4.9				
	Exposition	2	4.9				
	Sequential explanation	1	2.4				

Note: I=Introduction; L=Literature review; M=Methods; R=Results; D=Discussion; R&D=Results&Discussion; C=Conclusion; N=number; P=percentage

As shown in Table 4.8, the total number of elemental genres is marked under the abbreviations of each section. N and P represent the number of occurrences and their share in a given generic stage respectively. For example, there are altogether 59 instances of descriptive reports in the Introduction section, with a percentage of 51.3% (59/115). In general, descriptive reports still occur in large quantities throughout every generic stage. In addition, the physics ERAs also demonstrate the following three disciplinary characteristics.

First, in the Introduction section, reviews rank second place, which is the same as that in the linguistics ERAs. However, compositional reports take third place in the physics ERAs. This finding is attributed to the fact many authors prefer to introduce the organization of their articles at the end of the Introduction section.

Second, in the Methods section, sequential explanations, sequential formula recounts, direct formula recounts, and procedural recounts have similar percentages. This feature can be explained by the preponderance of formulas in the Methods section of the physics ERAs. Besides, writers of the physics ERAs tend to employ sequential explanations to state the purpose of their writing directly.

Third, in the macro stages of Results and Results&Discussion, figure expositions play a crucial role. This finding may be ascribed to the overwhelming instances of figures in the Results or R&D sections of the physics ERAs. Figure expositions are utilized for describing and commenting on those figures.

The following presents the major elemental genres in each main macro generic stage of the physics ERAs. The percentages of each elemental genre in every major stage are shown in Table 4.8.

In the stage of Introduction, descriptive reports remain in the leading position with 51.3% of the total share, followed by reviews, which contribute 16.5% of the overall distribution. Compositional reports take up 9.6% of the general allocation. Sequential explanations and factorial explanations each occupy 6.1% of the total distribution.

In the Literature review, descriptive reports still inhabit the predominant role in elemental genre deployments, with 40% of the total share. Sequential explanations stand in second place, with 20% of the distribution. Direct formula recounts and reviews each take up 13.3% of the general distribution and classifying reports account for 6.7%.

In the Methods, descriptive reports also take the lead, occupying 32.8% of the total share. Sequential explanations and sequential formula recounts demonstrate similar percentages, with 12.3% and 11.9% of the overall distribution respectively. Direct formula recounts and procedural formula recounts occupy 9.8% and 8.9% of the total share correspondingly.

In the Results, figure expositions contribute 32.8% of the total share. Descriptive reports occupy 23.9% of the general distribution and factorial explanations possess 14.9% of the share. Sequential explanations and direct formula recounts take up 9% and 6% of the general dispersion respectively.

In the Discussion, expositions take the dominant role in the elemental genre deployments with 38.7% of the total share. Figure expositions and sequential explanations demonstrate 19.4% and 16.1% of the general distribution respectively. Descriptive reports occupy 6.5% of the total dispersion.

In the R&D, figure expositions display the leading distribution with 30.2% of the total allocation. Descriptive reports take second place with 18.9% of the general distribution. Factorial explanations and sequential explanations dwell in 11.3% and 9.4% of the total share correspondingly while expositions take up 7.5% of the overall distribution.

In the generic stage of Conclusion, descriptive reports demonstrate a predominant role with 73.2% of the total distribution and factorial explanations take up 12.2% of the general dispersion. Classifying reports and expositions each occupy 4.9 % of the total.

4.3.3 Elemental genre deployments in each macro generic stage of ERAs in literary studies

The macro generic structure of the literature ERAs is Introduction - Argumentation-Conclusion. Table 4.9 presents the elemental genre deployments in the three macro generic stages of the literature sub-corpus.

Table 4.9 Summary of major elemental genres in each macro generic stage of the literature ERAs

	Elemental genres	N	P		Elemental genres	N	P
I	Descriptive report	74	37.8	A	exposition	169	19.4
196 cases	Sequential explanation	19	9.7	871 cases	Descriptive report	158	18.1
	Exposition	17	8.7		Exposition review	135	15.5
	Factorial explanation	15	7.7		Review	79	9.1
	elucidation	14	7.1		Sequential explanation	69	7.9
C	Descriptive report	9	56.3				
16 cases	Sequential explanation	2	12.5				
	Classifying report	1	6.3				
	Discussion	1	6.3				
	Challenge	1	6.3				

Note: I=Introduction; A=Argumentation; C=Conclusion; N=Number; P=Percentage

As illustrated in Table 4.9, the numbers below the macro generic stage indicate the total occurrences of elemental genres. In addition, N and P record the number of a specific elemental genre and its share in each macro stage. The distribution of elemental genres in each macro generic stage reveals similarities and differences with the other two sub-corpora.

In general, descriptive reports occur most frequently in the Introduction and Conclusion sections, which is the common point in the three sub-corpora. In addition, the literature ERAs showcase their own disciplinary characteristics, i.e., the profusion of expositions and exposition reviews in the Argumentation section. This plethora may stem from the purpose of the literature ERAs, which is to persuade the reader to accept certain points of view. The knowledge claim is established by convincing the reader with expositions rather than figures or formulas.

The major elemental genres in each macro generic stage are presented as follows. The specific numbers of percentages are illustrated in Table 4.9.

In the stage of Introduction, descriptive reports also take a predominant role, accounting for 37.8% of the total. Sequential explanations and expositions take up 9.7% and 8.7% respectively. Factorial explanations possess 7.7% and elucidations 7.1%.

In Argumentation, expositions, descriptive reports, and exposition reviews are the most regular elemental genres with percentages of 19.4%, 18.1%, and 15.5% respectively. Following the three elemental genres, reviews take up 9.1% of the whole distribution. Sequential explanations reside in 7.9% of the overall dispersion.

In Conclusion, descriptive reports take the lead, accounting for 56.3% of the total. Following descriptive reports are sequential explanations, which constitute 12.5% of the overall distribution.

4.3.4 Similarities and differences in elemental genre deployments in each macro generic stage

After summarizing the elemental genre deployments in each macro generic stage in the ERAs of the three disciplines, this sub-section focuses on analyzing and comparing the distribution of elemental genres in the same macro generic stage of the ERAs.

The same macro generic stages in the ERAs of the three disciplines are Introduction and Conclusion. Moreover, the same macro generic stages between ERAs of linguistics and ERAs of physics include Methods, Results, R&D, and

Discussion[①].

Methodologically, the normalized frequency of elemental genres is compared among the three sub-corpora. For the comparisons between the linguistics ERAs and the physics ERAs, the UAM CorpusTool 6.2e (O'Donnell, 2022) is used to analyze the similarities and meaningful differences. The operational process is illustrated in Figure 4.7.

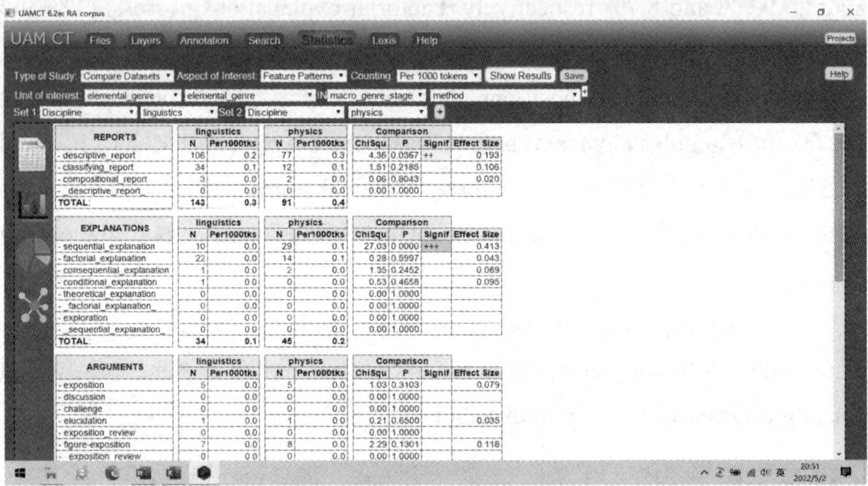

REPORTS	linguistics		physics		Comparison			
	N	Per1000tks	N	Per1000tks	ChiSqu	P	Signif	Effect Size
- descriptive_report	106	0.2	77	0.3	4.36	0.0367	++	0.193
- classifying_report	34	0.1	12	0.1	1.51	0.2185		0.106
- compositional_report	3	0.0	2	0.0	0.06	0.8043		0.020
- _descriptive_report_	0	0.0	0	0.0	0.00	1.0000		
TOTAL:	143	0.3	91	0.4				

EXPLANATIONS	linguistics		physics		Comparison			
	N	Per1000tks	N	Per1000tks	ChiSqu	P	Signif	Effect Size
- sequential_explanation	10	0.0	29	0.1	27.03	0.0000	+++	0.413
- factorial_explanation	22	0.0	14	0.1	0.28	0.5997		0.043
- consequential_explanation	1	0.0	2	0.0	1.35	0.2452		0.089
- conditional_explanation	1	0.0	0	0.0	0.53	0.4658		0.095
- theoretical_explanation	0	0.0	0	0.0	0.00	1.0000		
- _factorial_explanation_	0	0.0	0	0.0	0.00	1.0000		
- exploration	0	0.0	0	0.0	0.00	1.0000		
- _sequential_explanation_	0	0.0	0	0.0	0.00	1.0000		
TOTAL:	34	0.1	45	0.2				

ARGUMENTS	linguistics		physics		Comparison			
	N	Per1000tks	N	Per1000tks	ChiSqu	P	Signif	Effect Size
- exposition	5	0.0	5	0.0	1.03	0.3103		0.079
- discussion	0	0.0	0	0.0	0.00	1.0000		
- challenge	0	0.0	0	0.0	0.00	1.0000		
- elucidation	1	0.0	1	0.0	0.21	0.6500		0.035
- exposition_review	0	0.0	0	0.0	0.00	1.0000		
- figure-exposition	7	0.0	8	0.0	2.29	0.1301		0.118
- _exposition_review_	0	0.0	0	0.0	0.00	1.0000		

Figure 4.7 Sample of comparison of normalized elemental genre frequency between the linguistics ERAs and the physics ERAs

As demonstrated by Figure 4.7, the search conditions are set as "compare datasets", "feature patterns", and "per 1,000 tokens" at the first line. Then the unit of interest is chosen as "elemental genre in the macro generic stage of Method". After settling the comparing disciplines of linguistics and physics, the results of Chi-square tests and p-values are presented on the screen. The elemental genres with p<.05 are considered as being of statistical significance for further discussion. The results of the comparisons between the linguistics

① Though both the linguistics and the physics ERAs contain the macro generic stage of Literature review, there are only three physics ERAs that contain this macro generic stage. Therefore, the comparison of this macro generic stage is omitted.

ERAs and the physics ERAs are illustrated from Table 4.10 to Table 4.13.

As for the similarities in terms of elemental genre deployments in each macro generic stage, there are two points worthy of emphasizing.

Firstly, descriptive reports are found in all the macro generic stages of the ERAs. According to Rose and Martin (2012:130), the high frequency and diverse scattering of descriptive reports can be explained by the purpose of descriptive reports. In the Introduction section, descriptive reports can be used to describe the characters of related studies. In the Methods section, they are used for unfolding research participants or instruments whereas in the Results and Discussion sections, they are employed for stating the research results.

Secondly, for the linguistics ERAs and the physics ERAs, reviews occur frequently in the Introduction and Literature review parts. In these sections, related studies are analyzed and evaluated through reviews. Furthermore, expositions, which are used for arguing for a position, are frequently employed in the Results, R&D, and Discussion sections, where research results are evaluated and interpreted (Lewin, et al., 2001).

In terms of the differences in elemental genre deployments in each macro generic stage, the comparisons are conducted through two aspects. One is the observation of normalized frequency of elemental genres in Introduction and Conclusion macro generic stages among the three sub-corpora and the other is the Chi-square tests on normalized frequency of elemental genres in the linguistics ERAs and the physics ERAs.

Regarding the comparisons among the three sub-corpora, the differences lie in the macro generic stage of Introduction, where the physics ERAs use more elemental genres in the genre family of Reports (0.3 per 1,000 tokens), while the literature ERAs employ more various elemental genres, including those in Explanations, Arguments, and Recounts.

For the comparisons between the linguistics ERAs and the physics ERAs, the results in the Methods, Results, R&D, and Discussion sections are listed in Tables 4.10-4.13 respectively.

Table 4.10 Comparison between the linguistics ERAs and the physics ERAs in Methods

Type of elemental genres	Linguistics		Physics			
	N	F	N	F	Chi-Square	p-value
Descriptive report	106	0.2	77	0.3	4.36	0.0367
Sequential explanation	10	0.0	29	0.1	27.03	0.0000
Direct formula recount	0	0	23	0.1	43.24	0.0000
Conditional formula recount	0	0	10	0.0	18.8	0.0000
Sequential formula recount	0	0	28	0.1	52.64	0.0000
Review	0	0	3	0.0①	5.64	0.0176

Note: N=Number; F=Frequency per 1,000 tokens

Table 4.10 illustrates the results of Chi-Square tests on the frequency of elemental genres in Methods, which show that the physics ERAs use more descriptive reports, sequential explanations, and three types of formula recounts than the linguistics ERAs. This fact reflects the physics ERAs are knowledge-code oriented. According to Maton (2014), disciplines with knowledge codes emphasize what you know about and how. In other words, knowledge is legitimatized through following adequate procedures and rigorous methods (Hu&Cao, 2015). In the methods section, descriptive reports are used to describe the preparation of experiments, including instruments and tools. Sequential explanations explain the aims of the experiments. The three types of formula recounts are used for interpreting the meaning of formulas.

Table 4.11 Comparison between the linguistics ERAs and the physics ERAs in Results

Type of elemental genres	Linguistics		Physics			
	N	F	N	F	Chi-square	p-value
Sequential explanation	4	0.0	6	0.1	7.21	0.007 3
Factorial explanation	6	0.0	10	0.1	13.18	0.000 3
Exposition review	44	0.1	0	0	13.77	0.000 2
Figure exposition	18	0.1	22	0.2	21.41	0.000 0
Direct formula recount	0	0	4	0.0	12.78	0.000 3

Note: N=Number; F=Frequency per 1,000 tokens

① Since the data in UAM CT 6.2e only retains one decimal point, 0.0 is displayed here. The same situation occurs in Table 4.11-4.13.

In Table 4.11, the Chi-square tests on elemental genres in Results indicate that there are differences among five elemental genres. Because of the different knowledge-knower structures, the linguistics ERAs use more exposition reviews than the physics ERAs. However, the latter utilizes markedly more sequential explanations, factorial explanations, figure expositions, and direct formula recounts than the former. Physics, a knowledge-code-oriented discipline, presents a precise description of the physical world with formulas and figures. In addition, various elemental genres in explanations genre families are used to explore the reasons behind specific physical phenomena. Linguistics, which belongs to the social science (cf. Martin, et al., 2010:438), proceeds by adding new knowledge. Therefore, the reader can be convinced of the writer's point of view through expositions.

Table 4.12 Comparison between the linguistics ERAs and the physics ERAs in R&D

Type of elemental genres	Linguistics		Physics			
	N	F	N	F	Chi-Square	p-value
Descriptive report	7	0.1	30	0.2	9.87	0.001 7
Sequential explanation	2	0.0	15	0.1	7.41	0.006 5
Factorial explanation	2	0.0	18	0.1	9.69	0.001 9
Exposition	21	0.2	12	0.1	4.85	0.027 7
Exposition review	12	0.1	1	0.0	11.98	0.000 5
Figure exposition	3	0.0	48	0.4	30.93	0.000 0
Direct formula recount	0	0	8	0.1	6.44	0.011 2

Note: N=Number; F=Frequency per 1,000 tokens

Table 4.12 demonstrates the results of Chi-square tests on elemental genres in the stage of R&D. Similar to the situation in the Results section, the linguistics ERAs use more expositions and exposition reviews than the physics ERAs. However, the physics ERAs use more descriptive reports, sequential explanations, factorial explanations, figure expositions, and direct formula recounts than the linguistics ERAs. This may be due to the different emphasis on knowledge in the two disciplines. The linguistics ERAs tend to persuade readers to accept positions through arguments and defend the arguments through expositions and exposition reviews. The physics ERAs use direct formula recounts and figure expositions to describe and evaluate formulas and figures. Furthermore, descriptive reports are used to present research results, and explanations are employed to explain the reasons.

Table 4.13 Comparison between the linguistics ERAs and the physics ERAs in Discussion

Type of elemental genres	Linguistics		Physics			
	N	F	N	F	Chi-Square	p-value
Sequential explanation	3	0.0	5	0.1	11.31	0.000 8
Figure exposition	0	0	6	0.1	28.46	0.000 0
Direct formula recount	0	0	1	0.0	4.74	0.029 4

Note: N=Number; F=Frequency per 1,000 tokens

Table 4.13 illustrates the results of comparisons of elemental genres in the stage of Discussion, where the physics ERAs employ more sequential explanations, figure expositions, and direct formula recounts than the linguistics ERAs. The writers of the physics ERAs use these elemental genres to talk about figures and formulas. Moreover, sequential explanations are used to explore the reasons behind the physical experiments.

To sum up, concerning the three disciplines, the similarities lie in the frequency distribution of descriptive reports in all the sub-sections of ERAs. Besides, for the linguistics and physics ERAs, reviews occur frequently in the Introduction and Literature review parts. Additionally, expositions are frequently used in the Results, R&D, and Discussion sections.

The prevalence of descriptive reports throughout the ERAs of the three disciplines is in line with the previous studies on generic complexity in linguistics ERAs and bachelor's theses of English majors (Lai&Wang, 2018; Zhang&Pramoolsook, 2019). This finding could be attributed to the functions of descriptive reports. They are employed for introducing the features of related literature in the Introduction, describing research participants and instruments in the Methods, and presenting study findings in the Results and Discussion sections. Moreover, the similar allocation of expositions and reviews in the linguistics and the physics ERAs might also be explained by the functions of two elemental genres. Particularly, expositions are employed for assessing and interpreting research findings in the Results, R&D, and Discussion sections. Reviews are used to analyze and evaluate related studies in the Introduction and Literature review sections.

The disparity among the three sub-corpora lies in the Introduction section, where the physics ERAs employ more elemental genres (0.3 per 1,000 tokens) in the genre family of Reports while the literature ERAs use a larger diversity of elemental genres. This finding may be explained by the different knowledge-and-knower structures of the two disciplines. As a discipline operated by knowledge codes, physics tends to use more reporting genres for describing related studies in the Introduction. Literature, as a knower-code-focused discipline, puts more emphasis on highlighting the knowers' tastes and judgment (Doran, 2018, 33). Therefore, various elemental genres, especially arguing genres are used for validating authors' opinions toward literary works.

The macro-generic-stage-based differences in elemental genre distribution between the linguistics and the physics research papers are calculated by Chi-square tests. Briefly speaking, the physics ERAs boast noticeably more sequential explanations, figure expositions, and direct formula recounts than the linguistics ERAs do in the Methods, Results, R&D, and Discussion sections. The linguistics research papers utilize more exposition reviews than the physics ERAs do in the Results and R&D parts.

The higher instances of sequential explanations, formula recounts, and figure expositions in the four macro generic stages seem to be influenced by the knowledge code. Knowledge claims in the disciplines dominated by the knowledge code are legitimated by the empirical authority that is established from applying universally accepted principles of inquiry and methods of validation (Hu&Cao, 2015). Consequently, there would be a need for physicists to employ elemental genres that could help in increasing procedural adequacy and methodological rigor to strengthen epistemic conviction. In the physics sub-corpus, sequential explanations are used in Methods for explaining the direct reason for conducting certain experimental processes. Figure expositions are frequently used in the Results or R&D sections for summarizing, analyzing, and interpreting experimental results. Formula recounts mainly scatter in the Methods section, describing the meaning of formulas in physics papers. In a word, these elemental genres tend to increase the seriousness of experimental processes, making the knowledge claims persuasive by highlighting the hard facts, including data and formulas. In contrast, linguists' relatively stronger orientation to the knower code implies that knowledge claims are legitimated by the knowers' personal voice or expertise (Hu&Cao, 2015). Consequently, linguists tend to use elemental genres that would increase their authorial voice in research papers. Exposition reviews, with their schematic structure of Thesis ^ Evidence ^ Evaluation, serve the purpose of supporting the authors' thesis statements in the ERA. Thus, they would be employed more frequently by linguists to boost epistemic belief.

4.4 Chapter summary

This chapter focuses on the elemental genre distribution in the ERAs from three aspects. First, the types and major macro generic stages of the ERAs are analyzed. Second, the overall elemental genre deployments in the ERAs are explored. Third, the deployments of various elemental genres in the same macro generic stage are studied.

With regard to the ERA types, the linguistics ERAs can be divided into empirical ERAs and review ERAs. Most physics ERAs are empirical ERAs with a distinct Methods section. ERAs of literary studies are "opinion-stating" types with the macro generic structure of "Introduction-Argumentation-Conclusion".

As far as the major macro generic structures are concerned, the most frequent macro generic structure in the linguistics ERAs is ILMRDC while in the physics ERAs, IM[RD]C is the most common macro generic sequence. In the ERAs of literary studies, the most frequent macro generic structure is (I)A.

In the overall elemental genre deployments in the ERAs, on the one hand, six types of new elemental genres are emerging, including exposition reviews, elucidations, figure expositions, direct formula recounts, conditional formula recounts, and sequential formula recounts. On the other hand, the linguistics ERAs and the physics ERAs follow the same order of genre families, i.e., Reports > Arguments > Explanations > Recounts > Text responses. Yet, the ERAs of literary studies adhere to the order of Arguments > Reports > Explanations > Recounts > Text responses. As to specific elemental genres, the linguistics ERAs possess more classifying reports than the physics ERAs and the literature ERAs. The physics ERAs have direct, conditional, and sequential formula recounts and use more figure expositions than the linguistics ERAs and the literature ERAs. However, the literature ERAs adopt more exposition reviews than the ERAs of the other disciplines.

Regarding the deployment of elemental genres in the same macro generic stage, descriptive reports are dominant in the Conclusion stage of the ERAs of the three disciplines. In the Methods, Results, R&D, and Discussion sections, the physics ERAs demonstrate significantly more factorial explanations, sequential explanations, figure expositions, and three types of formula recounts than the linguistics ERAs. In the Results and R&D sections, the linguistics ERAs use more exposition reviews than the physics ERAs.

The above-mentioned exploration of generic complexity in the ERAs presents some theoretical, methodological, and pedagogical implications.

Firstly, the current study enriches the extant knowledge of generic complexity in the ERAs by discovering six emerging types of elemental genres, which sharpen the analytical framework for exploring generic complexity. Moreover, the discussion of generic complexity of the literature ERAs and the physics ERAs broadens the scope of the existing generic-complexity-related studies.

Secondly, by combining the statistical analysis of SPSS and UAM CT, the present chapter provides statistically significant differences in the genre deployments of the ERAs. Given that the previous discussions on the generic complexity are based on the counting of numbers of elemental genres in the ERAs or the undergraduate thesis of a single discipline, the statistical analysis of the genre deployments offers more convincing results for uncovering the differences and similarities among the three disciplines.

Finally, the findings of the present chapter also provide several implications for the teaching of academic writing. First, the generic complexity in the ERAs should be given deserved attention in courses in English academic writing. As indicated by previous studies, the research on ERAs focuses either on global features such as structures and organizations or on local characteristics like metadiscourse (e.g., Hyland&Jiang, 2018; Swales, 2004). However, the results of the current chapter show that the issue of generic complexity exists in the construction of ERAs. Therefore, it is necessary to raise the student writers' awareness of generic complexity in writing research articles. Second, disciplinary differences in the elemental genre deployments in the ERAs should be emphasized in the courses of academic writing. As suggested by the current study, the ERAs of the three disciplines show distinct differences in either the overall elemental genre deployments or the generic-stage-based genre allocation. Consequently, student writers should be given special instructions on the use of elemental genres.

In the current chapter, knowledge-knower structures offer a plausible explanation for the differences among the ERAs. In the next chapter, the elemental genre combining strategies among the three sub-corpora are discussed.

Chapter 5 Elemental Genre Combining Strategies

As the other main analytical dimension of the current study, genre combining strategies are the resources for organizing the instances of elemental genres into whole research articles. According to Martin (1994, 1995) and Halliday and Matthiessen (1999), these strategies include extension, elaboration, enhancement, projection, and embedding.

This chapter investigates how elemental genres in each main macro generic stage of the ERAs are combined and how they differ across three disciplines. It is composed of eight sections. Section 5.1 briefly summarizes the types and total numbers of genre linking patterns in the three sub-corpora. Section 5.2 to Section 5.6 elaborate on the elemental genre combining strategies in each discipline. Section 5.7 compares the similarities and differences among the three disciplines. Section 5.8 is the summary of this chapter.

5.1 Overview of elemental genre combining strategies

Following Martin (1994, 1995) and Halliday and Matthiessen (1999), the elemental genre combining strategies are identified and counted. The types and total numbers of the elemental genre linking patterns in the corpora are illustrated in Table 5.1.

Table 5.1 Types and total numbers of elemental genre combining patterns (1)

	Intra-elemental genre families								
	Lin			Phys			Lite		
	T	N	P	T	N	P	T	N	P
Extension	20	167	91.26%	29	126	92.65%	47	239	92.28%
Elaboration	6	13	7.10%	4	8	5.88%	11	19	7.34%
Enhancement	3	3	1.64%	1	2	1.47%	1	1	0.39%
Total	29	183	100%	34	136	100%	59	259	100%

Note: Lin=Linguistics; Phys=Physics; Lite=Literary studies; T=Types; N=Total numbers; P=Percentage

Table 5.2 Types and total numbers of elemental genre combining patterns (2)

	Inter-elemental genre families								
	Lin			Phys			Lite		
	T	N	P	T	N	P	T	N	P
Extension	45	160	86.02%	74	260	84.14%	118	453	93.40%
Elaboration	6	6	3.23%	5	6	1.94%	8	8	1.65%
Enhancement	9	20	10.75%	17	43	13.92%	14	24	4.95%
Total	60	186	100%	96	309	100%	140	485	100%

Note: Lin=Linguistics; Phys=Physics; Lite=Literary studies; T=Types; N=Total numbers; P=Percentage

Table 5.3 Types and total numbers of elemental genre combining patterns (3)

	Lin	Phys	Lite
Projection	31	95	10
Embedding	11	0	30

Note: Lin=Linguistics; Phys=Physics; Lite=Literary studies

Before presenting the general results of elemental combining patterns, two points need to be explained. First, as illustrated in Tables 5.1–5.2, three strategies of genre expansion are divided into combinations within or across the elemental genre families. Second, as for genre projection, the current study only discusses the projection of ideas represented by figure expositions. On the one hand, according to Martin (1995:34), figure expositions themselves, and the Figures[①] they project form the typical example of genre projection. On the other hand, focusing on the figure exposition can reduce the influence of subjectivity in the coding process since Figures in the research articles, with their visual presentation, are easier to identify. Similarly, to reduce the coding burden and increase the annotating reliability, overt embedding, which means the obvious font and typological differences between the embedded and embedding texts, is focused on in the present study.

Results show both similarities and differences in terms of genre combining strategies across the three sub-corpora. Concerning similarities, there are three points worthy of mentioning.

First, extension takes a predominant position in the genre linking strategies. As illustrated by Table 5.1, for the genre expansion strategies within the same elemental genre families, the cases of extension occupy 91.26% (167 cases), 92.65% (126 cases), and 92.28% (239 cases) in the linguistics, physics, and literature sub-corpora respectively. Moreover, the distribution of genre-expanding methods across elemental genre families displays a similar trend, i.e., extension takes up 86.02% (160 cases), 84.14% (260 cases), and 93.40% (453 cases) in the linguistics, physics, and literature ERAs respectively.

Second, for genre expansion within the same elemental genre families, the three strategies demonstrate the trend of extension > elaboration > enhancement. To be specific, elemental genre enhancement within the same elemental genre families is rare, with the linguistics, physics, and literature sub-corpora only

① To avoid terminological confusion, a Figure (the initial letter being capitalized) refers to a number drawing or diagram in RAs., while figures (the initial letter being in lower case) is a term in SFL, meaning a representation of experience in the form of a configuration, being composed of a process, participants, and circumstances (Halliday&Matthiessen, 1999:52).

seeing three, two, and one case of genre enhancement correspondingly.

Third, regarding genre expansion across elemental genre families, the three sub-corpora display the tendency of extension > enhancement > elaboration. Specifically speaking, inter-generic elaboration takes only a very small fraction in the linguistics (six cases, 3.23%), physics (six cases, 1.94%), and literature (eight cases, 1.58%) ERAs.

As for the variations, the three sub-corpora differ in the following three aspects.

Firstly, the sub-corpus of literary studies has the most elemental types and numbers in the three disciplines. According to the data in Table 5.1 and within the same elemental genre families, the types of extension in the literature ERAs (47 types) are 2.35 times higher than that in linguistics (20 types), and 1.62 times that in the physics ERAs (29 types). The total number (239 cases) of intra-genre extension is 1.43 times greater than that in linguistics (167 cases), and 1.89 times that in physics (126 cases).

For the inter-genre extension, the combining types of literary studies (118 types) are 2.62 times and 1.59 times greater than those in the linguistics (45 types) and physics (74 types) ERAs. Additionally, the literature sub-corpus possesses 485 inter-generic extension instances, 1.87 times more than those in physics (260 cases) and 3.03 times greater than those in linguistics (160 cases).

The overwhelming types and quantities of genre extension in the literature sub-corpus may be attributed to the abundance of elemental genres in Recounts, which show 13 types of various recounting elemental genres (see Table 4.4), compared with eight types in the linguistics sub-corpus and five types in the physics one. Those recounting genres can form a plentiful number of genre extensions with other recounting genres or genres from other genre families.

Second, the physics sub-corpus (74 types, 260 instances) also boasts more inter-generic types and numbers of extensions than the linguistics ERAs (45 types, 160 cases). This finding may be explainable from the profusion of figure expositions and formula recounts in the physics RAs.

Third, different disciplines favor different genre combining strategies. The physics ERAs see the most frequent use of inter-genre enhancement (43 cases), being twice that in linguistics (20 cases) and literary studies (24 cases) sub-corpora. A close examination of these enhancement patterns (see Table 5.9) reveals that four out of the top five enhancement patterns demonstrate that one reporting or arguing genre is enhanced by an explaining genre. Besides, the physics sub-corpus possesses more projection (95 cases) than the other two disciplines, with 31 cases and 10 instances in linguistics and literature ERAs respectively.

On the other hand, the literature sub-corpus demonstrates the highest number of extension patterns, with 453 inter-generic extensions and 239 cases of intra-generic extensions. In addition, the literature ERAs (30 cases) have more instances of overt genre embedding than the linguistics (11 cases) and the physics (0 cases) sub-corpora.

As for the linguistics ERAs, the three corpora show only several cases of elaboration. The percentage of inter-generic elaboration in the linguistics ERAs (3.23%) is higher than that in physics (1.94%) and literary studies (1.65%).

In the following sections, the specific elemental genre combining patterns in each sub-corpus are presented with typical examples.

5.2 Elemental genre extension

Extension is originally used in the formation of clause complexes, indicating that one clause extends the meaning of another by adding something new to it (Halliday&Matthiessen, 2014:471). In essence, extension is one of the major motifs of the ideation base (Halliday&Matthiessen, 1999:222). As one of the fractal meaning expansion strategies, extension is applied by Martin (1994, 1995) in the formation of macrogenres, showing that one instance of an elemental genre is extended by another instance of the same or other elemental genres.

The top five extension patterns within and across elemental genre families are counted. The results are shown in Tables 5.4 and 5.5. Because the two tables only show the top five extensions of each corpus, the total number of percentages in the tables is less than 100%.

Table 5.4 Top five elemental genre extension patterns: intra-genre families

Disciplines	Intra-elemental genre families		
	Types	N	P
Linguistics (167 cases)	descriptive report+descritpive report	45	26.95%
	exposition+exposition	20	11.98%
	classifying report+descriptive report	19	11.38%
	exposition review+exposition review	18	10.78%
	descriptive report+classifying report	14	8.38%
	Total	116	69.47%
Physics (126 cases)	descriptive report+descriptive report	32	25.40%
	figure exposition+figure exposition	21	16.67%
	descriptive report+compositional report	8	6.35%
	sequential explanation+sequential explanation	8	6.35%
	factorial explanation+sequential explanation	6	4.76%
	Total	75	59.53%
Literature (239 cases)	exposition+exposition	35	14.64%
	descriptive report+descriptive report	34	14.23%
	exposition review+exposition review	23	9.62%
	exposition+exposition review	16	6.69%
	review+review	12	5.02%
	Total	120	50.20%

Note: N=number; P=Percentage

Table 5.5 Top five elemental genre extension patterns: inter-genre families

Disciplines	Inter-elemental genre families		
	Types	N	P
Linguistics (160 cases)	factorial explanation+descriptive report	11	6.88%
	exposition+descriptive report	11	6.88%
	descriptive report+exposition	10	6.25%
	procedural recount+descriptive report	10	6.25%
	descriptive report+figure exposition (descriptive report+procedural recount)①	9	5.63%
	Total	51	31.89%
Physics (260 cases)	sequential explanation+descriptive report	18	6.92%
	formula recount+descriptive report	17	6.54%
	review+descriptive report	17	6.54%
	descriptive report+sequential explanation	10	3.85%
	formula recount+figure exposition	10	3.85%
	Total	72	27.70%
Literature (453 cases)	descriptive report+exposition	27	5.96%
	sequential explantion+descriptive report	19	4.19%
	descriptive report+sequential explanation	18	3.97%
	exposition+descriptive report	18	3.97%
	factorial explanation+descriptive report	14	3.09%
	Total	96	21.18%

Note: N=number; P=Percentage

As illustrated by Tables 5.4–5.5, the similarities and differences in terms of genre extensions are summarized as follows.

For similarities, there are four points to be emphasized.

Firstly, for the extension patterns in the intra-elemental genre families, the top five extension patterns account for more than half of the whole distribution, with 69.47% in the linguistics sub-corpus, 59.53% in the physics sub-corpus

① The patterns of descriptive report+figure exposition and descriptive report+procedural recounts are tied to the fifth place according to quantities in inter-genre extensions in the linguistics sub-corpus.

and 50.2% in the literature one. The reasons may be attributed to the intensive combination of the arguing genres and the reporting genres.

Secondly, for the extensions between inter-elemental genre families, although the top five extension patterns amount to a relatively lower proportion, they still take up a proportion of the total share. The linguistics sub-corpus takes up 31.89%, while the physics and the literature sub-corpus mount for 27.7% and 21.18% respectively. The decrease in the proportion may be explained by the increase in the types of genre extension patterns. Since the inter-elemental extension patterns involve more elemental genres, it is assumed that more types of inter-generic extension patterns exist.

Thirdly, from the specific extension patterns, descriptive report + descriptive report constitutes an important proportion in the three sub-corpora. It ranks first in the linguistics and the physics sub-corpus, with a proportion of 26.95% and 25.4% in the intra-elemental genre extension respectively. It is still listed as the second highest intra-elemental genre combining strategies in the literature sub-corpus, with an occurrence of 14.23%. This finding can be explained by the abundance of descriptive reports (see Table 4.3) among ERAs from the three disciplines. Descriptive reports run through the whole research article, describing the background information in the Introduction, and depicting related studies in Literature review, and introducing experiment participants and instruments in Methods.

Fourthly, some frequent combining patterns are shared by ERAs of different disciplines. In the intra-genre elemental genre extension, the linguistics and the literature sub-corpora share three patterns, i.e., descriptive report + descriptive report, exposition + exposition, and exposition review + exposition review. This finding may possibly be explained by the knower-code orientation of literary studies and the mixing characters of linguistics. Literary studies, as a typical knower-code-centered discipline, tend to persuade readers to accept the writers' point of view by arguing genres. Linguistics, as a discipline situated in the middle of the knowledge structure continuum, shows its mixing features of both knower-code and knowledge-code orientations. The writers' arguments are also convinced through arguing genres.

In the inter-generic extension, the linguistics and literature sub-corpus share two extension patterns, namely exposition + descriptive report and descriptive report + exposition. Two extension patterns, i.e., sequential explanation + descriptive report and descriptive report + sequential explanation, are shared by the ERAs for physics and literary studies.

Regarding differences, each discipline demonstrates its distinctive genre extension patterns.

Firstly, the pattern descriptive report + descriptive report is most prevalent in the linguistics sub-corpus. Intra-generically, three out of the top five extension patterns come from the reporting genre family. In addition, the most frequent inter-genre extension type is factorial explanation + descriptive report (11 cases, see Table 5.5), accounting for 6.88% of the extension patterns across genre families.

Secondly, the physics ERAs demonstrate their preference for using the pattern figure exposition + figure exposition (21 cases, 16.67%, see Table 5.4). Besides, the extensions between explaining genre families see their prominence in the physics sub-corpus. Two out of five top intra-generic extension patterns are explaining genre-based, i.e., sequential explanation + sequential explanation (eight cases, 6.35%, see Table 5.4) and factorial explanation + sequential explanation (six cases, 4.76%, see Table 5.4). For the extensions across genre families, formula recount + descriptive report (17 cases, 6.54%, see Table 5.5) is the type that ranks second and shows disciplinary exclusiveness.

Thirdly, the literature sub-corpus is characterized by the extensions guided by arguing genre families. Three out of the top five intra-generic extension patterns are from the genre family of Arguments. Moreover, exposition + exposition (35 cases, 14.64%, see Table 5.4) and descriptive report + exposition (27 cases, 5.96%, see Table 5.5) are the most frequent extension types within or across genre families.

The following sub-sections take a close look at the extension patterns in each discipline through elaboration on the examples of typical extending types.

5.2.1 Extension in the linguistics ERAs

The overall results of the genre extension strategies in the linguistics ERAs can be summarized from three aspects.

First of all, for the extension patterns within the elemental genres in the same genre family, the top five types are descriptive report+descriptive report, exposition+exposition, classifying report+descriptive report, exposition review+exposition review, and descriptive report+classifying report (see Table 5.4). These major combining patterns are located in the genre families of Reports and Arguments, which is different from Zhao's (2014) study on middle school textbooks, where extension is limited to Reports and Explanations. The reasons for the difference may be attributed to the choice of the research object. The research article, as the major channel for communicating research results and findings (Pang&Chen, 2022:1), uses the Report genre family to describe the related literature, research methods, and research results. In addition, the genre family of Arguments is utilized for establishing and consolidating authors' positions. On the contrary, the major purpose of textbooks is to impart certified knowledge to students (Deng, 2012:52). Thus, Report and Explanation genre families are abundant in middle school science textbooks.

Secondly, regarding the related patterns across genre families, the results are encapsulated from the types and quantities of the elemental genre combining patterns. It can be seen from the elemental genre combining types in the corpus that Reports+Explanations and Reports+Arguments are the two major combining patterns of genre families, with each accounting for 13 types. This may be explainable from the purpose of the research articles. After describing the phenomenon by using Reports, ERA writers tend to explain the reasons leading to the phenomenon by Explanations or persuade readers to accept a certain point of view through Arguments.

From the perspective of quantities, the five most frequent inter-elemental genre extension patterns include factorial explanation+descriptive report, exposition+descriptive report, descriptive report+exposition, procedural recount+descriptive report, descriptive report+figure exposition, and descriptive report+procedural recount (see Table 5.5).

The exploration of elemental genre extension patterns shows that extension exists not only within elemental genres in the same genre family but also among those from different genre families. The most common types of genre extension in the two categories are descriptive report+descriptive report and factorial explanation+descriptive report. The following analysis is unfolded through the detailed expounding from genre, field, and discourse semantics resources.

Firstly, the most common elemental genre combining pattern in the same elemental genre family is descriptive report+descriptive report, which can be illustrated by Example 5.1.

Example 5.1

Phenomenon	Self-Efficacy for Reading French. We measured reading self-efficacy ...
Description	The questionnaire was completed ... It asked about very specific aspects... Cronbach's alpha was .82... We therefore calculated...
Phenomenon	Phonological decoding. This was measured using a pen-and-paper 'sound-alike task'(SALT) ...
Description	In the SALT, each of the items presented participants with... Using knowledge of sublexical SSCs, learners had to... Pseudowords were created by... All words were monosyllabic... One point was awarded... Piloting showed acceptable reliability... In the final dataset in the main study, Cronbach's alpha was...

(Lin 202004) (Graham et al., 2020:702)

Example 5.1, taken from the Methods section of a linguistics ERA, is a combination of two descriptive reports that describe two measurement instruments, i.e., a questionnaire for self-report efficacy and a "sound-alike" task for measuring phonological decoding ability.

From the aspect of the genre stratum, the elemental genre is mainly identified through stages. The two reports spread through the schematic structure of Phenomenon ^ Description. In the first, the phenomenon to be described is the self-efficacy questionnaire. The description stage depicts three dimensions of this questionnaire, including the time for completion, the specific content, and the reliability of the instruments. The second instance of a descriptive report follows the same generic stage with the phenomenon of a "sound-alike" task and the description stage focuses mainly on the specific items and reliability of this task.

At the register stratum, the two reports revolve through two items, i.e., a questionnaire and a SALT task. The two items are taxonomized through various dimensions, such as the specific content of the task and the reliability testing.

The two items are realized as thing entities at the discourse semantics stratum. According to Hao (2020:143), both of the thing entities are instrumentally defined because they are all used for depicting the instruments. Experientially, the phenomenon stages in both texts are realized by material clauses which emphasize "measure". In the first text instantiation, the author uses *we measured reading self-efficacy*. And in the second text instance, a clause of passive voice *this was measured using a pen-and-pencil 'sound-alike' task* is employed.

Moreover, the two descriptive reports provide a wealth of material and relational clauses. The former is employed for depicting the measurement process while the latter is used for describing the validity and reliability of the tests.

Textually, the themes of the first report are "we–the questionnaire–it–Cronbach's alpha–we". Except for the first and last theme, which refers to the people who conduct the questionnaire. The other three themes keep focusing on the thing entity "questionnaire" either through directly mentioning the singular form or pronominal form or through the reliability index of this entity.

Although the second report uses many unmarked themes, a close examination of these themes reveals that they are mainly divided into two groups, with *in the SALT*, *pseudowords*, and *all words* being grouped as one set indicating the content of the task, and *one point*, *piloting*, *in the final dataset in the main study, Cronbach's alpha* stating the reliability testing of the task.

Given that the two major entities are both defined as subtypes of instruments used in the study, the thematic development patterns strengthen the extension relation between the two descriptive reports.

In addition to the extension between two elemental genres from the same genre family, elemental genres in different genre families can also be combined via extension. This can be illustrated by Example 5.2, which follows the combining pattern of factorial explanation+descriptive report.

Example 5.2

Phenomenon	Of the eight learning outcomes, only four learning outcomes maintained averages ... These were learning outcomes...
Factor	One explanation for the transfer of these learning outcomes is that... One explanation for the low student-identified transfer of (3) and (8) is that... Another explanation is that...
Phenomenon	As for the other four learning outcomes, ...these did not demonstrate sustained transfer ...,
Description	although learning outcome (1) did score just below... learning outcome (5) technical definition stands apart from...

(Lin 202010) (Hill et al., 2020: 9-10)

Example 5.2, taken from the Discussion section of a linguistics ERA, is an illustration of an extension of a factorial explanation with a descriptive report.

At the genre stratum, the two elemental genres are identified through stages. The first text is centered on the four strong-transferred learning outcomes. The factor stage explains the reasons for the strong transfer which is realized by three relational clauses. The second text is an instance of a descriptive report with the phenomenon stage summarizing the other four learning outcomes which show minor transfer and the description stage elaborating on the situation of the two learning outcomes.

At the register stratum, the factorial explanation is realized by an itemized activity of implication relation. The implication sequence is demonstrated in Figure 5.1.

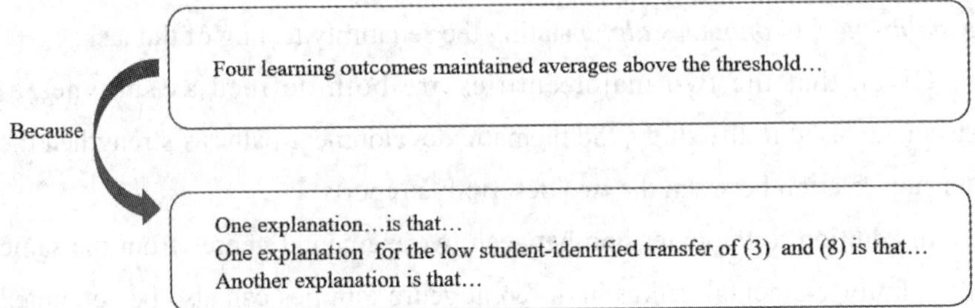

Figure 5.1 Implication sequence in interpreting learning outcomes

Here, the implication relation is recognized by the three relational clauses with "explanation" as participants. Besides, the learning outcome, which is the key item, is realized in the two instances.

In fact, the item is taxonomized into two groups, one demonstrates strong transfer while the other does not. These items are realized as entities at the discourse semantics stratum, which are finally instantiated by nouns or nominal groups at the lexicogrammatical stratum, such as learning outcomes and explanations.

The thematic development of the two texts indicates that the two clips are of extension relation. In the first clip, the themes progress in the chain of "of eight learning outcomes - these (the four learning outcomes which show strong transfer) - one explanation - one explanation - another explanation". The text revolves around the thing entity of four learning outcomes that display strong transfer. In the second clip, the thematic pattern is "the other four learning outcomes - learning outcome 1 - learning outcome 5". The text is centered on the thing entity *the other four learning outcomes*. Since the two entities are categorized as two aspects of the eight learning outcomes, they and the text clips are of equal status. Given the schematic structure and the thematic progressing pattern, Example 5.2 is a genre complex with a factorial explanation being extended by a descriptive report.

To sum up the above discussion, two points are highlighted. First, the extension between the elemental genres within the same genre family mainly scatters in Reports and Arguments, which is different from Zhao's (2014) study on middle school textbooks, where the extension is located within Reports and Explanations. The difference may be explainable from the various purposes of textbooks and RAs. The textbooks aid students in understanding and learning disciplinary knowledge (Wang, 2012:41), while RA, according to Hyland (2005:89-90), focuses on disseminating academics' work and assembling arguments that will go through a laborious and time-consuming process of peer review and ratification to offer the rationale that converts beliefs into knowledge. Thus, Reports and Arguments are two major elemental genre families in the linguistics ERAs (see Section 4.1).

Second, extension is discovered between elemental genres from different genre families. In addition, extension occurs predominantly between Reports and Arguments, or between Reports and Explanations. As illustrated in Table 5.2 (2), factorial explanation+descriptive report is the most frequent inter-generic extension pattern. Besides, three out of the five top inter-generic patterns involve Reports and Arguments, amounting to 30 cases, occupying 18.75% of the total inter-genre extension cases. It may be attributed to large quantities of Reports in the linguistics corpus. Reports are combined mainly with Arguments or Explanations via an extension for proposing the writers' positions or explaining the reasons behind certain phenomena.

5.2.2 Extension in the physics ERAs

Elemental genre extension in the physics ERAs can also be divided into genre extension within the same genre family and across genre families.

The most frequent elemental genre extension patterns within the same genre families are descriptive report+descriptive report (32 instances) and figure exposition+figure exposition (21 instances). Compared with the linguistics sub-corpus, the extension between two descriptive reports still takes a leading position in the physics ERAs. This is illustrated by Example 5.3.

Example 5.3

Description	**A. Materials** In this investigation, **PEO**, …, was purchased from Sigma Aldrich (Poole, UK). **Distilled water** was used as a solvent.
Description	**B. Preparation and characterization of solutions** **PEO** was completely dissolved at concentration 21 wt.% … **The polymer solution** was magnetically stirred for 24h and kept at ambient temperature…

(Phys 201901) (Alenezi et al., 2019:2)

Example 5.3 is extracted from the section of Methods in a physics ERA. As illustrated by the sub-section titles of the two text clips, the two descriptive reports focus on the materials and solution preparation respectively.

As far as genre is concerned, the title functions as the phenomenon stage while the content under the title belongs to the description stage. Viewed from the aspect of the field resources, the first descriptive report interprets the item—materials. The second one explicates the itemized activity–the preparation and characterization of solutions. The item is realized at the discourse semantics stratum as two thing entities—PEO and distilled water. The activity is realized by two figures of material processes.

The two descriptive reports are combined through the logico-semantic relation of extension in that they are all affiliated with the Methods section. The first descriptive report presents the materials in experiments first. Then the second descriptive report adds new information to the preparation of one of the materials—solutions. In other words, the second descriptive report extends the meaning of the first one.

Besides the extension between two descriptive reports, figure exposition+figure exposition ranks second place (21 cases, 16.67%, see Table 5.4) in intra-genre extension strategies in the physics sub-corpus, which is demonstrated by Example 5.4.

Example 5.4

Figure presentation	**C. Numerical analysis** **1. Effects of rotational speed at 7000 rpm without gas pressure** …In general, a higher spinning speed at a constant pressure leads to higher centrifugal force, which promotes higher solution deformation, **as shown in Fig.4. …**
Figure description	In the initial condition, the height of the PEO solution was 5 mm, … blue indicates the air gas fraction as shown in **Fig. 4(a).** ... **Figure 4(b) illustrates** the surface profile of the PEO solution … … **Finally, Figure 4(c) shows** how the PEO solution…
Figure description	**2. Effects of rotational speed at 8500 rpm without pressure gas** **Figure 4(d) shows** that the behavior of the polymer solution at a higher speed, … **In Fig.4 (e)**, it is evident that the polymer solution passed the orifices …

(Phys201901) (Alenezi et al., 2019: 6-7)

As illustrated in Example 5.4, the two text clips form an instantiation of figure exposition+figure exposition. These text clips are selected from the R&D section of a physics ERA. The first one possesses a schematic structure of Figure presentation ^ Figure description. In the figure presentation stage, the purpose of this elemental genre is shown as to demonstrate the effect when the rotational speed is at 7000 rpm. Furthermore, the figure description stage aims to depict *Fig. 4(a)* and *Fig. 4(b)*. However, the second clip only displays the figure description stage, which describes *Fig. 4(d)* and *Fig. 4(e)*.

Seen from field resources, both texts center on the taxonomized item—*Figure 4*. The relation between the item and its dimension is composition. For instance, in the first instance, the figure description stage focuses on *Fig. 4 (a)*, *Figure 4 (b)*, and *Figure 4 (c)*, which are components of *Figure 4*. Similarly, the second text also expounds the taxonomized item *Figure 4* in terms of composition relations. However, in this case, the components *Fig. 4 (d)* and *Figure 4 (e)* are emphasized.

At the stratum of discourse semantics, the figures and components of figures are realized as semiotic entities. Experientially, they are considered actors in the material clauses. For instance, *Figure 4 (b) illustrates...* is a relational clause with the entity *Fig. 4(b)* as the carrier. Additionally, these entities can also be realized as circumstances. For example, in the clause *In Fig. 4 (e), it is evident that*..., *In Fig. 4 (e)* functions as the circumstance in the clause.

The relation between the two text clips is an extension and can be explained from two aspects. On the one hand, they all belong to the section *numerical analysis*, which shows the results and discussion of numerical computation. On the other hand, from the titles of each text clip, it is discovered that they discuss results under different conditions. From the field and discourse semantics resources, they focus on different parts of the same Figure. Therefore, it is rcasonablc to say that thcy arc integrated by extension relation.

Apart from the extension between elemental genres from the same genre families, genres of various genre groups can also be combined through extension. The identification from the physics sub-corpus shows that sequential explanation+descriptive report (18 cases, 6.92%, see Table 5.5) and formula recount+descriptive report (17 cases, 6.54%, see Table 5.5) are the two most common relating patterns in the physics ERAs.

5.2.3 Extension in the literature ERAs

Similar to the linguistics and physics sub-corpora, elemental genre extension in the literature ERAs can be divided into two groups. One is the extension between elemental genres in the same genre family, with exposition+exposition (35 instances, 14.64%, see Table 5.4) as the most frequent pattern. The other is the extending between elemental genres across different genre families, with descriptive report+exposition (27 instances, see Table 5.5) being the most common form. The statistical analysis reflects the important role of the arguments genre family in shaping the literature ERAs. Genres in Arguments can be extended with elemental genres from other genre families such as Reports or Explanations in forming the ERAs of literary studies.

As illustrated by Example 5.5, two text excerpts instantiating expositions are extended by the logic-semantic relation of extension.

Example 5.5

Thesis	...I am interested in how Woolf's descriptions of tiredness evoke a sense of incurable and meaningless weariness.
Arguments	Such ongoing **weariness**..., mediates between the dualism of ability and disability. ... Woolf's reiterated **wish** to lie down reveals how modernism's hegemonic narratives of production and motion rely on the presumed ability of bodies to move...
Thesis	Woolf's idleness, ..., rebuffs the terms of production and labor that inflect modern ideologies ...
Arguments	We have only to look at the work of Henri Bergson and his influence on modernist studies to see his philosophy of ...

(Lite 201906) (Oakey, 2020:209-210)

Example 5.5 is selected from the implicit introduction of a literature ERA. The first exposition concentrates on the ways through which Woolf's description of tiredness arouses a sense of incurable and meaningless weariness. The writer in the arguments stage of this exposition first explains weariness and then analyzes the implication of Woolf's reiteration of weariness. The second exposition argues that Woolf's idleness rejects the concept of work and production that inform contemporary ideologies. Furthermore, the arguments stage supports the thesis with the viewpoints proposed by Henri Bergson.

In terms of the field resources, the two expositions explicate the item—weariness. In the first exposition, this item is realized as semiotic entities *weariness* and *wish* at the discourse semantics stratum. The two entities function as actors in two material clauses. In the second exposition, the thesis stage is realized by a material process *rebuff*. In the arguments stage, the source entity *we* and the thing entity *the work of Henri Bergson* are presented. This argument is used to provide background information. Given that the first exposition argues for the features of weariness directly. The second exposition reveals its features from the negative side. It can be said that the second exposition adds something new to the first exposition. In other words, the relation between them is extension.

Apart from the extension between elemental genres in the same genre family, the extension also appears within elemental genres across different genre families. The most frequent pattern in the literature ERAs is descriptive report+exposition (27 cases, 5.96%, see Table 5.5). This can be exemplified in Example 5.6.

Example 5.6

Description	The series, however, faces a bit of a challenge: the systemic violence and environmental devastation… is legendary, and oil barons have come under criticism...
Thesis	The series undermines these critiques ...
Arguments	It portrays the boomtown as a cheerful carnival, strung with glows of colored light… It also softens its petro-hero…

(Lite 202006) (Crosby&Willow, 2020:87)

Example 5.6 is extracted from the Argumentation section of a literature ERA. It is an example of an extension between a descriptive report and an exposition. In fact, the two elemental genres in this example do not follow the standard schematic structure of the genre. The descriptive report only includes the description stage, which aims to report the challenges faced by the TV series. The exposition contains the thesis and arguments stage, which serves the purpose of supporting the position that the series undercuts these criticisms by softening the setting and characters in it. The arguments support the two claims made by the thesis, setting, and character, respectively.

At the field stratum, the descriptive report is realized by the taxonomized item—challenge. This item is classified into systemic violence, environmental devastation, and criticism of oil barons whereas the exposition is complicated at the field stratum. To some extent, this exposition is constructed by the item: the point of view about the TV series.

At the discourse semantics stratum, experientially, the activity entities *systemic violence*, *environmental devastation*, and *criticisms to oil barons* are realized as participants in clauses. *Systemic violence* and *environmental devastation* serve as identifiers in relational clauses. *Oil barons* is the actor in a material clause.

The two elemental genres are combined by extension relation in that the descriptive report describes the criticism and extends the exposition arguing for the rejection of criticisms.

5.3 Elemental genre elaboration

Genre elaboration, according to Martin (1994, 1995), refers to one text which instantiates one elemental genre and reinterprets the other text clips. Based on the analysis of the current study, it is discovered that the elaboration can be either exemplification or specification. Exemplification means the text instance is used as an example for supporting the previous elemental genre. Specification refers to the elaborating genre particularizes the entities realized by the elaborated genres. The specific examples of the two sub-types of genre elaboration are presented in the following sub-sections. Besides, the similarities and differences in elemental genre elaboration strategies among the three sub-corpora are summarized in Table 5.6 and Table 5.7. Following Halliday and Matthiessen's (2014:461) discussion on elaboration, "=" is the symbol indicating extension.

Table 5.6 Elemental genre elaboration patterns: intra-genre families

Disciplines	Intra-elemental genre families		
	Types	N	P
Linguistics (13 cases)	descriptive report=descriptive report	5	38.46%
	classifying report=classifying report	2	15.38%
	factorial explanation=factorial explanation	2	15.38%
	procedural recount=procedural recount	2	15.38%
	descriptive report=classifying report	1	7.69%
	classifying report=descriptive report	1	7.69%
	Total	13	100.00 %
Physics (8 cases)	descriptive report=descriptive report	3	37.50%
	descriptive report=classifying report	2	25.00%
	exposition=exposition	2	25.00%
	sequential formula recount=formula recount	1	12.50%
	Total	8	100.00 %
Literature (19 cases)	exposition=exposition review	4	21.05%
	elucidation=exposition	4	21.05%
	sequential explanation=factorial explanation	2	10.53%
	elucidation=exposition review	2	10.53%
	classifying report=descriptive report	1	5.26%
	historical recount=biographical recount	1	5.26%
	figure exposition=figure exposition	1	5.26%
	factorial explanation=factorial explanation	1	5.26%
	exposition review=exposition review	1	5.26%
	descriptive report=descriptive report	1	5.26%
	conditional explanation=conditional explanation	1	5.26%
	Total	19	100.00 %

Note: N=Number; P=Percentage

Table 5.7 Elemental genre elaboration patterns: inter-genre families

Disciplines	Inter-elemental genre families		
	Types	N	P
Linguistics (6 cases)	factorial explanation=descriptive report	1	16.67%
	classifying report=figure exposition	1	16.67%
	classifying report=historical recount	1	16.67%
	classifying report=review	1	16.67%
	exposition=anecdote	1	16.67%
	exposition=review	1	16.67%
	Total	6	100.00 %
Physics (6 cases)	descriptive report=review	2	33.33%
	descriptive report=sequential explanation	1	16.67%
	exposition=descriptive report	1	16.67%
	descriptive report=formula recount	1	16.67%
	classifying report=review	1	16.67%
	Total	6	100.00 %
Literature (8 cases)	descriptive report=exposition review	1	12.50%
	descriptive report=exposition	1	12.50%
	exposition=descriptive report	1	12.50%
	exposition review=descriptive report	1	12.50%
	factorial explanation=exposition review	1	12.50%
	exposition=historical recount	1	12.50%
	exposition review=observation	1	12.50%
	factorial explanaiton=review	1	12.50%
	Total	8	100.00 %

Note: N=Number; P=Percentage

Regarding similarities, there are two points worthy of being highlighted.

First, genre elaboration takes up a small fraction of the overall genre combining patterns in the three sub-corpora. As illustrated in Table 5.1, intra-generically, the linguistics ERAs have 13 cases (7.10%) while the physics and literary studies sub-corpora have eight instances (5.88%) and 19 cases (7.34%) respectively. Inter-generically, genre elaboration occupies a smaller proportion, with 3.23% (six cases) in the linguistics ERAs. 1.94% (six cases) and 1.65% (eight cases) are genre elaborations in physics and literature ones.

Second, intra-generic genre elaborations are more frequent than inter-generic ones in the three sub-corpora. The proportions of intra-generic genre elaborations are 2.20 (7.10% vs. 3.23%), 3.03 (5.88% vs. 1.94%), and 4.45 (7.34% vs. 1.65%) times greater than inter-generic genre elaborations in the linguistics, physics, and literature ERAs (see Table 5.1). Furthermore, as demonstrated in Table 5.7, various patterns of inter-generic elaborations occur only once or twice across the three corpora.

In terms of variations, the three sub-corpora differ in their most common genre elaboration patterns. The linguistics and the physics ERAs share the most frequent pattern, i.e., descriptive report=descriptive report. This pattern occurs five times, accounting for 38.46% of the intra-generic elaboration in the linguistics sub-corpus (see Table 5.6). Three cases of this pattern are found in the physics ERAs. On the contrary, the literature sub-corpus possesses more elaborations between arguing genres, with exposition=exposition and elucidation=exposition being the most frequent elaboration types, each appearing four times.

The following sub-sections describe the typical elaboration types in the three corpora.

5.3.1 Elaboration in the linguistics ERAs

Compared with the various patterns of elemental genre extension in the linguistics sub-corpus, elemental genre elaboration only appears in several cases. As illustrated by Tables 5.6–5.7, elaboration can occur within the same elemental genre family, such as descriptive report=descriptive report (five cases), classifying report=classifying report (two cases), or across different elemental genre families with the pattern of factorial explanation=descriptive report (one case). Example 5.7 is a case of genre elaboration between descriptive reports.

Example 5.7

Phenomenon	**The data analyzed in this article were collected** as part of a larger study focused on the implementation and outcomes of ...
Description	The study involved explicit instruction about... Data were collected during one-on-one meetings... These meetings were audio- and video-recorded...
Phenomenon	The current analysis focuses on **one data source** used to document and support development in performance abilities ...
Description	...

(Lin 201901) (Van Compernolle, 2019: 876-877)

Example 5.7 is extracted from the Methods section of a linguistics ERA. Firstly, the elemental genres are identified through the schematic structures of the text clips. Both texts instantiate descriptive reports with the generic structure of Phenomenon ^ Description. The first focuses on the general data of the larger study. In the description stage, different dimensions of the data are introduced, such as the instruction and communicative tasks, and the tutoring meetings used for collecting data. The second descriptive report centers on one data source of the larger study, which is stated clearly by the first clause in the phenomenon stage of the genre.

Because the second descriptive report focuses on one part of the data mentioned by the first one, it is reasonable to conclude that the relation between the two descriptive reports is an extension. To be specific, the second descriptive report particularizes the first one.

5.3.2 Elaboration in the physics ERAs

There are altogether eight cases of intra-generic elaboration and six inter-generic elaborations in the physics sub-corpus (see Tables 5.6–5.7). The elaboration can either occur between genres from the same genre family or across different genre families. Example 5.8 illustrates the elaboration between two descriptive reports, which ranks as the most frequent genre elaboration pattern in the physics ERAs (three cases, 37.50%, see Table 5.6).

Example 5.8

Phenomenon	**The triboelectric nanogenerator (TENG)** is a newly developed technology that has the advantages of …
Description	The operation principle is based on … In a recent report, an advanced TENG unit …produced an average power density… Recently, Lin et al. presented a pendulum-inspired spherical TENG.
Phenomenon	Here, **we proposed an operation-duration-extended cylindrical TENG…**
Description	Compared to the pendulum-like TENG, a cylindrical TENG can achieve denser and more stable power outputs… … Under one excitation, the cylindrical TENG can oscillate for about 85s…

(Phys 20200103) (Feng et al., 2020:1-2)

Example 5.8 presents the elaboration between two descriptive reports. The separate elemental genre is identified through aims and generic stages. Both of them follow the generic stage of Phenomenon ^ Description. The first one focuses on introducing TENG. The second one specifies a particular TENG: an operation-duration-extended cylindrical TENG.

In terms of the field aspect, the first descriptive report concentrates on the taxonomized item—TENG. The description stage unfolds to introduce different dimensions of TENG. The second one centers on another taxonomized item—a specific type of TENG. Furthermore, the following description stage depicts the advantages of this kind of triboelectric nanogenerator.

The items are realized at the discourse semantics stratum as semiotic entities. For instance, the identifier *the triboelectric nanogenerator* in the first relational clause is the direct realization of the items.

Furthermore, the taxonomized dimensions of the items are realized as different participants experientially. For example, one aspect of the item—the operation principle is realized as the agent in the clause *The operation principle is based on….* The other dimension, a sub-type of this TENG—a spherical one, is realized as the goal in a material clause *recently, Lin et al. presented a pendulum-inspired spherical TENG*.

As for the second descriptive report, the taxonomized item "cylindrical TENG" is represented as an actor in the clause *a cylindrical TENG can achieve denser and more stable power outputs* and *the cylindrical TENG can oscillate for about 85s*. The modality shows the ability of this type of TENG.

From the above analysis, it is discovered that the first descriptive report focuses on the general TENG. However, the second descriptive report revolves around one specific type of TENG. In other words, the second text clip particularizes the first one. Therefore, the relation between them is elaboration.

5.3.3 Elaboration in the literature ERAs

In the previous section, one type of elemental genre elaboration—specification is analyzed, i.e., the elaborating genre particularizes one aspect of the elaborated genre. In this section, another type of elaboration—exemplification, is discussed. Following Halliday and Matthiessen (2014:463), exemplification refers to the process in which the second clause develops the thesis of the primary clause by becoming more specific about it, often citing an actual example. Concerning elemental genre combining strategies, exemplification means that the elaborating genre works as an example for supporting the elaborated genre.

Besides, the elaboration, though scarce in the literature sub-corpus, can also be found within the same genre family or across various genre families. Among them, the elaboration within the genre family of Arguments is relatively higher, with elucidation=exposition and exposition=exposition review each appearing four times in the corpus (see Table 5.6).

Example 5.9

Thesis	The idea of "suffisaunce" outlines the problematic biopolitics of ...
Arguments	As Agamben observes, … The personified Fortune concurs in this poem's reworking of ... …as J. Allan Mitchell puts it, …
Thesis	We can better understand the interaction between "suffisaunce" and "haboundance" in "Fortune" by examining a formally simpler lyric,
Description	Here Chaucer's lyricism takes on something like the voice of Lady Philosophy, … Here is its first stanza…
Analysis (evaluation)	Perhaps this sound-bite quality accounts for the popularity of this poem... Modally, the maxims shift between imperatives and indicatives…

(Lite 201905) (Nelson, 2019:78-79)

Example 5.9 demonstrates an exposition elaborated by an exposition review. Firstly, the elemental genre is identified through the schematic structure and purpose of the text clips. The exposition spreads with the schematic stage of Thesis ^ Arguments. The thesis states that "suffisaunce" outlines the poem "fortune". The arguments stage employs the viewpoints of literary critics about fortune. In addition, the exposition review followed further illustrates the interaction between suffisaunce and haboundance by analyzing the first stanza of the poem. In other words, the second text clip is used as an exemplification of the first text clip.

In addition to the elaboration between elemental genres within a single genre family, elemental genres within several genre families also exhibit elaboration. The elemental genres are mainly located in the genre families of Reports and Arguments. As is shown in Table 5.7, four out of the six inter-generic elaborations occur between reporting and arguing genres. Example 5.10 is an illustration of the genre combining pattern of descriptive report = exposition.

Example 5.10

Description	In Italy itself, Italian travel reports mainly from the Asian region, …, were being widely read. … The reports were written in a stylish, rational, systematic and scholarly manner…
Thesis	These primary emplotments…are also characterized by a genre-dependent intertextuality ...
Arguments	They drew on numerous Italian travel accounts from the mid-century onwards, ..., these travel accounts contain various observations about the foreign lands visited.
Restatement of thesis	This recording tradition of Italian travelers, …, is thus a legacy of the notarial-documentary culture of civic life in central and northern Italy...

(Lite 202003) (Tiller, 2020:364)

As is shown in Example 5.10, the description aims at introducing various dimensions of Italian travel reports, which include its scope or readers, content, and writing styles. The exposition particularizes one aspect of the written styles of those travel logs through the schematic structure of Thesis ^ Arguments ^ Restatements of arguments. The thesis explicates clearly what is going to be discussed is the genre-dependent intertextuality of the travel logs. The arguments stage further supports the author's position on intertextuality by referring to the fact that those travel logs draw on previous Italian travel accounts. The final stage of restatement of the thesis recaps the topic again by emphasizing that the recording of those travelers is a legacy of the notarial-documentary culture of civic life.

Given that the exposition focuses on one aspect of the written style of the travel log. It makes sense to draw the conclusion that the descriptive report and the exposition form an elaboration relation. Specifically, the exposition particularizes one aspect of the descriptive report.

5.4 Elemental genre enhancement

Genre enhancement, for Martin (1994, 1995), refers to the case in which one text instantiation of one elemental genre embellishes another text with circumstantial features of time, place, cause, or condition. The overall results of genre enhancement strategies are presented in Table 5.8, Table 5.9, and Table 5.10.

Table 5.8 Elemental genre enhancement patterns: intra-genre families

Disciplines	Intra-elemental genre families		
	Types	N	P
Linguistics	classifying report×descriptive report	1	33.33%
	classifying report×classifying report	1	33.33%
	sequential explanation×factorial explanation	1	33.33%
	Total	3	100.00 %
Physics	sequential explanation×factorial explanation	2	100.00 %
Literature	factorial explanation×sequential explanation	1	100.00 %

Note: N=Number; P=Percentage

Table 5.9 Elemental genre enhancement patterns: inter-genre families (1)

Disciplines	Inter-elemental genre families		
	Types	N	P
Linguistics (20 cases)	descriptive report×factorial explanation	8	40.00%
	exposition×factorial explanation	3	15.00%
	classifying report×sequential explanation	2	10.00%
	classifying report×factorial explanation	2	10.00%
	descriptive report×consequential explanation	1	5.00%
	figure exposition×factorial explanation	1	5.00%
	elucidation×factorial explanation	1	5.00%
	review×factorial explanation	1	5.00%
	historical recount×sequential explanation	1	5.00%
	Total	20	100%
Physics (43 cases)	descriptive report×factorial explanation	14	32.56%
	descriptive report×sequential explanation	5	11.63%
	exposition×factorial explanation	4	9.30%
	figure exposition×factorial explanation	3	6.98%
	sequential formula recount×review	3	6.98%
	exposition×sequential explanation	2	4.65%
	formula recount×sequential explanation	2	4.65%
	classifying report×factorial explanation	1	2.33%
	descriptive report×exposition	1	2.33%
	classifying report×exposition	1	2.33%
	classifying report×figure exposition	1	2.33%
	formula recount×descriptive report	1	2.33%
	figure exposition×sequential explanation	1	2.33%
	formula recount×factorial explanation	1	2.33%
	sequential formula recount×sequential explanation	1	2.33%
	sequential formula recount×elucidation	1	2.33%
	sequential explanation×review	1	2.33%
	Total	43	100%

Note: N=Number; P=Percentage

Table 5.10 Elemental genre enhancement patterns: inter-genre families (2)

Disciplines	Inter-elemental genre families		
	Types	N	P
Literature (24 cases)	descriptive report×sequential explanation	3	12.50%
	exposition×factorial explanation	3	12.50%
	descriptive report×factorial explanation	2	8.33%
	elucidation×factorial explanation	2	8.33%
	descriptive report×review	2	8.33%
	elucidation×factorial explanation	2	8.33%
	narrative×sequential explanation	2	8.33%
	historical recount×factorial explanation	2	8.33%
	exposition×review	1	4.17%
	compositional report×exposition	1	4.17%
	exposition×sequential explanation	1	4.17%
	challenge×factorial explanation	1	4.17%
	exposition×conditional explanation	1	4.17%
	figure exposition×factorial explanation	1	4.17%
	Total	24	100.00 %

Note: N=Number; P=Percentage

The similarities in elemental genre enhancement across the three sub-corpora lie in the following three aspects.

First, genre enhancement appears more frequently among different genre families. The linguistics, physics, and literature sub-corpora only see three, two, and one occurrences of intra-generic elemental genre enhancement (see Table 5.1). On the contrary, 20, 43, and 24 cases of inter-generic enhancement appear in the linguistics, physics, and literature ERAs respectively.

Second, the three corpora share the patterns exposition × factorial explanation and descriptive report × factorial explanation. In fact, the latter enhancement pattern is listed as the most frequent enhancing type in the linguistics (eight cases, 40.00%) and the physics (14 instances, 32.56%) research papers (see Table 5.9).

Third, the elemental genres in the genre family of Explanations often act as enhancing genres. As is shown in Table 5.9, all the four most frequent enhancement patterns in the linguistics sub-corpus include explanations. Furthermore, four out of the top five enhancing patterns in the physics ERAs and the literature ones contain explaining genres (see Table 5.9).

As for the differences, different disciplines favor different genre-enhancing patterns.

First, the linguistics sub-corpus witnesses the abundance of Reports × Explanations. Three out of the top four enhancement patterns follow the type of reporting genres enhanced by explaining genres. They are descriptive report × factorial explanation (eight cases, 40.00%), classifying report × sequential explanation (two cases, 10.00%), and classifying report × factorial explanation (two cases, 10.00%) (see Table 5.9).

Second, except for the genre enhancement between the genre families of Reports and Explanations, the physics ERAs show the exclusive enhancing pattern, i.e., sequential formula recount × review (three cases, 6.98%, see Table 5.9).

Third, the literature sub-corpus displays the enhancement patterns between genre families of Arguments and Explanations. As illustrated in Table 5.10, the enhancing patterns of exposition × factorial explanation and elucidation × factorial explanation occur three times and twice respectively. Besides, the enhancement patterns between genre families of Recounts and Explanations also exist in the literature corpus, with the patterns narrative × sequential explanation and historical recount × factorial explanation occurring twice. This finding can be attributed to the knower-code-orientation of literary studies, where arguing genres are employed to persuade readers to accept writers' viewpoints. The following sub-sections unfold with the analysis of typical enhancement patterns in the ERAs from each discipline.

5.4.1 Enhancement in the linguistics ERAs

The examination of the linguistics sub-corpus reveals that descriptive report × factorial explanation is the most common pattern (see Table 5.9).

Additionally, three out of the top four genre enhancement patterns belong to the type of reporting genres being enhanced by explaining genres. Example 5.11 is an illustration of this linking mode.

Example 5.11

Phenomenon	To investigate the impact of the age factor, the results of the adult group with L1 German were compared to the results of the child learners ...
Description	The children did not differ from the adult ... The more creative patterns, however, were mainly found in the adult learners. Furthermore, the child learners did not work on verb or noun inflection at all.
Phenomenon	The more uniform and less creative patterns found in the child data can be explained ...
Factors	It is thus plausible that the children's more restricted cognitive resources led to ... This interpretation would be compatible with the idea of processing determinism. It is also possible that children are less creative L2 users...

(Lin 201805) (Dimroth, 2018:898)

Firstly, the elemental genre of a descriptive report and a factorial explanation in Example 5.11 should be described, which can be identified through purpose and schematic structure. In this example, the descriptive report aims to convey the comparison results, while the factorial explanation seeks to explain the factors contributing to the findings. The descriptive report is initiated by a material clause with the marked theme *to investigate the impact of the age factor*, which emphasizes the aim of the comparison. The following clauses in the description stage of this descriptive report describe two aspects of the research results: one is that the child learners' uniform use of word order and preverbal negation; the other is their use of fewer creative patterns. The factorial explanation, on the other hand, starts with a verbal clause that contains the crucial process "explain". Furthermore, the following clauses explain the possible reasons for the children's more uniform and less creative patterns. The factor stage is mainly realized by two clause complexes initiating with two relational clauses *It is thus plausible that...* and *It is also possible that ....*

The realization of the elemental genres can be accomplished by using field and discourse semantics resources. The descriptive report focuses on the taxonomized item: results, which are semantically realized by entities, including *uniform use of word order* and *more creative patterns*. The two semiotic entities represent two aspects of the item.

The factorial explanation identifies the activity "explain". The explanation is mainly summarized in the relational clause of *the children's more restricted cognitive resources led to ....* Semantically, this clause is the grammaticalization of an implication sequence: The children have more restricted cognitive resources. Therefore, they have overly schematic linearization. In addition, two relational clauses also serve as the explanation for children's less creative use of linguistic patterns. One is *low processing cost is a ... state*. The other is *children are generally ... L2 users*.

Secondly, it should be approved that the logical-semantic relation between the descriptive report and the factorial explanation is enhancement. Semantically, this relation is implied in the meaning of the two text clips. The descriptive report depicts the comparison results, which indicate that the children use more uniform and less creative patterns than the adult learners. The factorial explanation aims for providing possible reasons attributing to the comparison findings. Lexicogrammatically, the relation is directly realized by the first clause of the factorial explanation, which is *the more uniform and less creative patterns found in the child data can be explained in several ways*. The subject of this clause is the summary of the results represented by the descriptive report.

If the descriptive report does not describe the results, it may be irrational to explain the reasons leading to the results. In other words, the descriptive report provides knowledge presupposition for the explanation. This dependency relation is a vital criterion for distinguishing enhancement from extension and elaboration. Given the above analysis, it is rational to claim that a descriptive report is enhanced by a factorial explanation in this case.

5.4.2 Enhancement in the physics ERAs

Similar to the situation in the linguistics corpus, elemental genre enhancement in the physics ERAs usually occurs between elemental genres from different genre families, which is illustrated in Table 5.1, where inter-generic genre enhancement in the physics ERAs amounts to 43 cases. In the corpus, the combining pattern of descriptive report × factorial explanation is the most frequent genre enhancement mode (see Table 5.9). This type of genre enhancement is illustrated by Example 5.12.

Example 5.12

Phenomenon	Similar shrinkage of the gap for inorganic nanotubes ... has been predicted theoretically, but confirmed **experimentally** for multiwall nanotubes WS_2 and MoS_2, only.
Description	Measurements..., show that the A-exciton transition energy of...is lower than the bulk value... Moreover, it becomes smaller with decreasing nanotube diameter...
Factorial explanation	**These results were ascribed to** enhanced strain, incorporated in the walls of TMDs' nanotubes with the reduction in size... **It was shown** that the strain energy in the rolled triple X-M-X layers follows roughly a $1/D^2$ behaviour, with D being the tube diameter. **The lowered D resulted in** increased strain and in a subsequent gap size shrinkage.

(Phys 202001) (Ghosh et al., 2020:2)

Example 5.12 is extracted from the Introduction section of a physics ERA. From the genre perspective, the first text clip is the instance of a descriptive report with the schematic structure of Phenomenon ^ Description, aiming at reporting the experiment results. The second text clip is an instantiation of a factorial explanation with a merged generic stage of both phenomenon and factors.

From the field perspective, the descriptive report is interpreted as a taxonomized item—result. The factorial explanation is realized by implication activity. These field resources are realized by various discourse semantics resources. For instance, the taxonomized item "results" is recognized by a clause complex *measurements show that the A-exciton transition energy of ... is lower than the bulk value*. Besides this clause complex embedded by a relational clause, the results are also interpreted by a relational clause *it becomes smaller with decreasing nanotube diameter*. On the other hand, the implication activity is realized by a clause and an implication sequence. The lexicogrammatical resources *be ascribed to* imply the purpose of the factorial explanation, which is to explain the reasons leading to the results.

Given the dependent relationship between the descriptive report and the factorial explanation, it is reasonable to claim that the descriptive report is enhanced by the factorial explanation.

5.4.3 Enhancement in the literature ERAs

In the literature sub-corpus, elemental genre enhancement can also be found, but it only makes up a minor portion of the entire corpus. As is shown in Table 5.1, there is only one case of intra-elemental genre enhancement in the literature ERAs. Moreover, 24 cases of inter-genre enhancement are discovered, which only accounts for 4.95% of total inter-generic combining strategies in the literature ERAs (see Table 5.1). Example 5.13 is an illustration of exposition × factorial explanation, which ranks as the most frequent enhancing type (three instances, 12.50%, see Table 5.10).

Example 5.13

Thesis	Intellectuals in T'ien Hsia Monthly adopted Goethe's concept of World Literature from a similar historical context.
Argument 1	...In January 1937, the journal published its own "Aim" and "Special Features" ...
Argument 2	..., it was apparent that the journal was inclined to publish content...
Phenomenon	Based on Goethe's concept, the cultural stance of T'ien Hsia Monthly had its own way of development, which was perhaps due to ...
Factor 1	As mentioned earlier, the editors of the journal were mainly returnees ...

(Lite 201903) (Liu, 2019: 399-400)

At the genre stratum, the elemental genres are identified through schematic structures. The exposition aims to argue the viewpoint that the editors of *T'ien Hsia Monthly* accept the notion of World Literature based on a similar historical background, which is proposed at the Thesis stage of this exposition. In the Arguments stage, this thesis is approved through the historical review of the journal's development, which is signified by the temporal circumstances.

The main idea of the exposition is summarized by the Phenomenon stage of the factorial explanation. Depending on the previous argument of the journal's stance, this factorial explanation enhances the exposition by analyzing the reasons attributed to the cultural identities of the journal. The key lexicogrammatical resources for identifying the factorial explanation lie in the phrase *was due to*.

Given the dependent relation between the two text clips, it is sensible to say that the factorial explanation enhances the exposition by explaining the factors leading to the thesis of the former exposition.

5.5 Elemental genre projection

According to Martin (1995:34), elemental genre projection can be divided into the projection of locutions and the projection of ideas. The former refers to the phenomenon in which one text is quoted by another while the latter indicates the phenomenon in which an alternative form of semiosis (graph, figure, drawing) reworks the content of the projecting text. Considering the heavy coding burden, the current study focuses on elemental genre projection, which is illustrated by figure expositions. Following Martin (1995:34), the figures and the elemental genre of "figure exposition" combined form the genre projection, where the verbal expression projects the visual figures.

As is shown in Table 4.3, the distribution of figure expositions in the three sub-corpora demonstrates the trend of Physics (95 cases, 12.5%) > Linguistics (31 cases, 3.3%) > Literary studies (10 cases, 0.9%). Moreover, the nonparametric tests confirm that the physics ERAs utilize figures expositions more frequently than the linguistics ERAs (p=.001) and the literature ones (p=.000). This discovery may be explained by the knowledge-code orientation of physics, where the validity of knowledge claims is determined by the application of generally recognized rules of inquiry and procedures of validation (Hu&Cao, 2015).

The ensuing sub-sections further discuss the genre projection strategies in the ERAs of the three disciplines respectively.

5.5.1 Projection in the linguistics ERAs

According to the statistics in Chapter 4, there are altogether 31 instances of figure expositions in the linguistics sub-corpus. Furthermore, the counting of the distribution of elemental genres in major generic stages shows that figure expositions mainly occur in the Results or R&D sections (see Table 4.7).

Example 5.14 illustrates a figure exposition. This excerpt is selected from the R&D section of a linguistics ERA. The whole *section 4.1 quantitative data: student practical reports* is considered a figure exposition which is composed of the description and evaluation of four figures. Example 5.14 is the illustration of *Figure 1*. These examples demonstrate multimodal resources. Visually, *Figure 1* is shown in the paper, which is an analytical process according to Kress and Leeuven (1996, 2006). Verbally, the description of this figure is shown by a figure exposition with the structure of Figure presentation ^ Figure description.

Example 5.14

Figure presentation	As can be seen in Figure 1,
Figure description	**the comparison** ... revealed that most students made valuable progress in terms of writing development, … There was **a significant increase** in the number of positive outcomes… **A similar pattern** was seen in all sections…

(Lin 201707) (Kelly-Laubscher et al., 2017:7)

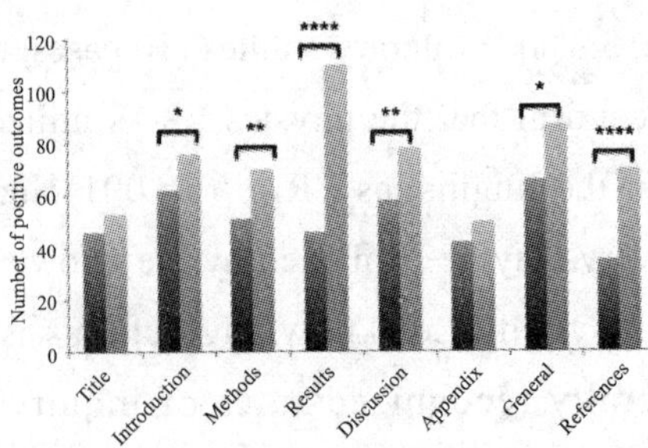

Figure 1. The number of positive outcomes in each section of the student reports for draft 1 (■) and draft 2 (■). *P< 0.05, **P < 0.01, ***P < 0.001.

Figure 5.2 Figure 1 in Lin 201707 (Kelly-Laubscher et al., 2017:7)

In other words, the text instance projects the content of a figure into verbal semiosis. As observed by Martin (1995:34), the figures are elaborated by titles and numbers to demonstrate their dependence on the verbal semiosis projecting them.

As shown in Figure 5.2, the title of *Figure 1* is *the number of positive outcomes in each section of the student report for draft 1 and draft 2*, which is the anaphoric reference of the unmarked theme *as can be seen in Figure 1* in the figure presentation stage.

At the register stratum and viewed from the field, the figure exposition focuses on the description of the item *Figure 1*. The item is touched upon by several dimensions, which are realized by the activity entity *comparison* and semiotic entity *a significant increase* and *a similar pattern*.

At the discourse semantics stratum, the figure is described by a relational process *the comparison of the first and final drafts of the reports revealed...*; an existential process *there was a significant increase", and a mental process "a similar pattern was seen....*

5.5.2 Projection in the physics ERAs

The physics sub-corpus is characterized by its relativeiy intensive use of figure expositions. As illustrated in Table 4.3, there are altogether 95 instances of figure projections in the physics sub-corpus. The normalized frequency of figure projections is 0.3/1000 tokens, which is higher than that in the linguistics sub-corpus (0.1/1000 tokens) and the literature one (0.0/1000 tokens). Moreover, according to the statistics in Table 4.8, figure exposition ranks first numerically in the Results (22 cases, 32.8%) and the R&D (48 cases, 30.2%) sections. Example 5.15 explains elemental genre projections in the physics ERAs.

Example 5.15

Figure description	**When R_1 equals 0.1**, the compensated rate of change…is almost as same as the decay rate of the excited population of the atom…, as illustrated in **figure 10 (a)**. … **When R_1 gets much larger**, the atom is almost decoupled from the pseudomodes, and almost none excitations transfer to the pseudomodes, as depicted in **figure 10 (c), …**
Figure evaluation	For a reservoir with a Lorantzian spectrum, one can utilize the above pseudomode theory to interpret the physics. However, this pseudomode method can not be used for sub-Ohmic, Ohmic or super-Ohmic reservoirs, as there exists no such poles in these reservoir spectrums …

(Phys 201705) (Zhang et al., 2017:11-12)

As illustrated by Example 5.15, the content of *Figure 10* is projected verbally by a figure exposition. Generically, this figure projection is composed of figure description and figure evaluation, providing description and comment on *Figure 10*. At the field stratum, the description stage focuses on identifying the taxonomized item—*Figure 10*. In this case, the taxonomized item is built up through a composition relation, i.e., the components are realized by several clause complexes. In the figure evaluation stage, the focus is still on *Figure 10*. However, this one centers on the application of *Figure 10*.

In fact, nearly every research article in the physics sub-corpus contains figure expositions (2.71 occurrences per article on average). It may be ascribed to the knowledge-orientation of physics, where the figures are used as the direct visual representation of experimental or numerical studies.

5.5.3 Projection in the literature ERAs

Compared with the linguistics and the physics sub-corpora, figure expositions appear in relatively small numbers (10 cases, see Table 4.3), i.e., 0.29 occurrences per article in the literature ERAs. The scrutinizing of the data shows that the figure expositions intensively scatter in the Lite 201705.

Example 5.16

Figure presentation	Using these two metrics..., it is possible to identify a typology of two different kinds of plays... Both kinds can be found in Shakespeare's oeuvre. The first is exemplified by Henry V **(Fig.1a).**
Figure description	**In this figure,** the nodes are sized for EC ... **At the center** of the play is the eponymous figure ... He **is the core** in a trinary king/core/periphery structure.
Figure evaluation	Echoing the pre-Enlightenment figure..., **Henry V is the character who focalizes the action of the play.** He not only interacts with more characters than any other, he interacts with all of the core characters.

(Lite 201705) (Algee-Hewitt, 2017:754)

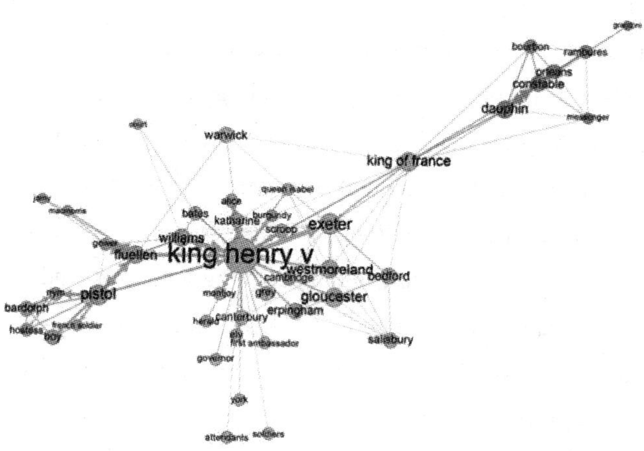

Figure 5.3 Figure 1a in Lite 201705 (Algee-Hewitt, 2017:755)

In the genre stratum, this figure exposition follows strictly the schematic structure of Figure presentation ^ Figure description ^ Figure evaluation. The figure presentation stage is used for providing the background information of the figure. The figure description stage is utilized for depicting the figure with the circumstance as the unmarked theme.

Seeing from Figure 5.3, the figure is projected through the figure exposition. Especially, the figure description stage intensively projects the content of Figure 5.3.

In terms of the register stratum, the figure description stage mainly focuses on the taxonomized item—Figure 1a. Here, the taxonomized dimension of the figure forms a part-whole relation, which is realized at the discourse semantics stratum by circumstances such as *in this figure*, and *at the center of.* The figure evaluation stage, on the other hand, resembles the structure of an exposition.

5.6 Elemental genre embedding

As pointed out by Martin (1994, 1995), elemental genre embedding refers to the fact that one stage of an elemental genre is realized by text instances from another elemental genre.

The close scrutinizing of the corpus reveals that there are two kinds of genre embedding. One is the implicit genre embedding, where the embedding genre is integrated into the embedded genre covertly (Martin, 1994, 1995; Lu&Yuan, 2022). The other is explicit elemental genre embedding, where the embedded genre is marked by a different typography to the genre it is embedded into.

Considering the heavy coding and identifying load, this study focuses only on explicit elemental genre embedding. These embeddings usually occur in qualitative studies, in which other texts are embedded into the RAs, serving as examples of illustration.

According to the analysis of the distribution of elemental genres in Tables 4.3–4.4, explicit genre embedding is discovered in the linguistics (11 instances) and the literature sub-corpora (30 instances). The physics sub-corpus, however, does not exhibit obvious genre embedding. This may be explained through the emphasis on knowledge claims of physics. To be specific, the physicists try to convince readers to accept their viewpoints through data derived from experiments or numerical analysis, rather than quoting excerpts from other texts.

The following two sub-sections present a detailed analysis of that overt genre embedding with examples.

5.6.1 Embedding in the linguistics ERAs

Following the summary of elemental genre distribution in Table 4.4, it is discovered that all of the 11 cases of embedding genres in the linguistics ERAs belong to the genre family of Recounts. Ten of the 11 instances of the embedding genres are observations and the remaining one instantiates a narrative.

Example 5.17 offers an example that an observation is embedded into an exposition.

Example 5.17

Thesis	Her second homestay...proved much more successful.
Argument 1	...there were frequent social outings with family members, such as... and even visiting a friend's baby shower.
Argument 2	The latter, gave Jana invaluable insights into the ways New Zealanders celebrate this tradition: EXCERPT 3 Interview 5 <observation> it was crazy it was like it was decorated like a wedding...

(Lin 201904) (Sauer&Ellis, 2019:749)

Example 5.17 is selected in the Discussion section of a linguistics ERA. Viewed from the schematic structure, it is an exposition with the generic structure of Thesis ^ Arguments. The embedding genre of observation demonstrates the untypical schematic structure, showing only the stage of Comment. This elemental genre is identified through its purpose, which concerns appreciating the influence of the event on the narrator (cf. Jorden, 2003:107; Martin&Rose, 2008:67). In this example, the observation is embedded into the exposition with different fonts and typologies.

5.6.2 Embedding in the literature ERAs

Elemental genre embedding is employed more in the literature ERAs (30 instances) than the linguistics (11 cases) and the physics EARs (0 cases) (see Table 5.3). This finding may be ascribed to the fact that the writers of the literature ERAs often quote the excerpts in the literary works as illustrations of their viewpoints.

In addition, elemental genre embedding is often related to exposition reviews. It usually occurs at the Example or Excerpt stage of an exposition review.

Example 5.18

Thesis	…Sepehri's subversion of ... would indicate otherwise.
Excerpt	The letter <when I read your letter, …, then you can return ...>.
Analysis	It would be quite remiss to interpret Sepehri's letter literally… The letter must be read with a view of his well-known humorous disposition… In the very first lines of the letter, we thus have a multiplicity of places…

(Lite 201907) (Shahmirzadi, 2019:318-319)

Example 5.18 is an illustration of a letter embedded at the Example stage of an exposition review. The thesis of this exposition review is that Sepehri shows his personal point of view. The letter with obvious topo and font characteristics is embedded in the excerpt stage of this exposition review. Then the analysis stage examines this letter to support the thesis of this exposition review.

5.7 Similarities and differences in elemental genre combining strategies

After the identification of the elemental genre combining patterns in the three sub-corpora, the similarities and differences among them are summarized as follows.

As regards similarities, extension dominates in quantity across the ERAs of the three disciplines. Other elemental genre combining strategies scatter sporadically in the corpus. Furthermore, the genre combining patterns involve both intra-generic and inter-generic families.

The differences in elemental genre combining strategies are discussed in terms of the various types of genre linking strategies.

For extension, the most frequent pattern in the linguistics and the physics sub-corpora is descriptive report+descriptive report. This finding may indicate the large quantities of descriptive reports in the ERAs of the two disciplines, where descriptive reports are combined in an extension to describe related studies, research methods, and study results. On the contrary, exposition+exposition is the most common genre extension type in the literature ERAs, where the writers' opinions are mainly expressed and convinced through expositions.

As for enhancement, the pattern of the Reports genre family enhanced by Explanations appears in all three sub-corpora. However, descriptive report × factorial explanation ranks as one of the top five inter-genre combining patterns in the physics sub-corpus. This finding again strengthens the characteristics of physics, which emphasizes the exploration of reasons behind physical phenomena.

As far as genre projection is concerned, the current study focuses on the projection of ideas represented by figure expositions. The analysis shows that figure expositions occur relatively more frequently in the physics sub-corpus. It may be ascribed to the abundance of figures in the EARs of physics, where figures are used for a visual presentation of experiment results.

In terms of elemental genre embedding, the present research centers on explicit genre embedding with obvious font or typography differences between the embedding and embedded genres. The results reflect that there is more elemental genre embedding in the literature ERAs. This may be attributed to the fact that excerpts from literary works are often embedded into the RAs as illustrations for analysis.

To sum up, the ERAs of the three disciplines mainly use the elemental genre of extension to expand the meaning potentials. At the same time, different disciplines show their distinctive features.

The linguistics ERAs show the most frequent pattern of descriptive report+descriptive report (45 cases, see Table 5.4) among the three sub-corpora. The physics sub-corpus prefers to use the pattern of figure exposition + figure exposition (21 cases, see Table 5.4) for presenting and analyzing experiments or numerical results. Besides, the physics ERAs show their exclusive use of formula-recount-related genre combining patterns, including formula recount + descriptive report (18 cases, see Table 5.5) and formula recount + figure exposition (10 instances, see Table 5.5). Obvious genre embedding, however, occurs more frequently in the literature ERAs (30 cases, see Table 5.3). Additionally, the literature sub-corpus boasts more arguing-genre-based combining strategies, including exposition + exposition (35 cases, see Table 5.4) and exposition + exposition review (16 cases, see Table 5.5).

5.8 Chapter summary

Based on Martin's (1994, 1995) discussion of genre complexing, the current chapter aims to explore the mechanism through which elemental genres are combined into a macrogenre. To accomplish this goal, this chapter closely examines the elemental genre combining patterns in the three sub-corpora. The examination of these patterns highlights at least four points.

Firstly, the mechanism for enlarging meaning potential in a macrogenre proposed by Martin (1994, 1995) can all be found in the ERAs.

Secondly, the most frequent strategy for elemental genre combining is extension, which reflects that the meaning is mainly enlarged by the addition of ERAs. In other words, the text clips instantiated various elemental genres are combined mainly through addition.

Thirdly, all these elemental genres combining strategies exist not only within the same genre family but also among various genre families, which shows more complicated situations in ERAs.

Fourthly, the combining patterns between elemental genres indicate disciplinary differences. The physics ERAs use more genre projection because of the preferences of figure expositions in this sub-corpus. In addition, the genre enhancement between descriptive reports and factorial explanation also demonstrates more occurrences in the physics sub-corpus, which indicates the emphasis on reasons ascribing to phenomena in physics. The literature ERAs, on the other hand, see their flourishing varieties of genre linking patterns within Arguments or between Arguments and other genre groups. Besides, genre embeddings appear more frequently in the literature sub-corpus. The linguistics ERAs, however, display a mixture of the first two sub-corpora. On the one hand, they resemble the physics ERAs, which employ many instances of descriptive report+descriptive report. On the other hand, they show a similar preference as the literature EARs in the use of obvious genre embedding.

The next chapter will further elaborate on the elemental genres that characterize disciplinary features through the analysis of genre, register, and discourse semantics strata.

Chapter 6 Particular Elemental Genres

In Chapters 4 and 5, the two major dimensions for exploring generic complexity in ERAs are conducted, which reveal the similarities and differences in elemental genre deployments and elemental genre combining strategies. In the analytical processes, certain elemental genres with disciplinary characteristics are emerging. This chapter aims to present a detailed description of these elemental genres from the aspects of genre, register, and discourse semantics. The reasons for the further exploration of certain elemental genres lie in two aspects. On the one hand, this chapter aims at testifying the analytical framework proposed in Chapter 3. Specifically, field resources at the register stratum can explicate genres, and the field resources such items and activities can be realized by different discourse semantics resources. On the other hand, the exploration of discipline-sensitive elemental genres can provide an in-depth understanding of generic complexity in the ERAs of the three disciplines.

This chapter is composed of four sections. Section 6.1 describes the particular elemental genres in the linguistics sub-corpus, followed by the description of discipline-sensitive elemental genres in the physics academic papers in Section 6.2. The specific elemental genres in the literature ERAs are discussed in Section 6.3. Finally, the summary of the current chapter is presented in Section 6.4.

6.1 Particular elemental genres in the linguistics ERAs

In the linguistics ERAs, classifying reports, expositions, and procedural recounts are chosen for a detailed analysis. The selection of the three elemental genres is determined by the statistical analysis in Chapter 4. In particular, there are three reasons for the selection, which are described as follows.

Firstly, the elemental genre of classifying reports is the only genre that shows noticeably more instances in the linguistics sub-corpus (114 cases, 12.2%, see Table 4.3) than in the other two sub-corpora (physics, 36 cases, 4.7%, p=.000; literary studies, 28 cases, 2.6%, p=.000; see Table 4.3 and Section 4.2.2). This can be explainable from the relatively more Literature review sections in the linguistics ERAs, where the previous studies are classified and described by classifying reports. Besides, the elemental genre is also employed in the Methods section for describing the participants and instruments of the experiments.

Secondly, the linguistics sub-corpus boasts more expositions (127 cases, 13.5%, see Table 4.3) than the physics one (42 cases, 5.5%, p=.010; see Table 4.3 and Section 4.2.2). However, it does not differ in using expositions with the literature sub-corpus (186 cases, 17.2%, p=.079; see Table 4.3 and Section 4.2.2). The finding shows that the writers of the linguistics research articles tend to convince the readers to accept their positions by utilizing expositions, which is a profile of knower-code-oriented disciplines.

Thirdly, the linguistics sub-corpus (46 instances, 4.9%, see Table 4.4) uses more procedural recounts than the literature one (three instances, 0.3%, p=.000; see Table 4.4 and Section 4.2.2), while there is no marked difference in the use of procedural recounts between the linguistics and the physics sub-corpora (34 instances, 4.5%, p=1.000; see Table 4.4 and Section 4.2.2). This may suggest that the linguistics ERAs, to some extent, employ the knowledge-building strategies used by the knowledge-code-oriented disciplines, where the knowledge claim is legitimated through the precise depiction of experimental procedures (Hu&Cao, 2015).

In the following sub-sections, classifying reports, expositions, and procedural recounts will be described in detail from the genre, register, and discourse semantics strata, to uncover how these elemental genres construct the knowledge in the discipline of linguistics.

At the genre stratum, the stage and phases are focused on. At the register stratum, field resources such as activities and items are elaborated on. At the discourse semantics stratum, the current study will follow Martin and Rose's (2014) analytical framework, describing the ideation, conjunction, identification, periodicity, and appraisal resources in construing elemental genres with specific examples.

6.1.1 Classifying reports

Classifying reports are used for classifying certain phenomena based on various classifying criteria with the schematic structure of Classifying system ^ Types (Martin&Rose, 2008:142). In the quantitative study of elemental genre deployments in Chapter 4, both the results in normalized frequency (114 cases, 0.3 /1000 tokens, see Table 4.3) and the nonparametric tests show that the linguistics ERAs employ more classifying reports than the physics (36 cases, p=.000) and the literature ones (28 cases, p=.000, see Section 4.2.2).

In this sub-section, the genre, register, and discourse semantics resources used for constructing the classifying reports are discussed in Example 6.1, which is included in Table 6.1.

At the genre stratum, this classifying report follows the standard schematic structure Classifying system ^ Types. As illustrated by the first two columns in Table 6.1, Stage 1 presents the classifying system, i.e., TBLT research focusing on cognitive processes and attentional resources. Stage 2 describes two different models that concentrate on the cognitive procedures and attentional properties in task completion.

At the register stratum, the field is focused on. Static items and dynamic activities are centered around. These items and activities can be realized as resources at the discourse semantics stratum. Therefore, the examination of the discourse semantics resources can help us sort out the items and activities in this classifying report.

Guided by Martin&Rose's (2014) analytical framework for depicting discourse semantics resources, ideationally, the ideation and conjunction systems are described. Textually, the identification and periodicity systems are discussed. Interpersonally, the appraisal resources are analyzed. For the explicit demonstration of the above-mentioned resources, Tables 6.1–6.3 present the summary of ideation, conjunction, and identification resources respectively.

The ideational resources of Example 6.1 are identified in Table 6.1. The entities, figures, and sequences are analyzed. Based on Martin&Rose (2014:95), the current study explores the relation within a clause through center, nuclear, and periphery. Process is considered as the center of a clause. The nuclear includes participants of a clause. And circumstances are taken as the periphery.

Table 6.1 Ideational resources of Example 6.1

Staging	Nuclear	Center	Nuclear	Periphery
Stage 1 (1)	The role of cognitive processes and attentional resources involved in L2 production during task completion	is	a key interest	in TBLT research
(2)	Two models of cognitive processes and complexity, Skehan and Foster's Limited Attentional Capacity Model … and Robinson's (2001, 2003) Cognition Hypothesis	have emerged		over the past twenty years...
Stage 2 Phase 1 (3)	Skehan and Foster's (2001) model	posits	that as tasks become more complex, learners' ability to focus on both content and form diminishes	since language complexity, accuracy and fluency vie for the same attentional resources
(4)	The three dimensions of task complexity, according to the Limited Attentional Capacity Model	are	code complexity…, cognitive complexity…, and communicative stress	
(5)	The presumption	is		when one type of complexity increases, attention is directed towards that area at the expense of the others
Phase 2 (6)	In contrast, Robinson's (2003) model—also called Triadic Componential Framework	differentiates	attentional resources between resource-directing and resource-dispersing variables	
(7)	Whereas increasing complexity via resource-directing vari ables…	may help	learners produce more complex and accurate language	
(8)	manipulating tasks along resource-dispersing variables…	may place	increased demands on participants' attentional resources…	

(Lin 201609) (Abrams&Byrd, 2016:2)

It can be seen from the ideational resources of Example 6.1 that the major activity sequences of this classifying report describe two types of models concerning cognitive processes and attentional resources in L2 production.

The chief processes are relational processes and material processes. The relational process belongs to the identifying type. For instance, clause (1) states that the main focus in TBLT research is the function of cognitive processes and attentional resources involved in L2 generation. Clause (4) categorizes three dimensions of task complexity. As for material processes, clauses (2), (6), (7), and (8), with the main process verbs as *have emerged*, *differentiates*, *may help*, and *may place* elaborate on the functions of the two models.

Taking the processes as a whole, it is rational to say that the classifying report is used for construing the static item—two models at the field stratum, which are realized by entities, figures, and sequences at the ideational base of the discourse semantics level.

In the second column on the left, the entities identified are summarized, such as *the role of cognitive processes and attentional resources involved in L2 production*, *two models of cognitive processes and complexity*, *Skehan and Foster's model*, *the three dimensions of task complexity*, and so on. The entities are mainly semiotic entities. Furthermore, the relation between them forms two taxonomies. One is the classification one: the research on the role of cognitive processes and attentional resources in L2 production can be divided into two types, which are represented by two models. Within each model, the entities can be further explicated through composition relation or classifying relation. For composition relations, the task complexity is composed of three dimensions. For classifying relations, the variables are divided into resource-dispersing and resource-directing ones.

After the ideational resources of this text clip are analyzed, the conjunction resources are examined to uncover the logical relations between figures and sequences.

According to Martin and Rose (2003, 2014:116), the conjunction system interacts with the ideation system, construing experiences as logically organized sequences of activities. The conjunction resources can be separated into external and internal ones. The former links events in an activity sequence while the latter relates logical steps that are internal to the text itself. The two conjunction resources can be subdivided into addition, comparison, time, and consequence. Except for the four major relations, Lai (2012:126) uses a type of reworking conjunctions, which depicts the details of a general feature.

Table 6.2 summarizes the conjunction resources employed in this classifying report.

Table 6.2 Conjunction resources of Example 6.1

Staging	Internal	Clause/Clause complex	External
Stage 1		(1)	
	Additive to (1)	(2)	
Stage 2 Phase 1		(3)	
	(4)-(5) reworking (3)	(4)	
	Additive to (4)	(5)	
Phase 2		(6)	
	(7)-(8) reworking (6)	(7)	
	Additive to (7)	(8)	

Two points are worthy of mentioning for the features of conjunction resources in this classifying report. One is that all the conjunctions belong to the internal ones, which indicates that they are used to organize the text itself rather than relate the activities. On the other hand, reworking conjunction relation is employed in the *type* stage of this genre. For instance, in Phase 1 of Stage 2, the authors first present the major characteristics of Skehan and Foster's model in sequence (3) [realized by clause complex (3) in Table 6.1]. Figures (5) and (6) [realized by clauses (5) and (6) in Table 6.1] further elaborate on this point by explicating the three components of task complexity and the major presumption of this viewpoint.

Textually, the identification and periodicity systems are explored. Identification, according to Martin and Rose (2014:155), is concerned with "introducing people and things into a discourse and keeping track of them once there". To put it simply, the identification system is divided into introducing resources and tracking resources. The former is realized by presenting references, which are represented by indefinite articles or proper nouns at the lexicogrammatical stratum (Martin&Rose, 2014:168). The latter is recognized by tracking resources, which are realized by definite articles or pronouns lexicogrammatically (Martin&Rose, 2014:168). Moreover, the identity of a participant is presumed through different reference methods, including anaphora, cataphora, cxophora, homophora, and esphora (Martin&Rose, 2014:169-172). The following summarizes the main entities presented and presumed in Example 6.1. Furthermore, the reference strategies through which these entities are introduced or tracked are also discussed briefly.

Table 6.3 Identification resources of Example 6.1

Staging	Studies on the role of cognitive processes and attentional resources	Two models	One model	The other model
Stage 1 (1)	Studies on the role of cognitive processes			
Stage 2 (2)		Two models		
(3)			Skehan and Foster's model	
(4)			The three dimensions of task complexity	
(5)			The presumption	
(6)				Robinson's model
(7)				Increasing complexity via resource-directing variables
(8)				Manipulating tasks along resource-dispersing variables

As for the identification resources, this classifying report centers on four major entities, i.e., studies on the role of cognitive processes and attentional resources, two models, one model, and the other model. It is worth mentioning, that the entities are all presented, without referring to the previous knowledge, which reflects that knowledge is added intensively in research articles.

In terms of the periodicity system, the current study focuses on the unfolding process of the text, which is displayed by theme and rhemes. According to periodicity, there are basically two ways of text progressing, i.e., hierarchies and series (Martin&Rose, 2014:199). A hierarchy of periodicity means that the macro-Themes or hyper-Themes can predict the meaning of the following texts. On the contrary, serial expansion means that discourse is added to what comes before without being foreseen by a higher-level Theme (Martin&Rose, 2014:199).

Regarding the periodicity resources, this classifying report is organized hierarchically. Stage 1 can be considered as the macro-Theme, which predicts the content of the following stages. Actually, Stage 1 presents the two models of cognitive attention in TBLT studies. The following stages dwell on the two models respectively.

To sum up, this sub-section describes the genre, field, and discourse semantics resources of a specific classifying report in the linguistics ERAs. In the next sub-section, an instance of an exposition will be depicted.

6.1.2 Expositions

The previous statistical analysis of elemental genre deployments shows that the linguistics ERAs (127 instances, p=.000; see Table 4.3 and Section 4.2.2) possess markedly more expositions than the physics ones (42 cases, see Table 4.3). The linguistics ERAs and the literature ERAs (186 cases, p=.079, see Section 4.2.2 and Table 4.3), however, do not demonstrate a significant difference in the use of expositions.

This sub-section provides a detailed analysis of an exposition in the linguistics corpus. At the genre stratum, the purpose and the schematic structure of the exposition are discussed. At the register stratum, the field resources, which include items and activities, are explored. At the discourse semantics stratum, the analysis unfolds through experiential, textual, and interpersonal meanings. Experientially, ideation and conjunction systems proposed by Martin and Rose (2003, 2014) are applied to reveal the ideational realization of this genre. Textually, identification and periodicity systems are used for unveiling the textual construal of expositions. Interpersonally, the appraisal resources are touched upon to reflect the interpersonal meanings.

In the linguistics sub-corpus, expositions usually occur in the Discussion or the R&D sections (see Table 4.7), ranking as the top elemental genres in Discussion (56 cases, 40.9%) and in R&D (21 cases, 37.5%), aiming for supporting the writer's point of view after presenting the research results. Example 6.2, which is included in Table 6.4, is an excerpt chosen from the Discussion section of a linguistics ERA. The text is segmented and coded by the clauses or clause complexes for the convenience of analysis. It is important to note that since the clauses and clause complexes are the realization of figures and sequences, the sequential numbers of these clauses or clause complexes are reserved for referring to figures and sequences at the discourse semantics stratum. For instance, clause (1) in Table 6.4 is at the same time the realization of the figure (1).

Table 6.4 Ideational resources of Example 6.2

Staging	Nuclear	Center	Nuclear	Periphery
Stage 1: Thesis (1)	A comparison of the distinctive bundles in this move	revealed	key differences	between abstracts in hard and soft science fields...
Stage 2: Arguments Phase1: Argument 1 (2)	First, many of the research-oriented bundles in this move	were found to be used	by writers in the hard fields	to specify the physical attributes of the following noun...
(3)	These nouns	were found to be	research objects/ contexts...	
(4)	Example 1 and 2 below	show	how these bundles are used in context	
Phase 2: Argument 2 (5)	In addition, hard science writers	had a preference		for using text-oriented bundle types in this move, compared to writers in the soft sciences
(6)	The majority of these bundles	were found to be employed		to situate arguments within a specific context

(Lin 201810) (Omidian et al., 2018:10)

From the genre stratum, this exposition follows the schematic structure of Thesis ^ Arguments, attempting to summarize and analyze the differences between abstracts in hard and soft sciences. The differences between expositions and descriptive reports lie in the fact that expositions not only summarize authors' opinions but also analyze them, which gives a detailed explanation in the analysis at the discourse semantics stratum.

Given that the field resources are complicated in expositions, this subsection employs a bottom-up approach. The resources at the discourse semantics stratum are analyzed first, and then the resources at the register stratum are discussed.

At the discourse semantics stratum, the entities, figures, and sequences are focused on, which is illustrated in Table 6.4. The composing figures in sequences are separated with independent codes for the convenience of analysis.

Firstly, the second column from left to right shows the entities. Following Hao's (2020) classification of entities, the major entities in this exposition are mainly cut into three groups, including source entity (e.g., *hard science writers*), activity entity (e.g., *comparison*), and semiotic entities (e.g., *the research-oriented bundles, these nouns, the majority of these bundles, example*).

In terms of figures, this exposition contains relational figures with process verbs like *reveal*, *be*, and *had* [see clauses (1), (3), and (5) in Table 6.4 respectively]. Other figures belong to the material type, with key verbs like *use* [see clause (2)] and *employ* [see clause (6)].

The conjunction resources in Example 6.2 are summarized in Table 6.5.

Table 6.5 Conjunction resources of Example 6.2

Staging	Internal	Clause/clause complex	External
Thesis		(1)	
Argument 1	Additive to (2)	(2)	
	(3)-(4) reworking (2)	(3)	
	Additive to (3)	(4)	
Argument 2	Additive to (4)	(5)	
	Reworking (5)	(6)	

There are two points in the linguistics sub-corpus in terms of conjunction resources that need to be highlighted. Firstly, all the conjunctions belong to the internal type, which indicates that the connection between figures is dependent on the text-internal relations. Secondly, the reworking conjunction relation is working through the stage of arguments. For instance, the Stage of Argument 1 is initiated by figure (2) [realized by clause (1) in Table 6.4], which is the thesis of this argument. Figures (3) - (4) [realized as clauses (3) and (4) in Table 6.4] provide a detailed analysis of this thesis. Particularly, the meaning of figure (2) is explained through the following figures. To some extent, the stages of Argument 1 take the schematic structure of Thesis ^ Example, which is the structure of an elucidation. The stages of Argument 2 take a similar schematic structure.

Except for the analysis of experiential resources, the exposition in the linguistics ERAs can be examined through textual resources, which are divided into the identification system and the periodicity system.

In terms of the identification system, the key entity *comparison* is focused on. The introducing and tracking modes of this entity are identified. It is discovered that *comparison* is presented by homophora, i.e., the entity is referred to self-reliantly, being independent as a concept that is beyond the boundary of the text. However, the results of the comparison unfold in two aspects in this exposition. One is *the use of the research-oriented bundles*. The other is the employment of *text-oriented bundle types*. The two entities are presumed through anaphora, which is signaled by the use of *these.* This point is supported by the first Nuclear element in figures (3) and (6) [realized by clauses (3) and (6) in Table 6.4].

Regarding the periodicity system, this exposition employs the hierarchical mode of theme development. The macro-Theme is proposed in Stage 1, which is intensively reflected in figure (1) [realized by clause (1) in Table 6.4]—*a comparison of the distinctive bundles in this move revealed key differences....* This macro-Theme forecasts the content of Stage 2, which revolves around introducing and analyzing the results of the comparison.

Lastly, the interpersonal resources are identified by finding out the appraisal resources. A few appreciation resources occur in this exposition. They are *distinctive* and *key*, which describe the features of bundles and differences respectively.

In summary, this sub-section takes a close look at the genre structure, field resources, and discourse semantics features of an exposition in the linguistics ERA. The next sub-section will examine another elemental genre—a procedural recount in the same corpus.

6.1.3 Procedural recounts

Procedural recounts are chosen for detailed analysis for two reasons. On the one hand, they are statistically more frequently used in the linguistics ERAs (46 cases, p=.000, see Section 4.2.2) than in the literature sub-corpus (three cases, see Table 4.4). On the other hand, they do not differ significantly in quantity from the physics ERAs (34 cases, p=1.000, see Table 4.4 and Section 4.2.2). In this aspect, the linguistics ERAs are similar to the physics ERAs, where the experimental processes are described rigidly through procedural recounts.

Following the analytical framework, the genre, field, and discourse semantics resources used for construing a typical procedural recount are described as follows.

As illustrated by the first column in Table 6.6 (Example 6.3), the analysis of the schematic structure of this text shows that it is an instance of a procedural recount embedded by a procedural recount. Overall, this procedural recount is composed of two stages: Stage 1 (objectives) and Stage 2 (steps). In Stage 1, the purpose of the semi-structured interview is explicated. In Stage 2, the four phases record the three steps of the interview: recording and transcribing the interviews, checking the accuracy of the transcriptions, content analysis, and determining key themes of the transcriptions. The three steps occur in a temporal order. Looking closely, it is discovered that Phase 4 of Stage 2 is itself a procedural recount. Sequence (6) [realized by clause complex (6) in Table 6.6] is the realization of the objective stage, which illustrates the purpose of Phase 4. Sequences (7) and (8) [realized by clause complexes (7) and (8) in Table 6.6] clarify the steps of conducting content analysis and extraction of themes. Thus, the schematic structure of this procedural recount is Objective ^ Step 1 ^ Step 2 ^ Step 3 <Objective ^ Sub-step1 ^ Sub-step 2>.

Next, the field resources of this procedural recount are examined phase-by-phase. The procedural recount is realized by two major field resources: the item of the semi-structured interview and the analytical procedures of this interview. The former is realized by figure (1) and figure (5) [realized by clauses (1) and (5) in Table 6.6], which divide the semi-structured interview following the part-whole relation. Figure (1) [realized by clause (1) in Table 6.6] presents the purpose of the interview as a whole while figure (5) [realized by clause (5) in Table 6.6] shows the participants of the interview.

The latter permeates through figure (2) to sequence (8) [realized by clause (2) to clause complex (8) in Table 6.6]. Following Martin and Doran's (2021) system network of activity, this activity of conducting interviews belongs to linear activity, with the process of audioing, transcribing, checking, and coding for themes linearly. From the aspect of momenting, this activity is momented through expectancy relation, which means the former event predicts the happening of the latter one.

At the discourse semantics stratum, experientially, the item and activity are realized in the ideation system through entities, figures, and sequences. The analysis of ideation resources is shown in Table 6.6.

Table 6.6 Ideational resources of Example 6.3

Staging	Nuclear	Center	Nuclear	Periphery
Stage 1: objectives (1)	A semi-structured interview	was used		to extend the themes identified in the COLT (e.g., content and activities)
(2)		and underpin	the teacher's beliefs and knowledge about teaching and learning and the TOEFL iBT	
Stage 2 Phase 1 (3)	The interviews	were audio recorded and transcribed		
Phase 2 (4)	The participants	were given	copies of the transcripts	to check for accuracy, …
Phase 3 (5)	All the interview data	was checked	by participants	with no amendments made
Phase 4 (6)	The COLT, field notes and transcriptions	were then used		to perform a content analysis and determine key themes…
Phase 4 Sub-phase 1 (7)	The raw data	were first organized into	preliminary categories	which were then given codes or themes
Phase 4 Sub-phase 2 (8)	This process	was	ongoing	until the researcher was content with the amount of description…

(Lin 201710) (Barnes, 2017:5-6)

The second column from left to right shows the major entities of this procedural recount. According to Hao (2020), those entities are divided into three types, including activity entities (e.g., *a semi-structured interview, the interviews*), semiotic entities (e.g., *all the interview data, the COLT, field notes and transcriptions, the raw data, this process*), and source entity (e.g., *the participants*). These entities interpret the taxonomized item—interview at the field stratum. Specifically, the entities categorize different dimensions of the taxonomized item: the interview as a whole, its participants, and its analytical process.

At the level of figures and sequences, it is interesting to discover that nearly all the material processes are represented through passive voice. For instance, the major process verbs include *was used to*, *were audio recorded*, *were given*, and *was checked*. This finding may indicate the authors' deliberate emphasis on the goal (i.e., the interview) of the material process. Furthermore, the fact that the figures and sequences are all initiated by the same entity makes the whole text more coherent.

As for the conjunction system, the procedural recounts, which are different from expositions, employ the external conjunction for connecting the activity sequences. In this case, the connection between figure (3) [realized by clause (3) in Table 6.6] to sequence (8) [realized by clause complex (8) in Table 6.6] is the time relation.

Textually, the identification system and the periodicity system of this procedural recount are discovered. The identification system examines the mechanism through which resources are introduced and tracked in texts. In figure (1) [realized by clause (1) in Table 6.6], the entity *a semi-structured interview* is introduced. In the following figures and sequences, this entity is presumed through anaphora, such as *the interviews* and *the raw data*.

The identification of the themes in this procedural recount shows that it progresses in a linear manner, which implies that there is no macro-New. In fact, the themes of all the figures and sequences, except figure (4) [realized by clause (4) in Table 6.6], converge to the entity *the interview*.

Interpersonally, two instances of appraisal resources are found in the text clip. One is in figure (4) [realized by clause (4) in Table 6.6], which describes the checking of accuracy. The data are checked to ensure that it is an appropriate representation of the teachers' attitudes and beliefs. The other is in sequence (8) [realized by clause complex (8) in Table 6.6], which depicts the ending condition of the coding process through the clause *The researcher was content with* .... The former adjective *appropriate* is appreciation while the latter *content* is judgment.

To sum up, this section analyzes three distinctive elemental genres in the linguistics sub-corpus. In the next section, the particular elemental genres in the physics ERAs are focused on.

6.2 Particular elemental genres in the physics ERAs

Based on the statistical analysis of elemental genre deployments in Chapter 4 (see Table 4.3), the physics ERAs possess markedly more figure expositions (95 cases, 12.5%) than the other two sub-corpora (linguistics, 31 cases, 3.3%; literary studies, ten cases, 0.9%). Moreover, the three types of formula recounts appear exclusively in the physics corpus, with direct formula recounts (50 cases, 6.6%, see Table 4.4) occurring relatively more frequently (conditional formula recounts, 11 cases, 1.4%; sequential formula recounts, 43 cases, 5.6%). Besides, the physics sub-corpus boasts significantly (77 cases, $p=.000$, see Section 4.2.3 and Table 4.3) more sequential explanations than the linguistics one (40 cases, see Table 4.3).

In this sub-section, these three elemental genres are explored with regard to their genre, field, and discourse semantics resources.

6.2.1 Figure expositions

Figure expositions are used for describing and analyzing Figures with the schematic structure of Figure presentation ^ Figure description ^ Figure analysis. The latter two stages are sometimes fused into one stage. Furthermore, the figure expositions in physics usually include a series of figures. Example 6.4 in Table 6.7 shows an illustration of a figure exposition in the physics corpus.

Table 6.7 Ideational resources of Example 6.4

Staging	Nuclear	Center	Nuclear	Periphery
Stage 1 (1)	The electrical characterizations of the individual components ...	are shown		in Fig.3.
Stage 2 Phase 1 (2)	For the photodetector, the energy diagram of the ITO/MPB/Au sandwich structure	is shown		in Fig.3(a)
(3)	The Au electrode	is widely used		to form Ohmic contact with perovskite
(4)	while a Schottky junction	is expected		at the ITO/ perovskite interface
Phase 2 (5)	Figure 3(b)	shows	the current-voltage (I-V) characteristic measured in the dark and under illumination	
(6)	Because of the asymmetric electrode, the photodetector	is	self-biased	under illumination with a rectification ratio of around 10^{3}...
(7)	It	should be noted	that the photodetector does not show any RS behavior ...	
Phase 3 (8)	Figure 3 (c)	displays	the switching of the device under a positive bias of 0.5 V	
(9)	and no performance degradation	was observed		
(10)	It	should be mentioned here	that the performance of the photovoltaic-type photodetector can be further improved ...	

(Phys 20200102) (Guan et al., 2020:3)

As illustrated by the first column of Table 6.7, this figure exposition is composed of two stages. Stage 1 is figure presentation. Stage 2 is figure description and analysis. It is important to note that Stage 2 can be broken down into three phases, each of which depicts one component of *Figure 3*, namely *Figure 3(a)*, *Figure 3(b)*, and *Figure 3(c)*. Since the physics ERAs usually employ this form of figure representation, it is common to see the figure description stage of a figure exposition includes several phases that describe part-figures involved in a figure.

Secondly, implicit genre embedding can also be found in figure expositions. It is determined by the purpose of this elemental genre. Since the analysis of the research result represented by the figures usually involves the exploration of the cause-and-effect relation between phenomena, it is common to find sequential explanations embedded in the stage of figure analysis. For instance, Phase 2 of Stage 2 in Example 6.4 is made up of two sequential explanations. One is realized by figure (6) [realized by clause (6) in Table 6.7], where the cause is contracted in the prepositional group *because of the asymmetric electrode*. The other sequential explanation is realized by sequence (7) [realized by clause complex (7) in Table 6.7], where the cause-and-effect relation is in the projecting clause *the photodetector does not show any RS behavior because ....*

Regarding the field resources, figure expositions center on the taxonomized item—a certain figure in the text. In this case, *Fig. 3* is the item, and the components part of *Fig.3* [i.e., *Fig. 3(a)*, *Fig. 3(b)*, and *Fig. 3(c)*] are described respectively in different phases of Stage 2. The identification of the item is approached through a bottom-up method. Strictly speaking, the analysis of entities of this text clip can reveal its key item.

At the discourse semantics stratum, entities, figures, and sequences are identified. Firstly, the second column of Table 6.7 demonstrates the entities of this figure exposition. These entities can be divided into thing entities (e.g., *the bottom photodetector, the photodetector, the Au electrode*), and semiotic entities [e.g., *the energy diagram, a Schottsky junction, Figure 3 (b), Figure 3 (c), performance degradation, and the performance of the photodetector*].

As for the relationship between these entities, some of the entities form a part-whole relation. For example, *Figure 3 (b)* and *Figure 3 (c)* are parts of *Figure 3*.

At the figure level, the main process verbs are *show* and *display*. These relational processes take the figures as carriers, aiming to show the content of the figures. At the sequence level, two projection clauses are used. *It should be noted that...* and *It should be mentioned that ...* reflect the writers' emphasis on the analysis of the figure. Moreover, the cause-and-effect is included in the projecting clause.

After the ideational resources of Example 6.4 are analyzed, the conjunction resources of the figure exposition are examined in order to reveal the logical organization of the ideational resources.

Table 6.8 Conjunction resources of Example 6.4

Staging	Internal	Clause	External
Stage 1		(1)	
Stage 2 Phase 1	(2)-(10) reworking (1)	(2)	
	(3)-(4) reworking (2)	(3)	
	Additive to (3)	(4)	
Phase 2	Additive to (4)	(5)	
	(6)-(7) reworking (5)	(6)	
	Additive to (6)	(7)	
Phase 3	Additive to (7)	(8)	
	(9)-(10) reworking (8)	(9)	
	Additive to (9)	(10)	

The conjunction relation in this figure exposition can be analyzed from two layers. From the perspective of stages, Stage 1 initiates the whole text by explaining the purpose of this elemental genre, i.e., showing the electrical characterization of the individual components of the photodetector. All the figures and sequences in Stage 2 expatiate the main content of Stage 1. In other words, Stage 2 reworks the meaning of Stage 1.

From the perspective of phases, the conjunction relations in the three phases of Stage 2 follow the same pattern. The first figure elucidates the purpose of this phase and the following figures and sequences rework the semantics of the first figure.

As for the identification system, the whole of *Fig. 3* and its components are introduced into the text through homophora, which means that the introduction of these figures is presented by proper nouns, such as *Fig 3*, *Fig 3(a)*, and *Fig 3(b)*. On the other hand, the referred entity in *Fig 3* (i.e., *the photodetector*) is presumed through anaphora in the text.

With regard to the periodicity system, this figure exposition runs in a linear manner. The first stage serves as the macro-Theme of the text clips. However, there are no macro-New in the instance.

For the appraisal resources, the two relational clauses are put into focus. One is *The photodetector is self-biased*. The other is *The Au electrode is widely used*. *Self-biased* and *widely* belong to the appreciation resources.

6.2.2 Direct formula recounts

There are three types of formula recounts in the corpus, i.e., direct formula recounts, sequential formula recounts, and conditional formula recounts. According to the statistical analysis in Chapter 4, direct formula recounts (50 instances, 6.6%, see Table 4.4 and Section 4.2.3) occur more frequently than the other two formula recounts (conditional formula recounts, 11 cases, 1.4%; sequential formula recounts, 43 cases, 5.6%; see Table 4.4). The analysis of these recounts reveals that direct formula recount adheres to a formalized pattern, with the stage of formula presentation being started with a circumstance indicating purpose followed by formula description which is abundant in relational clauses. The following explicates an example of a formula recount through genre, field, and discourse semantics stratum.

Table 6.9 Ideational resources of Example 6.5

Staging	Nuclear	Center	Nuclear	Peripheral
Stage 1 (1)	For the activation analysis described below, we	define	the effective projectile fluence for each reaction product	by the following equation
Stage 2 (2)	where the sum	is	over each step of the multichannel scaler assuming constant flux ...	
(3)	$_{\lambda}$x	is	the decay constant of thc given isotope	

(Phys 201908) (Szücs et al., 2019:4)

From the genre perspective, the direct formula recount follows the schematic structure of Formula presentation ^ Formula description. In the first stage, the formula is presented. In the second stage, the meanings of the parameters in the formula are clarified.

The direct formula recount is realized at the field stratum as the taxonomized item—formula. This item is realized at the discourse semantics stratum as an entity.

Viewed from the second column of Table 6.9, the entities constructed by this formula recount belong to two types. One is the source entity (i.e., *we*). The other is the semiotic entity (e.g., *the sum and* λ_x). The source entity refers to the writers who formulate the formula while the semiotic entities illustrate individual parts of the formula.

At the ranks of figures and sequences, figure (1) and figure (2) [which are coded as (1) and (2) in Table 6.9] form a sequence. Figure (1) is a material process. It is noteworthy that the circumstance is located as the marked theme, which highlights the aim of the formula recount. Figure (2) is an identifying relational process, detecting the meaning of the parameters of the formula. Similarly, figure (3) [realized by clause (3) in Table 6.9] employs the same identifying relational process for explaining the meaning of $\lambda_{x.}$ For the conjunction system, the three figures in the formula recount are combined through addition.

Regarding the identification system, this formula recount uses a homophoric way of introducing resources. In other words, the formula and the parameters of the formula are referred to through homophora in this elemental genre.

For the periodicity system, the formula recount develops linearly. Alternatively speaking, there is no macro-New in the formula recount. Additionally, appraisal resources are not found in this formula recount.

6.2.3 Sequential explanations

Another feature in the elemental genre deployments in the physics ERAs is the profusion of sequential explanations. There are altogether 77 instances of sequential explanations in the physics sub-corpus (10.1%, see Table 4.3), which is distinctly more than that in the linguistics ERAs (40 cases, 4.3%, p=.000; see Table 4.3 and Section 4.2.3). However, the literature (90 cases, 8.3%, see Table 4.3) and the physics sub-corpora do not show a significant difference in terms of the use of sequential explanations (p=1.000, see Section 4.2.3).

Table 6.10 Ideational resources of Example 6.6

Staging	Nuclear	Center	Nuclear	Periphery
Stage 1 (1)	Given that this work	is	a proof-of-concept of the methods proposed	
Stage 2 (2)	we	use	a single test value	within the parameter space
(3)	and we	created	a template bank	…

(Phys 201803) (Astone et al., 2018:6)

Example 6.6 in Table 6.10 is extracted from the Methods section of a physics ERA. It is a typical example in the physics sub-corpus which discloses the causes of the specific methods taken by the researchers.

From the genre perspective, this sequential explanation contains two stages. Stage 1 is the cause, which shows the features of the methods. Stage 2 is the effect, which displays specific procedures of the experiment.

At the field stratum, the sequential explanation is realized by the activity of implication relation. The activity is built up by one relational figure [see figure (1), which is realized by clause (1) in Table 6.10] and two material figures [see figures (2) and (3), which are realized by clauses (2) and (3) in Table 6.10] at the discourse semantics stratum which will be expounded in the following paragraphs.

At the discourse semantics stratum, the entities, figures, and sequences are identified. The entities construed by this sequential explanation can be divided into source entity (e.g., *we*) and semiotic entity (e.g., *this work*). At the figures and sequences rank, this sequential explanation is composed of two material processes and one relational one. Figure (1) [realized by clause (1) in Table 6.10] depicts the reason for using a single test and creating a template bank whereas figures (2) and (3) [realized by clauses (2) and (3) in Table 6.10] present the effect of a proof-of-concept method.

As for the conjunction system, the text clip is combined through internal relations. Figure (3) is additive to figure (2). Furthermore, figure (2) and figure (3) are consequences of figure (1).

In terms of the identification system, esphora is used for the repeated references of the source entity *we*. As for the appraisal resources, the adjective *single* belongs to the resources of appreciation, which is used to summarize the test value of the experiment.

In a nutshell, figure expositions and direct formula recounts are formulated by items at the register stratum. The former centers on Figures, which are realized by thing entities and semiotic entities semantically. The thing entities focus on the materials or containers used in the experiments while the semiotic entities are employed for construing the Figures. The latter is realized mainly by semiotic entities, which show the various parameters in the formula.

Besides, source entities appear in sequential explanations to highlight the people who conduct experiments. The physics ERAs employ sequential explanations for signaling the reasons for using particular experiment methods.

The next section examines elemental genres with disciplinary characteristics in the literature sub-corpus.

6.3 Particular elemental genres in the literature ERAs

After the exploration of the discipline-sensitive elemental genres in the linguistics and physics sub-corpora, the particular elemental genres in the literature corpus are under examination. According to the statistical results in Chapter 4, the writers of the literature ERAs use noticeably more exposition reviews (138 cases, 12.7%; see Table 4.3 and Section 4.2.4) than the authors of the other two research articles (linguistics, 59 instances, 6.3%, p=.000; physics, one case, 0.1%, p=.000; see Table 4.3 and Section 4.2.4). Moreover, they employ more expositions (186 cases, 17.2%) than physicists (42 instances, 5.5%, see Table 4.3) in writing their papers. The finding indicates the special convincing methods used by authors of the literature ERAs, i.e., their viewpoints are supported through main elemental genres in the genre family of Arguments. The detailed analysis of the two types of elemental genres is displayed in the following sub-sections, aiming to reveal the specific genre, field, and discourse semantics resources used for building the two arguing genres.

6.3.1 Exposition reviews

Exposition reviews are used to support the authors' viewpoint through examples of literary works. They usually follow the schematic structure of Thesis ^ Evidence ^ Evaluation. This can be shown in Table 6.11 and Example 6.7.

Table 6.11 Ideational resources of Example 6.7

Staging	Nuclear	Center	Nuclear	Periphery
Stage 1: Thesis (1)	As a publication aimed at promoting cultural exchanges ..., T'ien Hisia Monthly	had	a clear cultural stance	from its inception
Stage 2: Evidence (2)	In its first issue, Yuanning Wen	pointed out	that "Perhaps the best we can do to define our attitude is 'world literature'..."	
(3)	Meanwhile, in the editorial commentary, Fo Sun	wrote	that "Physical contiguity has not brought about ...	
(4)	we	should strive to bring about	a friendly atmosphere, in which physical contiguity ...	
Stage 3: Evaluation (5)	This	was imbued with	the same spirit as ...	

(Lite 201903) (Liu, 2019:398-399)

From the genre perspective, this exposition review follows stringently the schematic structure of Thesis ^ Evidence ^ Evaluation. In the thesis stage, the thesis that *T'ien Hsia Monthly* had a definite cultural stance since its inception is proposed. In the evidence stage, this thesis is supported by quotations from Yuanning Wen and Fo Sun. In the evaluation stage, the author comments on the viewpoints presented in the evidence stage by pointing out their similarity with Goethe's idea.

At the register stratum, one item—the *T'ien Hsia Monthly* and one activity, i.e., to convince the readers that the journal possesses a cultural stance, make up of the major field resource. The item is constructed by entities, whereas the activity is realized in a more complicated manner. In addition to entities, it can also be realized through figures and sequences.

At the discourse semantics stratum, the types of entity reveal an interesting trend in the literature ERAs. As shown by the second column from left to right, four out of the five entities are source entities, which either indicates the journal itself (e.g., *T'ien Hisa Monthly*) or the writers contributing to the journal (e.g., *Yuanning Wen, Fo Sun*). This finding suggests the knower-code-oriented tendency of literary studies. Literary critics try to make their positions convincing by explicitly quoting other people's voices.

As for figures and sequences rank, except for the material and relational processes, projection occurs. In this case, both figures (2) and (3) [realized by clauses (2) and (3) in Table 6.11] are projections. This finding can also be explained by the knower orientation of literary studies. The projected clause employs the source entity as the sayer, whose viewpoints are projected in the projecting clause. That is to say, the author's point of view is approved by quoting other people's opinions in the literature ERAs. Thus, the source entities, especially the people, are more visible.

As for the other system of experiential meaning, the conjunction system depicts the relations between figures and sequences. As illustrated by Table 6.12, the conjunction relation between the figures and sequences is of the external type, i.e., the selection of pieces of evidence is determined by the writers, not by the logical relationships within the text. In terms of stages, the evidence stage supports the thesis proposed in the first stage. Stage 3 adds the evaluation on Stage 2. Within the stage, figure (3) [realized by clause (3) in Table 6.11] adds to figure (2) [realized by clause (2) in Table 6.11] and is added by figure (4) [realized by clause (4) in Table 6.11].

Table 6.12 Conjunction resources of Example 6.7

Staging	Internal	Clause/Clause complex	External
Stage 1		(1)	
Stage 2		(2)	(2)-(4) reworking (1)
		(3)	Additive to (2)
		(4)	Additive to (3)
Stage 3		(5)	Additive to (4)

Regarding the identification system, the entity *T'ien Hsia Monthly* is presented in figure (1) [realized by clause (1) in Table 6.11]. Then, this entity is presumed in sequence (2) [realized by clause complex (2) in Table 6.11] through an anaphoric device *its*. In sequence (3) [realized by clause complex (3) in Table 6.11] and figure (4) [realized by clause (4) in Table 6.11], homophora is used for introducing the source entities *Yuanming Wen*, *Fo Sun*, and *we*. Finally, in figure (5) [realized by clause (5) in Table 6.11], anaphora *this* is used to refer to the previous shreds of evidence presented by the author.

In terms of the periodicity system, the exposition review uses the way of hierarchical progression. The thesis stage predicts the main ideas of the evidence stage. To some extent, the evaluation stage further enhances the evidence stage.

As for the appraisal resources, compared with the linguistics and the physics sub-corpora, the literature ERAs display the authors' attitude more visibly. For instance, all figures and sequences in this exposition review contain appreciation resources, such as *clear* in *a clear cultural stance* and *friendly* in *a friendly atmosphere*, and *genuine* in *a genuine respect for each other's point of view*.

To sum up, exposition reviews in the literature ERAs highlight the source entities at the discourse semantics stratum, which reflect the knower-orientation of the discipline of literary studies, where the views of the authors are presented by referring to other persons' opinions. In addition, the use of appraisal resources is used more explicitly than the other two disciplines, which is realized in the fact that adjectives used for expressing attitudes are employed more frequently. This finding also suggests that this discipline is knower-oriented, where the attitudes of writers are more overtly expressed.

6.3.2 Expositions

In addition to exposition reviews, expositions are another elemental genre prevalent in the literature ERAs (186 cases, 17.2%; see Table 4.3). Example 6.8 is an illustration of an exposition.

Table 6.13 Ideational resources of Example 6.8

Staging	Nuclear	Center	Nuclear	Periphery
Stage 1 (1)	In this context, a third and final intersection between Conrad and world-ecology	arises	that of the notion of extra-human revolt as discussed by ...	
Stage 2 Argument 1 (2)	Moore	focuses on	incidents of ecological revenge…	as moments in which life ...
Argument 2 (3)	Deckard	identifies	similar moments of extra-human revolt	as registered uncounsicously in gothic aesthetics, …
(4)	we	might link	such moments to the various storms…	

(Lite 201806) (Vandertop, 2018: 693-694)

Viewed from the genre stratum, this exposition follows the schematic structure of Thesis ^ Arguments. In the thesis stage, the theme of this exposition is articulated. In the arguments stage, this viewpoint is backed by resorting to other literary critics' positions.

As for the field stratum, the items and activities construed by expositions are not as clearly represented as explanations or descriptive reports. Therefore, a bottom-up approach is adopted here for delving into the entities, figures, and sequences at the discourse semantics first.

In the discourse semantics stratum, the entities are explored in the first place, followed by the discussion of figures or sequences. The main entities identified are demonstrated in Table 6.14.

Table 6.14 Main entities identified in Example 6.8

Sequence	Source entities	Semiotic entities
(1)		the notion of extra-human revolt
(2)	Moore	incidents of ecological revenge
(3)	Deckard	similar moments of extra-human revolt
(4)	we	such moment

As is shown in Table 6.14, one of the distinctive characteristics of the literature ERAs is the occurrences of source entities. In this example, *Moore* and *Deckard* are used as source entities for illustrating obviously the origin of positions, which reflects the feature of the discipline of literature. On the other hand, the semiotic entities are various alterations of the key entity—extra-human revolt.

Viewed from the rank of figures and sequences, superficially, the four figures or sequences belong to material processes. However, a close look at figure (2) [realized by clause (2) in Table 6.13] *Moore focuses on incidents of ecological revenge as*... and figure (3) [realized by clause (3) in Table 6.13] *Deckard identifies similar moments of extra-human revolts as*... can reveal that these two figures resemble relational processes. Specifically, figure (2) identifies the incidents of ecological revenge as life rebels. Furthermore, figure (3) considers the extra-human revolt as registered unconsciously in gothic aesthetics.

When the entities, figures, and sequences at the discourse semantics stratum are considered, it is reasonable to say that this exposition focuses on construing the item—extra-human revolt at the register stratum.

For the conjunction system, the relations between figures and sequences are displayed in Table 6.15.

Table 6.15 Conjunction relations in Example 6.8

Staging	Internal	Message	External
Stage 1		(1)	
Stage 2	(2)-(4) reworking (1)	(2)	
	Additive to (2)	(3)	
	reworking (3)	(4)	

Across stages, the figures and sequences in Stage 2 can be said to work out the viewpoint presented in the first stage. Within stages, figure (3) [realized by clause (3) in Table 6.13] is added to figure (2) [realized by clause (2) in Table 6.13] as another argument supporting the thesis. Figure (4) [realized by clause (4) in Table 6.13] *we might link such moments to the various storms...that...* reworks figure (3), which serves as an exemplification of figure (3).

Regarding the identification resources, homophora is employed in the source entities. The names of the literary critics are used as homophora. On the other hand, the semiotic resources are, to some extent, referred to with the method of esphora. To be specific, all the semiotic resources indicate the same entity with a slight change in the lexicogrammatical choices. For instance, *the notion of extra-human revolt* and *similar moments of extra-human revolt* are nearly the same except for the different qualifiers.

As for the periodicity system, the text progresses hierarchically. Figure (1) [realized by clause (1) in Table 6.13] in Stage 1 is used as a macro-Theme. The theme of *extra-human revolt* runs like a thread through the whole exposition, which envisages the themes of the following figures and sequences in Stage 2.

In addition, the literature ERAs are imbued with appraisal resources. For instance, in figure (3) [realized by clause (3) in Table 6.13], the qualities such as *similar*, *ubiquitous*, and *monstrous* depict the characteristics of natural disasters. In figure (4) [realized by clause (4) in Table 6.13], *various*, *becalmed*, and *shifting* belong to the appreciation resources describing the features of those natural phenomena.

In a word, this exposition also reveals the features of the literature ERAs, i.e., the explicit demonstration of source entities and the copious use of appraisal resources.

6.4 The influence of disciplinarity on particular elemental genres

From the previous discussion, it is noticed that the disciplinarity, which is embodied by Maton's (2014) knowledge-knower structure, can influence the building of particular elemental genres in the three sub-corpora.

Firstly, linguistics, which falls in the middle position of the discipline continuum, exhibits traits from both the knowledge-code and knower-code orientations.

On the one hand, driven by the knower-code positionings, researchers' attitudes and dispositions are displayed for establishing epistemic conviction (Maton, 2014:92). Consequently, the expositions in the linguistics sub-corpus are constructed by several pieces of appraisal resources.

On the other hand, motivated by the knowledge-code orientations, the precise processes for carrying out experiments are focused on (Hu&Cao, 2015), which may be attributed to the relatively more occurrences of procedural recounts (46 cases, 4.9%, see Table 4.4) in the linguistics sub-corpus than the literature one (three cases, 0.3%, p=.000; see Table 4.4).

Secondly, physics, which belongs to a discipline centering on knowledge-code, exerts an impact on both the distribution of particular elemental genres and the field and discourse semantics resources used to expound them.

Regarding the overall distribution of elemental genres, figure expositions in the physics sub-corpus display higher frequency than the other two sub-corpora (95 cases, 12.5%, see Table 4.3). Moreover, three types of formula recounts occur exclusively in the physics RAs, which can be possibly explainable by the emphasis on the fact that physics is knowledge-code oriented, where the empirical authority is consolidated by precision and accuracy (Hu&Liu, 2018). Additionally, sequential explanations, which occur more frequently in the Methods section (29 cases, 0.1 per 1,000 tokens, see Table 4.10), also reflect the features of physics, where the reasons for conducting experiments are summarized by this elemental genre to ensure the validation of methods.

In terms of the resources of these particular elemental genres, the disciplinarity of physics also excises influencing power. For figure expositions, the static items—figures are shaped at the register stratum. At the discourse semantics stratum, thing entities, which refer to the materials or containers used in experiments are employed. Furthermore, direct formula recounts are realized by semiotic entities (e.g., parameters in formulas). In addition, sequential explanations are highlighted by implication sequences in the Methods section. This finding may be plausibly attributed to the disciplinary characters of knowledge-code-oriented disciplines, where the rigor of methodology is emphasized to be epistemically persuasive (Hu&Cao, 2015). Thus, these thing entities, semiotic entities, and implication sequences are used for explicitly revealing the accurate procedure of the experimentation, the clear description of formulas needed, and the reasons for taking certain steps in experiments.

Thirdly, as a knower-code-centered discipline, literary studies may influence both the deployment and construing resources of certain elemental genres. The literature sub-corpus boasts significantly more arguing genres (see Table 4.5 and Figure 4.2). In particular, exposition reviews (138 cases, 12.7%; see Table 4.3) and expositions (186 cases, 17.2%; see Table 4.3) are witnessed with markedly more occurrences than the other two sub-corpora. This result can be accounted for by the characters of literary studies, where the researchers' authority and expertise are confirmed for legitimating disciplinary knowledge (Wang&Hu, 2023).

Besides, the disciplinarity of literary studies may also have an impact on the discourse semantics resources used to realize exposition reviews and expositions. The findings can be illustrated in two aspects. First, source entities (e.g., other literary critics) are employed for realizing exposition reviews and expositions, which demonstrates the knower-code orientation of literary studies, where other people's voices and tastes are given salient positions. Second, appraisal resources are used more explicitly than the other two disciplines. This result can also be explained by the disciplinary features of literary studies, which tend to express authors' appreciation towards literary works.

6.5 Chapter summary

This chapter analyzes eight elemental genres which possess disciplinary preference in the corpus. The analysis is conducted from three strata, namely, the purpose and schematic structure at the genre stratum, the field resources at the register stratum, and the discourse semantics properties. The focus of the study is on the discourse semantics stratum, where the experiential meaning of these elemental genres is portrayed through ideation and conjunction systems, the textual meaning is analyzed through identification and periodicity system, and the interpersonal meaning is identified by appraisal resources.

The findings can be shown in three aspects.

Firstly, the linguistics ERAs demonstrate the mixed characteristics in the physics and the literature ERAs. On the one hand, they possess more expositions (127 instances, 13.5%) than the physics articles (42 instances, 5.5%, p=.010; see Table 4.3 and Section 4.2.1). On the other hand, they boast markedly more procedural recounts (46 cases, 4.9%, see Table 4.4) than the literature ERAs (three cases, 0.3%, p=.000; see Table 4.4 and Section 4.2.2). Besides, the linguistics sub-corpus employs significantly more classifying reports (114 cases, 12.2%, see Table 4.3) than the other two sub-corpora (physics, 36 cases, 4.7%, p=.000; literary studies, 28 cases, 2.6%, p=.000; see Table 4.3 and Section 4.2.2). The examination of the genre, field, and discourse semantics resources reveals that classifying reports are primarily realized by items in terms of the field resources. In addition, expositions and procedural recounts can be realized either by items or activities. Furthermore, semiotic entities scatter across the three elemental genres.

Secondly, the physics ERAs are characterized by their large quantity of figure expositions (95 cases, 12.5%, see Table 4.3) and exclusive occurrences of three types of formula recounts (see Table 4.4), which shows that there are relatively more direct formula recounts (50 cases, 6.6%; compared to conditional formula recounts, 11 cases, 1.4%; sequential formula recounts, 43 cases, 5.6%; see Table 4.4). Moreover, sequential explanations (77 cases, 10.1%; compared to these in the linguistics sub-corpus: 40 cases, 4.3%, p=.000; see Table 4.3 and Section 4.2.3) are often utilized for specifying evidently the aims of experiments. From the perspective of field resources, figures expositions and direct formula recounts are basically realized by items. From the discourse semantics stratum, figure expositions highlight thing entities (e.g., the materials or containers used in the experiments) and semiotic entities (e.g., the figures). Direct formula recounts emphasize semiotic entities, i.e., various parameters in the formulas. Sequential explanations are realized by implication sequences.

Thirdly, the literature ERAs are abundant in the arguing genre, such as exposition reviews (138 cases, 12.7%; see Table 4.3) and expositions (186 cases, 17.2%; see Table 4.3). The analysis exposes that the two elemental genres in the literature ERAs prefer to use literary critics as the source entities and highpoint appraisal resources that directly express writers' appreciation.

The implication of the study of particular elemental genres lies in two folds. Theoretically, it tests the applicability of the three-strata framework for analyzing generic complexity proposed in this study. Practically, the results in this chapter disclose the fact that different discourse semantics resources are used in the same elemental genres across ERAs of different disciplines. It may provide a good reference for teaching academic writing to students from various disciplines.

Chapter 7 Linguistics ERAs vs CRAs

This chapter compares the generic features of linguistics ERAs and CRAs. Section 7.1 summarizes the overall elemental genre deployments and macro-generic-stage-based elemental genre allocation in linguistics ERAs. Section 7.2 explicates the generic characteristics of linguistics CRAs. Section 7.3 analyzes the similarities and differences between the two linguistics sub-corpora. Section 7.4 concludes this chapter.

7.1 Elemental genre deployment in linguistics ERAs

7.1.1 Overall elemental genre deployment in linguistics ERAs

In the previous chapters, the overall elemental genre deployment in linguistics ERAs is analyzed through two aspects: the overall distribution of elemental genre families and the allocation of specific elemental genres.

In terms of the overall deployment of elemental genre families, as illustrated by Figure 4.3, the elemental genre families show the following descending order according to numbers, i.e., Reports > Arguments > Explanations > Recounts > Text responses.

In terms of the specific elemental genres, the top ten elemental genres in linguistics ERAs are presented in Figure 7.1.

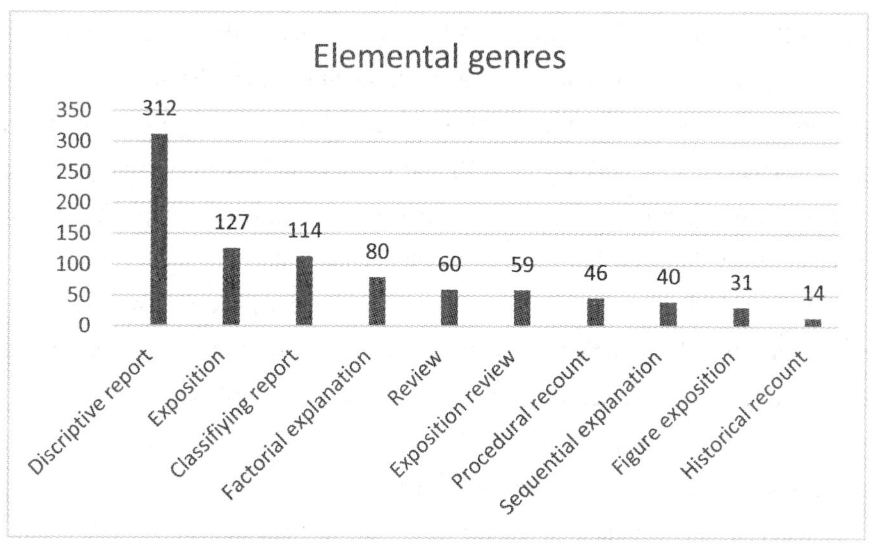

Figure 7.1 Top ten elemental genres in linguistics ERAs

As is shown in Figure 7.1, descriptive reports (312 instances, 33.1%) are employed most frequently in linguistics ERAs, followed by expositions (127 instances, 13.5%). Classifying reports (114 instances, 12.1%) rank third place in the specific elemental genre distribution.

It should be mentioned that classifying reports and descriptive reports amount to 426 instances, which accounts for 45.2% of the total elemental genres. The results coincide with the previous study on elemental genre distribution (Lai, 2018). This may be attributed to the disciplinarity of linguistics and the functions of Reports. On the one hand, descriptive reports are used for describing the attributes of entities in research. Classifying reports are utilized for classifying related literature and introducing subjects and instruments employed in experiments. On the other hand, linguistic research activities require descriptions of the properties, structures, categories, etc. of the entity in question (ibid.:41), which motivates authors' employment of Reports in RA writing.

Expositions are second only to descriptive reports in frequency. This is also consistent with Lai and Wang's (2018) findings. The utilization of expositions lies in the purpose of research articles, i.e., to persuade readers to accept authors' opinions through argumentation. In addition, two elemental genres in Arguments—exposition reviews (59 instances, 6.3%) and figure expositions (31 instances, 3.3%) rank at the fifth and ninth positions respectively. These three elemental genres work together to make the Arguments occupy the second place in the overall distribution of elemental genre families.

Factorial explanations (80 instances, 8.5%) occupy the fourth place. This may be attributed to the fact that authors need to analyze many factors leading to certain results. Besides, another elemental genre in Explanation—sequential explanation, ranks at the eighth position (40 instances, 4.2%), explaining the reasons for taking certain experiment procedures.

Reviews (40 instances, 4.2%) take up the fifth position. As the only elemental genre in Text responses entering the top-ten list, reviews appear primarily in the Literature review section, which evaluate the literature by combing through it.

Procedural recounts (46 instances, 4.6%) and historical recounts (14 instances, 1.5%) are the two elemental genres in Recounts that are included in the top-ten list. Procedural recounts mainly describe the specific procedures in experiments. Historical recounts describe the progress of research chronologically.

7.1.2 Macro-generic-stage-based elemental genre distribution in linguistics ERAs

With the help of UAM CT, the distribution of elemental genres in the major macro generic stages in linguistics ERAs is presented (see Table 4.7).

Generally, descriptive reports and classifying reports run throughout all the major macro generic stages. Besides, in each major section of ERAs, the authors tend to use certain elemental genres.

In the Introduction and Literature review sections, reviews rank second and third places respectively. This finding may be explainable by the functions of the Introduction and Literature review. Usually, a summary and evaluation of related literature are presented in these two sections. Reviews serve for commenting messages (Rose&Martin, 2012:128). Therefore, reviews occur relatively frequently in these two sections.

In the Methods section, procedural recounts (30 instances, 13.2%) rank third position, following descriptive reports and classifying reports. This may be due to the fact that in the methods section, authors need to present the research design, describe the experimental steps, and observe the experimental procedures. These objectives coincide with the main purpose of procedural recounts.

In the Results section, figure expositions (18 instances, 9.6%) are one of the five elemental genres that occur more frequently. This could be explained by the appearance of figures in the Results section. It is reasonable to see that figure expositions appear intensively in this section, as an elemental genre that describes and evaluates figures.

In the Discussion and "Results and Discussion" sections, expositions rank at the first position. This finding may be attributable to the purposes of Discussion, which analyze research results, explain the reasons, and persuade readers to accept the interpretation of results. Therefore, RA writers resort to expositions for achieving these objectives.

7.2 Generic complexity features in linguistics CRAs

7.2.1 Overall elemental genre deployments in linguistics CRAs

Table 7.1 Overall elemental genre deployments in linguistics CRAs

	N	%		N	%
REPORTS			EXPLANATIONS		
Descriptive report	363	33.5	Sequential explanation	54	5
Classifying report	60	5.5	Factorial explanation	95	8.8
Compositional report	32	2.9	Sub-total:	149	13.70
Sub-total:	455	41.90			
ARGUMENTS			RECOUNTS		
Exposition	63	5.8	Historical recount	2	0.2
Elucidation	42	3.9	Procedural recount	39	3.6
Exposition review	126	11.6	Sub-total:	41	3.80
Figure exposition	90	8.3			
Sub-total:	321	29.60			
TEXT RESPONSES					
Review	119	11			
Sub-total	119	11.00			
Total	1085	100			

Note: N=number of elemental genres; %=percentage

Table 7.1 presents the overall elemental genre deployments in linguistics CRAs. As for elemental genre families, the five elemental genre families show the order Reports > Arguments > Explanations > Text responses > Recounts. Similar to the English linguistics RA corpus, Reports take the lead, and followed by Arguments. Explanations rank third in terms of overall distribution. However, different from the ERAs, recounts are the least frequent elemental genre family.

As for specific elemental genres, the top ten elemental genres are listed in Figure 7.2.

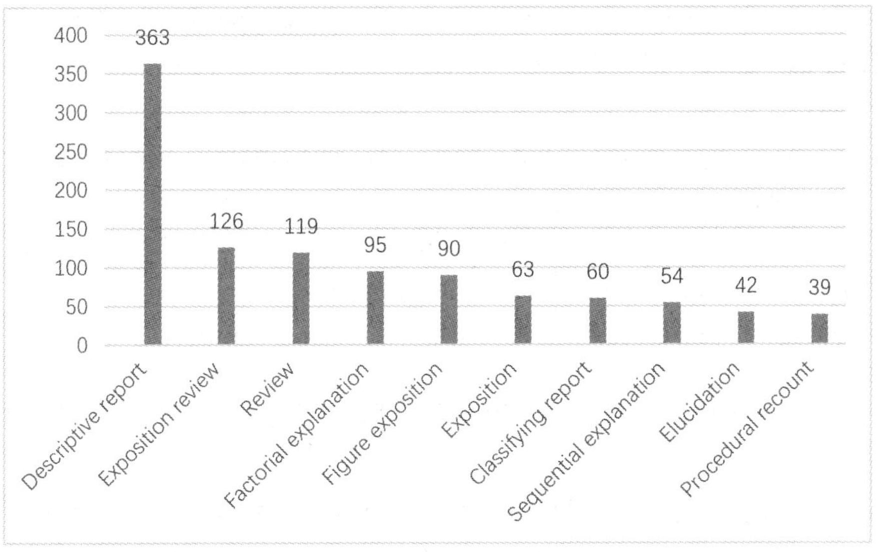

Figure 7.2 Top ten elemental genres in linguistics CRAs

Descriptive report (363 instances, 33.5%) is still the most frequent elemental genre in linguistics CRAs. Another elemental genre in this genre family—classifying report (60 instances, 5.5%) ranks at the seventh place. The frequent occurrences of the two elemental genres make Reports the predominant elemental genre family in the linguistics CRAs.

Exposition review (126 instances, 11.6%) is the second largest elemental genre in the corpus. In addition, the other three elemental genres in Arguments, expositions (63 cases, 5.8%), elucidations (42 cases, 3.9%), and figure exposition (90 cases, 8.3%) also enter the list of top−ten elemental genres. The large quantity of these elemental genres makes Arguments the second largest elemental genre family.

Review (119 cases, 11%) occupies the third place in the distribution of specific elemental genres. Since its relatively higher occurrences in the CRAs, Text responses show more frequent appearances than Recounts in the corpus.

Factorial explanation (95 cases, 8.8%) ranks at the fourth place. Another elemental genre in Explanations, sequential explanation (54 cases, 5%)

occupies the eighth place in the top−ten list. The combination of these two elemental genres makes Explanations the third largest elemental genre family in CRAs.

Procedural recount (39 cases, 3.6%) is the only elemental genre belonging to Recounts that enter the top−ten list.

To sum up, similar to the situation in linguistics ERAs, Reports, Arguments, and Explanations are three major elemental genre families. However, the linguistics CRAs witness more instances of Recounts.

7.2.2 Macro-generic-stage-based elemental genre distribution in linguistics CRAs

With the help of UAM CT (version 6.2e), the elemental genre distribution in the main macro generic stage is recorded. Table 7.2 demonstrates the top five elemental genres in terms of quantity in each major section of CRAs.

Table 7.2 Summary of major elemental genres in each macro generic stage of the linguistics CRAs

	Elemental genres	N	P		Elemental genre	N	P
I	Descriptive report	39	42.4	L	Review	89	50.6
92 cases	Review	28	30.4	176 cases	Descriptive report	28	15.9
	Sequential explanation	8	8.7		Classifying report	22	12.5
	Factorial explanation	7	7.6		Factorial explanation	11	6.3
	Classifying report	5	5.4		Compositional report	9	5.1
M	Descriptive report	151	67.1	R	Figure exposition	65	30.8
225 cases	Procedural recount	28	12.4	211 cases	Descriptive report	53	25.1
	Compositional report	15	6.7		Exposition review	36	17.1
	Classifying report	12	5.3		Elucidation	23	10.9
	Sequential explanation	6	2.7		Classifying report	16	7.6
	Factorial explanation	6	2.7				
D	Exposition review	58	27.4	R&D	Exposition review	29	29.3
212 cases	Factorial explanation	48	22.6	99 cases	Descriptive report	14	14.1
	Exposition	42	19.8		Factorial explanation	13	13.1
	Descriptive report	34	16		Elucidation	13	13.1
	Sequential explanation	19	9		Figure exposition	13	13.1
C	Descriptive report	36	94.7				
38 cases	Classifying report	1	2.6				
	Compositional report	1	2.6				

Note: I=Introduction; L=Literature review; M=Methods; R=Results; D=Discussion; R&D=Results&Discussion; C=Conclusion; N=number; P=percentage

Table 7.2 summarizes the top five elemental genres in each macro generic stage. The number under the abbreviations of each section represents the total number of elemental genres. The percentage indicates the proportion of a given elemental genre to the total number of elemental genres at that macro generic stage.

The elemental genre deployments in each macro generic stage of CRAs show the following characteristics.

First, descriptive reports rank as one of the top five elemental genres in each section. This finding coincides with the previous study on linguistics ERAs. This result may be explainable by the functions of descriptive report.

Second, similar to the situation in linguistics ERAs, reviews occur relatively frequently in the Introduction and Literature review parts. They rank second and third place in the Introduction and Literature review sections respectively.

Third, though there are a large number of descriptive reports in the Methods section, procedural recounts (28 instances, 12.4%) occupy the second place in this section. Likewise, this finding can also be attributed to the purposes of Methods and procedural recounts.

Fourth, figure expositions (65 instances, 30.8%) take a lead in the Results section. Similarly, in the linguistics ERAs, figure expositions are also listed as one of the top five elemental genres in Results. This may be attributable to the prevalence of figures in Results.

Fifth, exposition reviews are predominant in both the Discussion and R&D sections. This finding is also similar to the situation of the linguistics ERAs. The results can be explained by the purpose of the Discussion section, which interprets authors' opinions (Swales, 2004; 236).

The following parts provide detailed elaboration on the major elemental genres in each macro generic stage of linguistics CRAs.

The Introduction section sees the emergence of 92 cases of elemental genres. Among them, the descriptive report ranks first place with the occurrence of 39 cases, amounting to 42.4%. Following the descriptive report, review takes up the second place with the occurrence of 28 times (30.4%). Besides, sequential explanation, factorial explanation, and classifying report occupy the following three places, with the appearance of 8 (8.7%), 7 (7.6%), and 5 (5.4%) respectively.

In the Literature review part, the review amounts for 50.6% (89 cases). Descriptive report (28 cases) and classifying report (22 cases) each take up more than 10%. The remaining two elemental genres—factorial explanation (11 cases) and compositional report (9 cases) each occupy over 5%.

In the Methods section, descriptive report (151 cases) takes the lead with a proportion of 67.1%. Procedural recount ranks the second place with 28 instances (12.4%). Compositional report (15 cases, 6.7%) and classifying report (12 cases, 5.3%) occupy the third and fourth positions. Sequential explanation and factorial explanation occupy the fifth place with the occurrence of six times (2.7%).

The Results section witnesses the higher occupation of figure exposition (65 cases, 30.8%). Descriptive report (53 cases, 25.1%) ranks the second place. Exposition review (36 cases, 17.1%) and elucidation (23 cases, 10.9%) take up 28% of this part. Classifying report (16 cases, 7.6%) ranks at the fifth place.

In the Discussion section, exposition review (58 cases) takes the lead, with a proportion of 27.4%. Factorial explanation, with its occurrences of 48 times, ranks the second place. Exposition appears 42 times, accounting for 19.8%. Descriptive report (34 instances) and sequential explanation (19 cases) rank the fourth and fifth places respectively.

In the R&D section, exposition review (29 cases) shows the most frequent occurrences, accounting for 29.3%. The other four elemental genres—descriptive report, factorial explanation, elucidation, and figure exposition take similar proportion, ranging between 13.1% to 14.1%.

In the Conclusion section, 94.7% of total elemental genres belong to descriptive report.

7.3 Similarities and differences in generic complexity features between linguistics ERAs and CRAs

After the overall elemental genre deployments and generic-stage-based elemental genre allocation are analyzed, this section summarizes the similarities and differences in generic complexity features between linguistics ERAs and CRAs.

In terms of similarities, the linguistics ERAs and CRAs take on consistency in the top-three-ranked elemental genre families, i.e., Reports > Arguments > Explanations. Besides, descriptive reports present an overwhelming dominance in both ERAs and CRAs.

To reveal the meaningful differences in elemental genre deployments between linguistics ERAs and CRAs, the UAM Corpus Tool 6.2e (O'Donnell, 2022) is utilized.

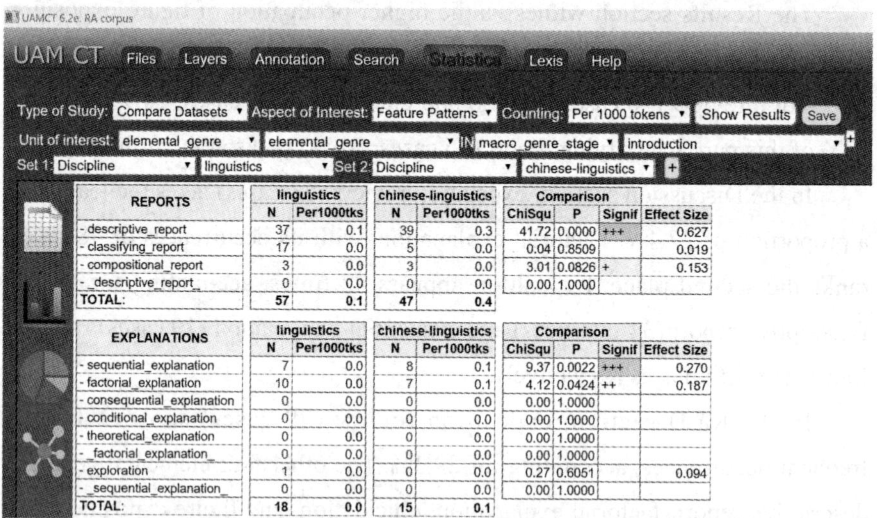

REPORTS	linguistics		chinese-linguistics		Comparison			
	N	Per1000tks	N	Per1000tks	ChiSqu	P	Signif	Effect Size
- descriptive_report	37	0.1	39	0.3	41.72	0.0000	+++	0.627
- classifying_report	17	0.0	5	0.0	0.04	0.8509		0.019
- compositional_report	3	0.0	3	0.0	3.01	0.0826	+	0.153
- _descriptive_report_	0	0.0	0	0.0	0.00	1.0000		
TOTAL:	57	0.1	47	0.4				

EXPLANATIONS	linguistics		chinese-linguistics		Comparison			
	N	Per1000tks	N	Per1000tks	ChiSqu	P	Signif	Effect Size
- sequential_explanation	7	0.0	8	0.1	9.37	0.0022	+++	0.270
- factorial_explanation	10	0.0	7	0.1	4.12	0.0424	++	0.187
- consequential_explanation	0	0.0	0	0.0	0.00	1.0000		
- conditional_explanation	0	0.0	0	0.0	0.00	1.0000		
- theoretical_explanation	0	0.0	0	0.0	0.00	1.0000		
- _factorial_explanation_	0	0.0	0	0.0	0.00	1.0000		
- exploration	1	0.0	0	0.0	0.27	0.6051		0.094
- _sequential_explanation_	0	0.0	0	0.0	0.00	1.0000		
TOTAL:	18	0.0	15	0.1				

Figure 7.3 Sample of comparison of normalized elemental genre frequency between linguistics ERAs and CRAs

As illustrated by Figure 7.3, the normalized frequency of elemental genres in the Introduction is compared between the linguistics ERAs and CRAs. Table 7.3 to Table 7.9 demonstrate the significant differences in the major macro-generic stages.

Table 7.3 Comparison between linguistics ERAs and CRAs in Introduction

	ERAs		CRAs			
Type of elemental genres	N	P	N	P	ChiSqu	P
Descriptive report	37	0.1	39	0.3	41.72	0.0000
Sequential explanation	7	0	8	0.1	9.37	0.0022
Factorial explanation	10	0	7	0.1	4.12	0.0424
Review	20	0	28	0.2	40	0.0000

Note: N=Number; F=Frequency per 1,000 tokens

Table 7.3 shows the normalized frequency and the results of Chi−Square in elemental genre allocation between linguistics ERAs and CRAs. It is noticed that CRAs possess significantly more descriptive reports, sequential explanations, factorial explanations, and reviews than ERAs. It reflects the diversity of Introduction in CRAs. Sequential explanations and factorial explanations are employed to explain why a certain research topic is chosen. Reviews are used to sort out the previous literature and figure out the research gap.

Table 7.4 Comparison between linguistics ERAs and CRAs in Literature Review

	ERAs		CRAs			
Type of elemental genres	N	P	N	P	ChiSqu	P
Descriptive report	41	0.1	28	0.3	11.6	0.0007
Classifying report	31	0.1	22	0.2	9.89	0.0017
Compositional report	0	0	9	0.1	29.7	0.0000
Factorial explanation	10	0	11	0.1	9.98	0.0016
Procedural recount	0	0	3	0	9.9	0.0017
Review	22	0.1	89	0.8	201.54	0.0000

Note: N=Number; F=Frequency per 1,000 tokens

In the Literature review part, CRAs display a noticeably higher frequency of reviews. Besides, Chinese authors tend to use more reports of elemental genres, factorial explanations, and procedural recounts in Literatrue review.

Table 7.5 Comparison between linguistics ERAs and CRAs in Methods

	ERAs		CRAs			
Type of elemental genres	N	P	N	P	ChiSqu	P
Descriptive report	106	0.2	151	1.2	219.12	0.0000
Compositional report	3	0	15	0.1	41.9	0.0000
Procedural recount	30	0.1	28	0.2	25.75	0.0000

Note: N=Number; F=Frequency per 1,000 tokens

As illustrated by Table 7.5, CRAs witness more occurrences of descriptive reports, compositional reports, and procedural recounts in Methods. Descriptive reports, in particular, demonstrate distinctly more appearances in CRAs (1.2/1000 tokens), which reveals the Chinese authors' preferences for describing instruments or participants in the Methods section.

Table 7.6 Comparison between linguistics ERAs and CRAs in Results

	ERAs		CRAs			
Type of elemental genres	N	P	N	P	ChiSqu	P
Descriptive report	46	0.1	53	0.6	51.09	0.0000
Classifying report	11	0	16	0.2	19.69	0.0000
Elucidation	5	0	23	0.2	54.56	0.0000
Exposition review	44	0.1	36	0.4	21.31	0.0000
Figure exposition	18	0.1	65	0.7	141.42	0.0000

Note: N=Number; F=Frequency per 1,000 tokens

Similarly, authors of CRAs show a significant preference for the utilization of descriptive reports, classifying reports, elucidations, exposition reviews, and figure expositions in Results. Among these elemental genres, figure expositions and descriptive reports demonstrate a clear advantage in quantity. This may be due to the relatively higher occurrences of figures in the Results of CRAs.

Table 7.7 Comparison between linguistics ERAs and CRAs in R&D

	ERAs		CRAs			
Type of elemental genres	N	P	N	P	ChiSqu	P
Descriptive report	7	0.1	14	0.6	31.48	0.0000
Sequential explanation	2	0	4	0.2	8.99	0.0027
Factorial explanation	2	0	13	0.6	45.21	0.0000
Elucidation	1	0	13	0.6	50.25	0.0000
Exposition review	12	0.1	29	1.3	72.37	0.0000
Figure exposition	3	0	13	0.6	40.83	0.0000

Note: N=Number; F=Frequency per 1,000 tokens

Table 7.7 demonstrates that CRAs show more occurrences of descriptive reports, sequential explanations, factorial explanations, elucidations, exposition reviews, and figure expositions. It should be mentioned that exposition reviews demonstrate a higher frequency (1.3/1000 tokens), which highlights Chinese authors' selection of expositions review in constructing the R&D section.

Table 7.8 Comparison between linguistics ERAs and CRAs in Discussion

	ERAs		CRAs			
Type of elemental genres	N	P	N	P	ChiSqu	P
Descriptive report	25	0.1	34	0.4	37.76	0.0000
Sequential explanation	3	0	19	0.2	47.95	0.0000
Factorial explanation	25	0.1	48	0.5	71.73	0.0000
Exposition	56	0.2	42	0.4	20.05	0.0000
Elucidation	1	0	4	0	8.8	0.0030
Exposition review	3	0	58	0.6	172.49	0.0000
Figure exposition	0	0	4	0	12.92	0.0003

Note: N=Number; F=Frequency per 1,000 tokens

In the Discussion section, CRAs demonstrate more appearances of elemental genres in the Arguments, including expositions, elucidations, exposition reviews, and figures expositions. In addition, elemental genres in Explanations also appear more frequently in CRAs.

Table 7.9 Comparison between linguistics ERAs and CRAs in Conclusion

	ERAs		CRAs			
Type of elemental genres	N	P	N	P	ChiSqu	P
Descriptive report	31	0.1	36	0.3	30.09	0.0000

Note: N=Number; F=Frequency per 1,000 tokens

As demonstrated by Table 7.9, CRAs also display relatively higher frequency in using descriptive reports in Conclusion. These descriptive reports summarize the main findings, research significance, and future directions.

7.4 Chapter summary

This chapter compares the linguistics ERAs and CRAs in terms of generic complexity features. As for similarities, the two sub−corpora show a consistent trend in the top−three−ranked elemental genre family sequence, which is Re ports−Arguments−Explanations. Besides, descriptive reports unfold with dominant numbers in both RAs. Moreover, factorial explanations and sequential explanations take the same rank in terms of quantity.

As for differences, the results of UAM CT show that CRAs demonstrate more occurrences of Reports and Arguments in the major generic stages of RAs. In the literature review section, CRAs display distinctly more reviews. Additionally, descriptive reports and figure expositions are highlighted in the Methods and Results sections respectively. In the Discussion section, CRAs present an the abundance of exposition reviews.

Chapter 8 Conclusion

The current study establishes a framework for exploring generic complexity and applies this framework to the analysis of generic complexity in the ERAs from three disciplines. Chapter 8 first summarizes the findings of the present study in relation to the RQs raised in Chapter 1. Then, the theoretical, methodological, and practical implications of the current study are pointed out. Finally, the limitations and suggestions for future studies are presented.

8.1 Major Findings

With the help of corpora, the present study has attained its purpose of exploring generic complexity in four aspects: (1) to establish a framework for exploring generic complexity in RAs; (2) to apply this framework in the analysis of the ERAs in the three disciplines; and (3) to figure out the influence of disciplinarity on the generic complexity of the ERAs. (4) to compare linguistics ERAs and CRAs in terms of generic complexity. The first aspect is realized through Chapter 3, where the theoretical framework is proposed. The second and fourth aspects are realized through Chapters 4 to 7. The study shows that the framework proposed in Chapter 3 can be used in the analysis of generic complexity. On the one hand, the exploration of elemental genres reveals that six elemental genres can be added to the original genre identification model. On the other hand, various elemental genre combining strategies are employed in the formation of macrogenres in the main stages of ERAs.

In terms of the specific research questions proposed in Chapter 1, Chapter

4 serves to answer RQ1, where the major generic structures, emerging elemental genres, and the overall and macro-generic-stage-based elemental genre distribution are discussed. Chapter 5 responds to RQ2, where the elemental genre combining strategies in the main generic stages are analyzed. Chapter 6 presents the answers to RQ3, which depicts the discipline-sensitive elemental genres mainly from the field and the discourse semantics strata. As for RQ4, the impact of disciplinary features on the generic complexity is integrated into the discussion of research findings through Chapter 4 to Chapter 6. The answers to RQ5 are presented in Chapter 7.

The following six sub-sections summarize the results of the current study following the order of research questions.

8.1.1 Major generic structure

As the preliminary procedure for identifying the elemental genres and elemental genre combining strategies, the macro generic stages in the ERAs are coded. The results in the three sub-corpora illustrate distinctive characteristics. ILMRDC (16 cases, 32%, see Table 4.1) is the most common generic pattern in the linguistics sub-corpus. IM[RD]C (14 cases, 28%, see Table 4.1) is favored by the physics RAs. In addition, the Methods section can be demarcated as two sections, with section titles like *Experiment, Simulated events, and Numerical methods*, etc. As regards the literature sub-corpus, the most frequent generic pattern is (I)A.

In summary, the physics ERAs exhibit an emphasis on the Methods section, which may be attributed to the knowledge-code orientation of physics, i.e., the physical phenomena are approached through rigorous descriptions of methodology. The literature sub-corpus, however, demonstrates the preferences of the Argumentation stage. This finding can possibly be explained by the knower-code orientation of literary studies, where the authors' judgements on literature works are convinced through a large number of arguing genres.

8.1.2 Emerging elemental genres

In the real operation of the analytical framework for exploring elemental genres proposed in Chapter 3, some elemental genres that are not included in the original genre identifying model are emerging. These elemental genres include exposition reviews, elucidations, figure expositions, direct formula recounts, conditional formula recounts, and sequential formula recounts. The first three are classified as elemental genres in the genre family of Arguments while the other three belong to the genre family of Recounts. The purpose, schematic structure, and specific instances of these elemental genres are discussed in detail in Chapter 4.

An exposition review is employed to support the writers' positions with the schematic structure of Thesis ^ Evidence ^ Evaluation. An elucidation is used for negotiating the authors' point of view with the schematic structure of Thesis ^ Example (Evidence). Figure expositions serve to describe and evaluate figures in the ERAs. They follow the schematic structure of Figure presentation ^ Figure Description ^ (Evaluation).

The remaining three burgeoning elemental genres occur exclusively in the physics ERAs. Direct formula recounts aim at describing a single formula with the schematic structure of Formula presentation ^ Description. Conditional formula recounts are characterized by the lexicogrammatical resource "if" in the formula presentation phase followed by the formula description phase which details the meanings of parameters. Sequential formula recounts are instantiated by a series of mutually-related formulas with the schematic structure of Formula presentation ^ Formula Description [1-n].

Under the guidance of macro generic stage identification and the summary of emerging elemental genres, the elemental genre deployments are investigated in the present study, and the results of this exploration are recapped in the next sub-section.

8.1.3 Elemental genre deployments

The current study explores the elemental genre deployments in the three sub-corpora from two aspects. On the one hand, the overall elemental genre deployments are discussed. On the other hand, the elemental genre deployments in each macro generic stage are analyzed.

Regarding the overall elemental genre deployments, the findings are elaborated on from the elemental genre families and the specific elemental genres. In terms of the elemental genre families, the physics sub-corpus and the linguistics one follow the same order of elemental genre families, i.e., Reports > Arguments > Explanations > Recounts > Text responses. As for the literature ERAs, Arguments take the lead followed by Reports. The remaining three elemental genre families adhere to the same order as the research papers from the other two disciplines.

Concerning the differences in elemental genre families, the results of one-way ANOVA or nonparametric tests show that the literature ERAs use significantly more Arguments than the research papers of the other two disciplines do. The physics sub-corpus possesses markedly more Recounts than the other two sub-corpora.

In terms of the specific elemental genres, the similarities and differences are summarized in Table 4.6. Regarding similarities, two points are emphasized. Firstly, within each elemental genre family, the elemental genres which favor more occurrences are the same. Secondly, factorial explanations scatter equally frequently among the three sub-corpora, which indicates that similar strategies are chosen when the writers list several reasons attributing to certain phenomena.

Regarding variations, the results demonstrate the influence of disciplinarity on the distribution of certain elemental genres. The physics EARs prefer to utilize formula recounts, figure expositions, and procedural recounts due to their emphasis on knowledge claims. The literature ERAs frequently use expositions and exposition reviews because they aim to persuade the reader to embrace their personal opinion or taste in literary works. The linguistics ERAs show a mixture of knowledge and knower code. On the one hand, the linguistics academic articles show more occurrences of expositions than the physics sub-corpus. On the other hand, the linguistics sub-corpus demonstrates a higher frequency of procedural recounts than the literature ones.

In addition to the exploration of overall elemental genre deployments, the distribution of elemental genres in major generic stages is also analyzed. The results are encapsulated as follows.

Regarding similarities, descriptive reports run through all the major generic stages among the three sub-corpora. Besides, as for the linguistics and the physics ERAs, expositions are frequently used in the Results, R&D, and Discussion sections, which assess and interpret research findings. In addition, reviews, which analyze and evaluate related studies, occur frequently in the Introduction and Literature review sections.

In terms of the differences, the disparity among the three sub-corpora lies in the Introduction section, where the physics ERAs employ more elemental genres (0.3 per 1,000 tokens) in the genre family of Reports while the literature ERAs use a larger diversity of elemental genres, including those in the genre families of Explanations, Arguments, and Recounts.

The differences in elemental genre distribution between the linguistics and the physics research papers in the Methods, Results, R&D, and Discussion sections are calculated by Chi-square tests.

The results are demonstrated in Tables 4.10–4.13. Briefly speaking, the physics ERAs boast noticeably more sequential explanations, figure expositions, and direct formula recounts than the linguistics ERAs do in the Methods, Results, R&D, and Discussion sections. The linguistics research papers utilize more exposition reviews than the physics ERAs do in the Results and R&D parts. This finding might also be attributed to the different knowledge structure orientations of the two disciplines. Physics, which is a knowledge-code-centered discipline, uses formula recounts and figure expositions to provide an accurate description of physical phenomena. Additionally, different elemental genres from the genre family of Explanations are utilized to investigate the causes of particular physical occurrences. Linguistics, which is a discipline in social science (see Martin et al., 2010:438) tries to interpret the research results through expositions.

8.1.4 Elemental genre combining strategies

As the other major analytical dimension of the current framework for exploring generic complexity, the mechanism through which elemental genres are combined within the major macro generic stages is coded and analyzed. The results are detailed in Chapter 5.

Concerning similarities, elemental genre extension predominates in terms of quantity across the three disciplines. Additionally, genre combining patterns include both intra-generic and inter-generic families.

The differences in elemental genre combining strategies among the three sub-corpora exist in extension, enhancement, projection, and embedding.

For extension, descriptive report+descriptive report is the most frequent pattern in the linguistics and physics sub-corpora. This discovery might be attributed to the vast number of descriptive reports that are integrated to describe related studies, research methodologies, and study outcomes in the ERAs of the two disciplines. Contrarily, the most prevalent genre extension type in literature ERAs is exposition+exposition, where the writers' viewpoints are mostly presented and persuaded through expositions.

In terms of enhancement, all three sub-corpora display the pattern of the Reports genre family being enhanced by Explanations. However, one of the top five inter-genre combining patterns in the physics sub-corpus is descriptive report×factorial explanation. The disciplinary features of physics, which emphasize the investigation of the causes of physical phenomena, are further supported by this finding.

Regarding genre embedding, the current research focuses on explicit genre embedding with glaring font or typographic disparities between the embedding and embedded genres. The findings show that the literature ERAs had a higher proportion of elemental genre embedding. This may be explained by the fact that ERAs of literary studies frequently use literary excerpts as examples for interpretation.

In conclusion, the ERAs primarily exploit the elemental genre of extension to increase the range of meaning potential. At the same time, various disciplines display their unique characteristics. The physics sub-corpus favors the descriptive report × factorial explanation pattern for elucidating the causes behind experiments or numerical results. However, the literature ERAs show more instances of overt genre embedding.

8.1.5 Discipline-distinctive elemental genres

Based on the statistical analysis in Chapter 4, eight elemental genres which display disciplinary preferences are chosen for further analysis. The eight elemental genres are classifying reports, expositions, and procedural recounts in the linguistics sub-corpus; figure expositions, direct formula recounts, and sequential explanations in the physics ERAs; exposition reviews and expositions in the literature research papers. The findings are summarized in three dimensions.

First, the linguistics ERAs show mixed features between the physics and literature ERAs. They have more expositions than physics articles, on the one hand. Yet, compared to the literature ERAs, they include noticeably more procedural recounts. Additionally, compared to the other two sub-corpora, the linguistics sub-corpus uses a larger number of classifying reports. The analysis of field and discourse semantics resources demonstrates that classifying reports are principally built up by items in terms of field resources. Expositions and procedural recounts, however, can be realized by either items or activities. In addition, semiotic entities are dispersed among the three elemental genres.

Second, the physics ERAs are featured for their abundance of figure expositions and unique appearances of three different types of formula recounts. Furthermore, sequential explanations are frequently used to clarify the objectives of experiments. From the perspective of field resources, direct formula recounts and figure expositions are primarily identified by items. Figure expositions highlight thing entities (e.g., the tools or containers used in the experiments) and semiotic entities (e.g., the figures) from the discourse semantics stratum. Direct formula recounts highlight semiotic entities (e.g., different formula parameters). Sequential explanations are realized by implication sequences semantically.

Third, the literature ERAs see an abundance of arguing genres, including exposition reviews and expositions. The analysis reveals that the two elemental genres favor using literary critics as the source entities and employing more evaluation resources that directly convey writers' attitudes.

8.1.6 Disciplinary features

The answer to RQ4 is actually woven throughout the discussion of the previous three questions from Chapter 4 to Chapter 6. The disciplines exert influence on generic complexity, which is realized in three aspects.

First, the disciplinary characteristics influence the overall elemental genre deployments. Physics, a knowledge-code-oriented discipline, possesses three types of formula recounts exclusively, which provide an accurate description of mathematical formulas. Besides, figure expositions (95 cases, 0.3 per 1,000 tokens, see Table 4.3), which present the analysis and evaluation of figures, show significantly more frequent occurrences than those in other disciplines (31 cases, 0.1 per 1,000 tokens in the linguistics sub-corpus; 10 cases, 0 per 1,000 tokens in the literature sub-corpus, see Table 4.3). The ERAs of literary studies, which is a knower-code-centered discipline, use markedly more exposition reviews (138 instances, 0.4 per 1,000 tokens, see Table 4.3) than the other two disciplines do (59 instances, 0.1 per 1,000 tokens in the linguistics

ERAs; one case in the physics sub-corpus, see Table 4.3). Linguistics, which lies in the middle of the discipline continuum, displays a somewhat mixture of both knowledge codes and knower codes. Procedural recounts (46 cases, 0.1 per 1000 tokens, see Table 4.4) and figure expositions (31 cases, 0.1 per 1,000 tokens, see Table 4.3) in the linguistics corpus are more than those in literature papers (3 cases for the procedural recounts, see Table 4.4; 10 cases for figure expositions, see Table 4.3). However, expositions (127 cases, 0.3 per 1,000 tokens, see Table 4.3) and exposition reviews (59 cases, 0.1 per 1,000 tokens, see Table 4.3) show more occurrences than those in the physics corpus (42 cases, 0.1 per 1,000 tokens for expositions; one case for exposition reviews, see Table 4.3).

Second, the disciplinary features can influence genre combining strategies. For the literature sub-corpus, the most frequent elemental genre combining pattern is exposition + exposition (35 cases, 14.64%, see Table 5.4). Furthermore, overt elemental genre embedding occurs more frequently (30 cases, see Table 5.3). These findings may be attributed to the abundance of expositions in the literature ERAs. Additionally, the direct quotation of the excerpts from literary works through overt genre embedding also reflects the features of knower-code-oriented disciplines, where the other person's voice and authority are emphasized.

For the physics sub-corpus, the genre enhancement pattern of descriptive report × factorial explanation (14 cases, 32.56%, see Table 5.9) can rank as one of the top five frequent elemental genre enhancing types, which indicates the emphasis on finding out the reasons behind certain physical phenomena of physics. Moreover, genre projection, which is realized by figure expositions (95 cases, see Table 5.3), also occurs more frequently in the physics ERAs.

Third, disciplines can also exert influence on the construction of specific elemental genres, which are revealed in the discipline-specific field and discourse semantics resources used for construing certain elemental genres. For the physics ERAs, figure expositions highlight thing entities, which include the containers or tools employed in conducting experiments. Furthermore, figures themselves, as semiotic entities, are also emphasized by figure expositions. For the literature ERAs, source entities (e.g., other literary critics) often realize expositions and exposition reviews in terms of the field resources. Besides, at the discourse semantics stratum, appraisal resources are employed more often by authors of the literature ERAs for expressing their attitudes.

8.2 Implications

The current study establishes a framework for exploring generic complexity in RAs. Furthermore, this framework is testified through the analysis of RAs from physics, linguistics, and literary studies. This study possesses a number of theoretical, methodological, and pedagogical implications.

Theoretically, the present project may contribute to the following three aspects.

First, this study enriches the research on RAs. Although RAs have attracted the attention of scholars from various academic backgrounds, the generic complexity of RAs is still underexplored. Therefore, the current project takes the RAs in three disciplines as research objects, exploring the overall elemental genre deployments and elemental genre combining strategies. Thus, this study provides a relatively thorough investigation of the generic complexity of RAs.

Second, the current study broadens the explanatory horizon of SFL-based genre theory. A framework catering to analyzing generic complexity in RAs is proposed and testified. The findings reveal six emerging elemental genres in the RAs. Furthermore, the study analyzes the mechanism through which elemental genres are combined.

Third, the current research deepens the understanding of generic complexity in different disciplines. The results of the present study show that some elemental genres possess statistically meaningful distribution in certain disciplines. Moreover, the elemental genre allocations differ in the same macro generic stage among the ERAs of the three disciplines. Additionally, ERAs from different disciplines favor different elemental genre combining patterns. All of the above-mentioned discoveries can strengthen our understanding of the generic features in three disciplines representing sciences, social sciences, and the humanities.

Methodologically, the current study presents statistically significant distinctions in the elemental genre deployments of the RAs by integrating the statistical analyses of SPSS and UAM CT. This statistical analysis of the genre deployments provides more convincing results for revealing the differences and similarities among the three disciplines because previous discussions on the generic complexity were based on counting the number of elemental genres in ERAs or undergraduate theses of a single discipline.

Pedagogically, the findings of the present study can provide guidance on the teaching of academic writing and the compiling of teaching materials for academic writing.

Regarding the academic writing courses, firstly, the generic complexity of RAs should be given due attention. Previous studies of the RAs focus either on local aspects like metadiscourse or global ones like structures and organizations (e.g., Hyland&Jiang, 2018; Swales, 2004). However, the findings of this study demonstrate that generic complexity is present in the design of RAs. Raising student writers' awareness of the generic complexity of writing research articles is therefore required. Moreover, in the teaching of academic writing, the differences in generic complexity in RAs of various disciplines should be emphasized. Based on the findings of the present research, the overall elemental genre deployments among the research papers representing humanities, natural sciences, and social sciences demonstrate variations. In addition, the linking patterns between two adjacent elemental genres also display differences. Furthermore, the RAs of the three disciplines show their preferred elemental genres, which are built up by distinctive field and discourse semantics resources. All the above-mentioned discoveries support the need to design academic writing courses catering to various disciplines.

As for the compiling of teaching materials for academic writing, disciplinary features in generic complexity among different disciplines should be emphasized. According to the findings of the current study, there are disparities between the three disciplines in the total elemental genre deployments, the generic-stage-based genre allocation, and elemental genre combining patterns. Moreover, various fields and discourse semantics are employed in the construction of discipline-sensitive elemental genres. Thus, specific guidance on the use of elemental genres in the different disciplines should be given to student authors.

8.3 Limitations and future directions

Given the implications listed above, it is safe to say that the present study is valuable in offering a thorough analysis of generic complexity in the RAs from the three disciplines. However, limitations have to be mentioned and can be followed up by future research.

The first limitation is that the scope of the disciplines selected can be enlarged. Even though the three chosen disciplines serve as generally typical representative subjects in sciences, social sciences, and the humanities, the disciplinary representation can still be improved by a larger range of disciplines. Moreover, it might be worthwhile to look into the paradigmatic influences on the generic complexity of RAs, which have not been considered either.

The second limitation is that the current study only focuses on English RAs and linguistics CRAs. The similarities and differences between ERAs and RAs in other languages can be analyzed and summarized so that a thorough understanding of generic complexity in research papers can be achieved.

Moreover, the following can be the focus of future work.

A wider range of disciplines can be examined for the disciplinary variation study to shed more light on how writers employ various elemental genres in RAs.

The results of the current study may be a reference for the study of a large range of disciplines, such as geology or historical linguistics, which are relatively less discussed than other disciplines. Besides, future studies can also pay attention to subjects like nursing, social work, and business studies that are more practice-oriented and require vocational abilities.

Appendices

Appendix 1: Research articles in the original corpus

Linguistics

	Code	
1	Lin 202001	Ganassin, S.,&Holmes, P. (2020). 'I was surprised to see you in a Chinese school': Researching multilingually opportunities and challenges in community-based research. *Applied Linguistics*, *41*(6), 827-854.
2	Lin 202002	Brainerd, C. J., Bialer, D. M.,&Chang, M. (2020). Norming retrieval processes. *Journal of Memory and Language*, *115*, 104143.
3	Lin 202003	Von Esch, K. S., Motha, S.,&Kubota, R. (2020). Race and language teaching. *Language Teaching*, *53*(4), 391-421.
4	Lin 202004	Graham, S., Woore, R., Porter, A., Courtney, L.,&Savory, C. (2020). Navigating the challenges of L2 reading: Self-efficacy, self-regulatory reading strategies, and learner profiles. *The Modern Language Journal*, *104*(4), 693-714.
5	Lin 202005	Lieberman, A. M.,&Borovsky, A. (2020). Lexical recognition in deaf children learning American sign language: Activation of semantic and phonological features of signs. *Language Learning*, *70*(4), 935-973.
6	Lin 202006	Wu, Z. (2020). Tracing EFL writers' digital literacy practices in asynchronous communication: A multiple-case study. *Journal of Second Language Writing*, *50*, 100754.
7	Lin 202007	Bancroft-Billings, S. (2020). Identifying spoken technical legal vocabulary in a law school classroom. *English for Specific Purposes*, *60*, 9-25.
8	Lin 202008	Prasad, G.,&Lory, M.-P. (2020). Linguistic and cultural collaboration in schools: Reconciling majority and minoritized language users. *Tesol Quarterly*, *54*(4), 797-822.
9	Lin 202009	Jeongyeon, K.,&Hye Young, S. (2020). Negotiation of emotions in emerging language teacher identity of graduate instructors. *System*, *95*, 102365.

Cont.

	Code	
10	Lin 202010	Hill, C., Khoo, S.,&Hsieh, Y.-C. (2020). An investigation into the learning transfer of English for specific Academic Purposes (ESAP) writing skills of students in Singapore. *Journal of English for Academic Purposes*, *48*, 100908.
11	Lin 201901	Van Compernolle, R. A. (2019). Constructing a second language sociolinguistic repertoire: A sociocultural usage-based perspective. *Applied Linguistics*, *40*(6), 871-893.
12	Lin 201902	Fehér, O., Ritt, N.,&Smith, K. (2019). Asymmetric accommodation during interaction leads to the regularisation of linguistic variants. *Journal of Memory and Language*, *109*, 104036.
13	Lin 201903	Lee, I. (2019). Teacher written corrective feedback: Less is more. *Language Teaching*, *52*(4), 524-536.
14	Lin 201904	Sauer, L.,&Ellis, R. O. D. (2019). The social lives of adolescent study abroad learners and their L2 development. *The Modern Language Journal*, *103*(4), 739-762.
15	Lin 201905	Uchikoshi, Y. (2019). Phonological awareness trajectories: Young Spanish–English and Cantonese–English bilinguals. *Language Learning*, *69*(4), 802-838.
16	Lin 201906	Jiang, J., Bi, P.,&Liu, H. (2019). Syntactic complexity development in the writings of EFL learners: Insights from a dependency syntactically-annotated corpus. *Journal of Second Language Writing*, *46*, 100666.
17	Lin 201907	Geng, Y.,&Wharton, S. (2019). How do thesis writers evaluate their own and others' findings? An appraisal analysis and a pedagogical intervention. *English for Specific Purposes*, *56*, 3-17.
18	Lin 201908	Kim, H. R.,&Bowles, M. (2019). How deeply do second language learners process written corrective feedback? Insights gained from think-alouds. *Tesol Quarterly*, *53*(4), 913-938.
19	Lin 201909	Lindstromberg, S. (2019). Ratings of the emotional valence and arousal of collocations and their constituent words: How can they be useful in L2 vocabulary research? *System*, *87*, 102144.
20	Lin 201910	Pun, J. K. H. (2019). Salient language features in explanation texts that students encounter in secondary school chemistry textbooks. *Journal of English for Academic Purposes*, *42*, 100781.
21	Lin 201801	Moody, S. J. (2018). Fitting in or standing out? A conflict of belonging and identity in intercultural polite talk at work. *Applied Linguistics*, *39*(6), 775-798.
22	Lin 201802	Keung, L.-C.,&Staub, A. (2018). Variable agreement with coordinate subjects is not a form of agreement attraction. *Journal of Memory and Language*, *103*, 1-18.
23	Lin 201803	Isabelli-García, C., Bown, J., Plews, J. L.,&Dewey, D. P. (2018). Language learning and study abroad. *Language Teaching*, *51*(4), 439-484.
24	Lin 201804	Teimouri, Y. (2018). Differential roles of shame and guilt in L2 learning: How bad is bad?. *The Modern Language Journal*, *102*(4), 632-652.

Cont.

	Code	
25	Lin 201805	Dimroth, C. (2018). Beyond statistical learning: Communication principles and language internal factors shape grammar in child and adult beginners learning Polish through controlled exposure. *Language Learning*, *68*(4), 863-905.
26	Lin 201806	McKinley, J.,&Rose, H. (2018). Conceptualizations of language errors, standards, norms and nativeness in English for research publication purposes: An analysis of journal submission guidelines. *Journal of Second Language Writing*, *42*, 1-11.
27	Lin 201807	Bremner, S.,&Costley, T. (2018). Bringing reality to the classroom: Exercises in intertextuality. *English for Specific Purposes*, *52*, 1-12.
28	Lin 201808	Kashiwa, M.,&Benson, P. (2018). A road and a forest: Conceptions of in-class and out-of-class learning in the transition to study abroad. *Tesol Quarterly*, *52*(4), 725-747.
29	Lin 201809	Ilieva, R.,&Ravindran, A. (2018). Agency in the making: Experiences of international graduates of a TESOL program. *System*, *79*, 7-18.
30	Lin 201810	Omidian, T., Shahriari, H.,&Siyanova-Chanturia, A. (2018). A cross-disciplinary investigation of multi-word expressions in the moves of research article abstracts. *Journal of English for Academic Purposes*, *36*, 1-14.
31	Lin 201701	Li, S. (2017). Identity constructions in bilingual advertising: A critical-cognitive approach. *Applied Linguistics*, *38*(6), 775-799.
32	Lin 201702	Jacobs, C. L., Dell, G. S.,&Bannard, C. (2017). Phrase frequency effects in free recall: Evidence for redintegration. *Journal of Memory and Language*, *97*, 1-16.
33	Lin 201703	Graves, K.,&Garton, S. (2017). An analysis of three curriculum approaches to teaching English in public-sector schools. *Language Teaching*, *50*(4), 441-482.
34	Lin 201704	Marsden, E.,&Kasprowicz, R. (2017). Foreign language educators' exposure to research: Reported experiences, exposure via citations, and a proposal for action. *The Modern Language Journal*, *101*(4), 613-642.
35	Lin 201705	Suzuki, Y.,&DeKeyser, R. (2017). The interface of explicit and implicit knowledge in a second language: Insights from individual differences in cognitive aptitudes. *Language Learning*, *67*(4), 747-790.
36	Lin 201706	Kibler, A. K. (2017). Becoming a "Mexican feminist": A minoritized bilingual's development of disciplinary identities through writing. *Journal of Second Language Writing*, *38*, 26-41.
37	Lin 201707	Kelly-Laubscher, R. F., Muna, N.,&van der Merwe, M. (2017). Using the research article as a model for teaching laboratory report writing provides opportunities for development of genre awareness and adoption of new literacy practices. *English for Specific Purposes*, *48*, 1-16.
38	Lin 201708	Hwang, J. K., Lawrence, J. F., Collins, P.,&Snow, C. (2017). Vocabulary and reading performances of redesignated fluent English proficient students. *Tesol Quarterly*, *51*(4), 757-786.

Cont.

	Code	
39	Lin 201709	Tracy-Ventura, N. (2017). Combining corpora and experimental data to investigate language learning during residence abroad: A study of lexical sophistication. *System*, *71*, 35-45.
40	Lin 201710	Barnes, M. (2017). Washback: Exploring what constitutes "good" teaching practices. *Journal of English for Academic Purposes*, *30*, 1-12.
41	Lin 201601	Louw, S., Watson Todd, R.,&Jimarkon, P. (2016). Teacher trainers' beliefs about feedback on teaching practice: Negotiating the tensions between authoritativeness and dialogic space. *Applied Linguistics*, *37*(6), 745-764.
42	Lin 201602	Mahowald, K., James, A., Futrell, R.,&Gibson, E. (2016). A meta-analysis of syntactic priming in language production. *Journal of Memory and Language*, *91*, 5-27.
43	Lin 201603	Ushioda, E. (2016). Language learning motivation through a small lens: A research agenda. *Language Teaching*, *49*(4), 564-577.
44	Lin 201604	Hiver, P.,&Al-Hoorie, A. H. (2016). A dynamic ensemble for second language research: Putting complexity theory into practice. *The Modern Language Journal*, *100*(4), 741-756.
45	Lin 201605	Darcy, I., Mora, J. C.,&Daidone, D. (2016). The role of inhibitory control in second language phonological processing. *Language Learning*, *66*(4), 741-773.
46	Lin 201606	Kyle, K.,&Crossley, S. (2016). The relationship between lexical sophistication and independent and source-based writing. *Journal of Second Language Writing*, *34*, 12-24.
47	Lin 201607	Nathan, P. (2016). Analysing options in pedagogical business case reports: Genre, process and language. *English for Specific Purposes*, *44*, 1-15.
48	Lin 201608	Humphrey, S.,&Macnaught, L. (2016). Functional language instruction and the writing growth of English language learners in the middle years. *Tesol Quarterly*, *50*(4), 792-816.
49	Lin 201609	Abrams, Z. I.,&Byrd, D. R. (2016). The effects of pre-task planning on L2 writing: Mind-mapping and chronological sequencing in a 1st-year German class. *System*, *63*, 1-12.
50	Lin 201610	Becker, A. (2016). L2 students' performance on listening comprehension items targeting local and global information. *Journal of English for Academic Purposes*, *24*, 1-13.

Physics

	Code	
1	Phys 202001	Ghosh, S., Brüser, V., Kaplan-Ashiri, I., Popovitz-Biro, R., Peglow, S., Martínez, J. I., Alonso, J. A.,&Zak, A. (2020). Cathodoluminescence in single and multiwall WS2 nanotubes: Evidence for quantum confinement and strain effect. *Applied Physics Reviews*, *7*(4), 041401.
2	Phys 20200102	Guan, X., Wang, Y., Lin, C.-H., Hu, L., Ge, S., Wan, T., Younis, A., Li, F., Cui, Y., Qi, D.-C., Chu, D., Chen, X. D.,&Wu, T. (2020). A monolithic artificial iconic memory based on highly stable perovskite-metal multilayers. *Applied Physics Reviews*, *7*(3), 031401.
3	Phys 20200103	Feng, Y., Jiang, T., Liang, X., An, J.,&Wang, Z. L. (2020). Cylindrical triboelectric nanogenerator based on swing structure for efficient harvesting of ultra-low-frequency water wave energy. *Applied Physics Reviews*, *7*(2), 021401.
4	Phys 202002	Stefani, C., Ponet, L., Shapovalov, K., Chen, P., Langenberg, E., Schlom, D. G., Artyukhin, S., Stengel, M., Domingo, N.,&Catalan, G. (2020). Mechanical softness of ferroelectric 180° domain walls. *Physical Review X*, *10*(4), 041001.
5	Phys 202003	Payne, E., Talbot, C., Lasky, P. D., Thrane, E.,&Kissel, J. S. (2020). Gravitational-wave astronomy with a physical calibration model. *Physical Review D*, *102*(12), 122004.
6	Phys 202004	Singleton, J., Schmidt, A. C., Bailey, C., Wigger, J.,&Krawczyk, F. (2020). Information carried by electromagnetic radiation launched from accelerated polarization currents. *Physical Review Applied*, *14*(6), 064046.
7	Phys 202005	Li, B., Lin, S., Wang, Y., Yuan, Q., Joo, S. W.,&Chen, L. (2020). Promoting rebound of impinging viscoelastic droplets on heated superhydrophobic surfaces. *New Journal of Physics*, *22*(12), 123001.
8	Phys 202006	Pan, Y.,&Dong, H. (2020). Computational analysis of hydrodynamic interactions in a high-density fish school. *Physics of Fluids*, *32*(12), 121901.
9	Phys 202007	Takashima, R., Ohira, M., Yokochi, H., Aoki, D., Li, X.,&Otsuka, H. (2020). Characterization of N-phenylmaleimide-terminated polys (ethylene glycol) and their application to a tetra-arm poly (ethylene glycol) gel. *Soft Matter*, *16*(48), 10869-10875.
10	Phys 202008	Haselschwardt, S. J., Kostensalo, J., Mougeot, X.,&Suhonen, J. (2020). Improved calculations of β decay backgrounds to new physics in liquid xenon detectors. *Physical Review C*, *102*(6), 065501.

Cont.

	Code	
11	Phys 202009	Tian, K., Ren, H.-P.,&Grebogi, C. (2020). Rössler-network with time delay: Univariate impulse pinning synchronization. *Chaos: An Interdisciplinary Journal of Nonlinear Science, 30*(12), 123101.
12	Phys 202010	Matzkin, A.,&Sokolovski, D. (2020). Wigner-friend scenarios with noninvasive weak measurements. *Physical Review A, 102*(6), 062204.
13	Phys 201901	Alenezi, H., Cam, M. E.,&Edirisinghe, M. (2019). Experimental and theoretical investigation of the fluid behavior during polymeric fiber formation with and without pressure. *Applied Physics Reviews, 6*(4), 041401.
14	Phys 20190102	Duim, H., Fang, H.-H., Adjokatse, S., ten Brink, G. H., Marques, M. A. L., Kooi, B. J., Blake, G. R., Botti, S.,&Loi, M. A. (2019). Mechanism of surface passivation of methylammonium lead tribromide single crystals by benzylamine. *Applied Physics Reviews, 6*(3), 031401.
15	Phys 201902	Salerno, G., Price, H. M., Lebrat, M., Häusler, S., Esslinger, T., Corman, L., Brantut, J. P.,&Goldman, N. (2019). Quantized hall conductance of a single atomic wire: A proposal based on synthetic dimensions. *Physical Review X, 9*(4), 041001.
16	Phys 201903	Yang, L., Randel, E., Vajente, G., Ananyeva, A., Gustafson, E., Markosyan, A., Bassiri, R., Fejer, M. M.,&Menoni, C. S. (2019). Investigation of effects of assisted ion bombardment on mechanical loss of sputtered tantala thin films for gravitational wave interferometers. *Physical Review D, 100*(12), 122004.
17	Phys 201904	Yang, Y., Zhao, Q., Liu, L., Liu, Y., Rosales-Guzmán, C.,&Qiu, C.-w. (2019). Manipulation of orbital-angular-momentum spectrum using pinhole plates. *Physical Review Applied, 12*(6), 064007.
18	Phys 201905	Grebenkov, D. S., Metzler, R.,&Oshanin, G. (2019). Full distribution of first exit times in the narrow escape problem. *New Journal of Physics, 21*(12), 122001.
19	Phys 201906	Cox, C., Najjari, M. R.,&Plesniak, M. W. (2019). Three-dimensional vortical structures and wall shear stress in a curved artery model. *Physics of Fluids, 31*(12), 121903.
20	Phys 201907	Breuer, A., Lauritsen, L., Bertseva, E., Vonkova, I.,&Stamou, D. (2019). Quantitative investigation of negative membrane curvature sensing and generation by I-BARs in filopodia of living cells. *Soft Matter, 15*(48), 9829-9839.
21	Phys 201908	Szücs, T., Mohr, P., Gyürky, G., Halász, Z., Huszánk, R., Kiss, G. G., Szegedi, T. N., Török, Z.,&Fülöp, Z. (2019). Cross section of α-induced reactions on ^{197}Au at sub-Coulomb energies. *Physical Review C, 100*(6), 065803.

Cont.

	Code	
22	Phys 201909	Sun, Q., Tang, Y.,&Zhao, C. (2019). Cycle-SfM: Joint self-supervised learning of depth and camera motion from monocular image sequences. *Chaos: An Interdisciplinary Journal of Nonlinear Science*, *29*(12), 123102.
23	Phys 201910	Bermudez, A., Xu, X., Gutiérrez, M., Benjamin, S. C.,&Müller, M. (2019). Fault-tolerant protection of near-term trapped-ion topological qubits under realistic noise sources. *Physical Review A*, *100*(6), 062307.
24	Phys 201802	Arvanitaki, A., Dimopoulos, S.,&Van Tilburg, K. (2018). Resonant absorption of bosonic dark matter in molecules. *Physical Review X*, *8*(4), 041001.
25	Phys 201803	Astone, P., Cerdá-Durán, P., Di Palma, I., Drago, M., Muciaccia, F., Palomba, C.,&Ricci, F. (2018). New method to observe gravitational waves emitted by core collapse supernovae. *Physical Review D*, *98*(12), 122002.
26	Phys 201804	Serikawa, T.,&Furusawa, A. (2018). Excess loss in homodyne detection originating from distributed photocarrier generation in photodiodes. *Physical Review Applied*, *10*(6), 064016.
27	Phys 201805	Guevara-Bertsch, M., Chavarría-Sibaja, A., Godínez-Sandí, A.,&Herrera-Sancho, O. A. (2018). Energy exchange between atoms with a quartz crystal μ-balance. *New Journal of Physics*, *20*(12), 123001.
28	Phys 201806	Singh, N. K.,&Premachandran, B. (2018). Mixed regime of film boiling over a horizontal cylinder in an upward flow of saturated liquid. *Physics of Fluids*, *30*(12), 122101.
29	Phys 201807	Zou, S., Therriault, D.,&Gosselin, F. P. (2018). Failure mechanisms of coiling fibers with sacrificial bonds made by instability-assisted fused deposition modeling. *Soft Matter*, *14*(48), 9777-9785.
30	Phys 201808	Ochala, I.,&Fiase, J. O. (2018). Symmetric nuclear matter calculations: A variational approach. *Physical Review C*, *98*(6), 064001.
31	Phys 201809	Jayaprasath, E., Wu, Z.-M., Sivaprakasam, S.,&Xia, G.-Q. (2018). Observation of additional delayed-time in chaos synchronization of uni-directionally coupled VCSELs. *Chaos: An Interdisciplinary Journal of Nonlinear Science*, *28*(12), 123103.
32	Phys 201810	Paraschiv, M., Miklin, N., Moroder, T.,&Gühne, O. (2018). Proving genuine multiparticle entanglement from separable nearest-neighbor marginals. *Physical Review A, 98*(6), 062102.
33	Phys 201702	Harshman, N. L., Olshanii, M., Dehkharghani, A. S., Volosniev, A. G., Jackson, S. G.,&Zinner, N. T. (2017). Integrable families of hard-core particles with unequal masses in a one-dimensional harmonic trap. *Physical Review X*, *7*(4), 041001.

Cont.

	Code	
34	Phys 201703	Collaboration, H., Alfaro, R., Alvarez, C., Álvarez, J. D., Arceo, R., Arteaga-Velázquez, J. C., Avila Rojas, D., Ayala Solares, H. A., Barber, A. S., Becerril, A., Belmont-Moreno, E., BenZvi, S. Y., Brisbois, C., Caballero-Mora, K. S., Capistrán, T., Carramiñana, A., Casanova, S., Castillo, M., Cotti, U., . . . Zhou, H. (2017). All-particle cosmic ray energy spectrum measured by the HAWC experiment from 10 to 500 TeV. *Physical Review D*, *96*(12), 122001.
35	Phys 201704	Zhang, Y., Song, Z., Wang, X., Cao, W.,&Au, W. W. L. (2017). Directional acoustic wave manipulation by a porpoise via multiphase forehead structure. *Physical Review Applied*, *8*(6), 064002.
36	Phys 201705	Zhang, R., Chen, T.,&Wang, X.-B. (2017). Deterministic quantum controlled-PHASE gates based on non-Markovian environments. *New Journal of Physics*, *19*(12), 123001.
37	Phys 201706	Joshi, P. S., Mahapatra, P. S.,&Pattamatta, A. (2017). Effect of particle shape and slip mechanism on buoyancy induced convective heat transport with nanofluids. *Physics of Fluids*, *29*(12), 122001.
38	Phys 201707	Wulfert, R., Seifert, U.,&Speck, T. (2017). Nonequilibrium depletion interactions in active microrheology. *Soft Matter*, *13*(48), 9093-9102.
39	Phys 201708	Schuetrumpf, B.,&Nazarewicz, W. (2017). Cluster formation in precompound nuclei in the time-dependent framework. *Physical Review C*, *96*(6), 064608.
40	Phys 201709	Yuan, T.,&Tanaka, G. (2017). Robustness of coupled oscillator networks with heterogeneous natural frequencies. *Chaos: An Interdisciplinary Journal of Nonlinear Science*, *27*(12), 123105.
41	Phys 201710	Correa, L. A., Perarnau-Llobet, M., Hovhannisyan, K. V., Hernández-Santana, S., Mehboudi, M.,&Sanpera, A. (2017). Enhancement of low-temperature thermometry by strong coupling. *Physical Review A*, *96*(6), 062103.
42	Phys 201602	Brawand, N. P., Vörös, M., Govoni, M.,&Galli, G. (2016). Generalization of dielectric-dependent hybrid functionals to finite systems. *Physical Review X*, *6*(4), 041002.
43	Phys 201603	Collaboration, X., Aprile, E., Aalbers, J., Agostini, F., Alfonsi, M., Amaro, F. D., Anthony, M., Arneodo, F., Barrow, P., Baudis, L., Bauermeister, B., Benabderrahmane, M. L., Berger, T., Breur, P. A., Brown, A., Brown, E., Bruenner, S., Bruno, G., Budnik, R., . . . Zhang, Y. (2016). XENON100 dark matter results from a combination of 477 live days. *Physical Review D*, *94*(12), 122001.
44	Phys 201604	Diallo, I. C.,&Demchenko, D. O. (2016). Native point defects in GaN: A hybrid-functional study. *Physical Review Applied*, *6*(6), 064002.
45	Phys 201605	Scholz, C., D'Silva, S.,&Pöschel, T. (2016). Ratcheting and tumbling motion of Vibrots. *New Journal of Physics*, *18*(12), 123001.

Cont.

	Code	
46	Phys 201606	Shang, X., Huang, X.,&Yang, C. (2016). Vortex generation and control in a microfluidic chamber with actuations. *Physics of Fluids*, *28*(12), 122001.
47	Phys 201607	Smith, E. R., Müller, E. A., Craster, R. V.,&Matar, O. K. (2016). A Langevin model for fluctuating contact angle behaviour parametrised using molecular dynamics. *Soft Matter*, *12*(48), 9604-9615.
48	Phys 201608	Logoteta, D., Bombaci, I.,&Kievsky, A. (2016). Nuclear matter properties from local chiral interactions with Δ isobar intermediate states. *Physical Review C*, *94*(6), 064001.
49	Phys 201609	Gavrilov, A., Mukhin, D., Loskutov, E., Volodin, E., Feigin, A.,&Kurths, J. (2016). Method for reconstructing nonlinear modes with adaptive structure from multidimensional data. *Chaos: An Interdisciplinary Journal of Nonlinear Science*, *26*(12), 123101.
50	Phys 201610	Guarnieri, G., Nokkala, J., Schmidt, R., Maniscalco, S.,&Vacchini, B. (2016). Energy backflow in strongly coupled non-Markovian continuous-variable systems. *Physical Review A*, *94*(6), 062101.

Literary studies

	Code	
1	Lite 202001	Hill, M. G. (2020). Reading distance: Port Louis, Cairo, Beijing. *PMLA/Publications of the Modern Language Association of America*, *135*(5), 859-876.
2	Lite 202002	Young, K. (2020). Joyce's Ulysses and the Neuroaesthetics of "Yes". *Narrative*, *28*(3), 269-288.
3	Lite 202003	Tiller, E. (2020). Humanist transfer of knowledge from foreign lands: Modes of cognitive perception of the world among Florentine travelers to America between 1490 and 1530. *Neohelicon*, *47*(2), 357-378.
4	Lite 202004	Banta, E. (2020). Agonistic audiences: Comic play in the early national theater. *American Literature: A Journal of Literary History, Criticism, and Bibliography*, *92*(3), 429-455.
5	Lite 202005	Kim, D. Y. (2020). Translations and ghostings of history: The novels of Han Kang. *New Literary History: A Journal of Theory and Interpretation*, *51*(2), 375-399.
6	Lite 202006	Crosby, S. L.,&Willow, A. J. (2020). Indigenous-washing and the petro-hero in genre fictions of the North American oil boom. *MFS: Modern Fiction Studies*, *66*(1), 78-100.
7	Lite 202007	Esonwanne, U. (2020). Hamlet and the people "Who Know Things". *The Cambridge Journal of Postcolonial Literary Inquiry*, *7*(3), 238-246.

Cont.

	Code	
8	Lite 202008	Chariandy, D., Crey, K., John, A. S., Nicholson, C., Nock, S., Okot Bitek, O. J., Reddon, M., Reder, D.,&McCall, S. (2020). Conversations at the crossroads: Indigenous and black writers talk. *ARIEL: A Review of International English Literature, 51*(2-3), 57-81.
9	Lite 202009	Wagoner, B. D. v. (2020). Perilous networks: Risk and maritime news in *The Merchant of Venice. Shakespeare Quarterly, 71*(1), 25-52.
10	Lite 202010	Freebury-Jones, D. (2020). Determining Robert Greene's dramatic canon. *Style, 54*(4), 377-398.
11	Lite 201901	Hollister, L. (2019). The green and the black: Ecological awareness and the darkness of Noir. *PMLA/Publications of the Modern Language Association of America, 134*(5), 1012-1027.
12	Lite 201902	Caracciolo, M. (2019). Form, science, and narrative in the Anthropocene. *Narrative, 27*(3), 270-289.
13	Lite 201903	Liu, Y. (2019). Overseas translation of modern Chinese fiction via T'ien Hsia Monthly. *Neohelicon, 46*(2), 393-409.
14	Lite 201904	McKelvey, S. (2019). Beyond protest: Voice and exit in contemporary American poetry. *American Literature: A Journal of Literary History, Criticism, and Bibliography, 91*(4), 841-870.
15	Lite 201905	Nelson, I. (2019). Poetics of the rule: Form, biopolitics, lyric. *New Literary History: A Journal of Theory and Interpretation, 50*(1), 65-89.
16	Lite 201906	Hornby, L. (2019). Downwrong: The pose of tiredness. *MFS: Modern Fiction Studies, 65*(1), 207-227.
17	Lite 201907	Shahmirzadi, A. A. (2019). "Where is the friend's home?": New world landscapes in Sohrab Sepehri's poetic geography. *The Cambridge Journal of Postcolonial Literary Inquiry, 6*(3), 313-328.
18	Lite 201908	Lim, T. Y. (2019). "Forgetting" and "remembering": The language of stuttering and the notion of "home" in Theresa Hak Kyung Cha's experimental writings. *ARIEL: A Review of International English Literature, 50*(4), 79-104.
19	Lie 201909	Jensen, P. (2019). Causes in nature: Popular astrology in *King Lear. Shakespeare Quarterly, 69*(4), 205-227.
20	Lite 201910	Tsur, R. (2019). Statistical versus structural-cognitive approaches to phonetic symbolism: Two case studies. *Style, 53*(3), 281-307.
21	Lite 201801	Ong, Y.-P. (2018). Anna Karenina reads on the train: Readerly subjectivity and the poetics of the novel. *PMLA/Publications of the Modern Language Association of America, 133*(5), 1083-1098.
22	Lite 201802	Andersson, G.,&Sandberg, T. (2018). Sameness versus difference in narratology: Two approaches to narrative fiction. *Narrative, 26*(3), 241-261.

Cont.

	Code	
23	Lite 201803	Ryan, M.-L. (2018). What are characters made of? Textual, philosophical and "world" approaches to character ontology. *Neohelicon, 45*(2), 415-429.
24	Lite 201804	Trigg, C. (2018). Islam, puritanism, and secular time. *American Literature: A Journal of Literary History, Criticism, and Bibliography, 90*(4), 815-839.
25	Lite 201805	Hanich, J. (2018). Great expectations: Cinematic adaptations and the reader's disappointment. *New Literary History: A Journal of Theory and Interpretation, 49*(3), 425-446.
26	Lite 201806	Vandertop, C. (2018). "The earth seemed unearthly": Capital, world-ecology, and enchanted nature in Conrad's *Heart of Darkness*. *MFS: Modern Fiction Studies, 64*(4), 680-700.
27	Lite 201807	Jolly, R. J.,&Fyfe, A. (2018). Introduction: Reflections on postcolonial animations of the material. *The Cambridge Journal of Postcolonial Literary Inquiry, 5*(3), 296-303.
28	Lite 201808	Menon, S. J. (2018). Highland tales in the *Heart of Borneo*: Postcolonial capitalism, multiculturalism, and survivance. *ARIEL: A Review of International English Literature, 49*(4), 163-188.
29	Lite 201809	Dahlquist, M. (2018). Hamlet and the snare of scandal. *Shakespeare Quarterly, 69*(3), 167-187.
30	Lite 201810	Ikeo, R. (2018). Unshared presuppositions and sssumptions in Flannery O'Connor's *Wise Blood*. *Style, 52*(3), 189-211.
31	Lite 201701	Calderwood, E. (2017). Franco's Hajj: Moroccan pilgrims, Spanish fascism, and the unexpected journeys of modern Arabic literature. *PMLA/Publications of the Modern Language Association of America, 132*(5), 1097-1116.
32	Lite 201702	Alber, J. (2017). Narratology and performativity: On processes of narrativization in live performances. *Narrative, 25*(3), 359-373.
33	Lite 201703	Oppermann, S. (2017). Nature's narrative agencies as compound individuals. *Neohelicon, 44*(2), 283-295.
34	Lite 201704	Barnard, J. L. (2017). The cod and the whale: Melville in the time of extinction. *American Literature: A Journal of Literary History, Criticism, and Bibliography, 89*(4), 851-879.
35	Lite 201705	Algee-Hewitt, M. (2017). Distributed character: Quantitative models of the English stage, 1550-1900. *New Literary History: A Journal of Theory and Interpretation, 48*(4), 751-782.
36	Lite 201706	Iler, D. R. (2017). Suicide and the afterlife of the Cold War: Accident, intentionality, and periodicity in Paul Auster's *Leviathan* and Jeffrey Eugenides's *The Virgin Suicides*. *MFS: Modern Fiction Studies, 63*(4), 737-758.
37	Lite 201707	Newell, S. (2017). The last laugh: African audience responses to colonial health propaganda films. *The Cambridge Journal of Postcolonial Literary Inquiry, 4*(3), 347-361.

Cont.

	Code	
38	Lite 201708	Ledent, B.,&O'Callaghan, E. (2017). Caryl Phillips' *The Lost Child*: A story of loss and connection. *ARIEL: A Review of International English Literature, 48*(3-4), 229-247.
39	Lite 201709	Lamb, J. (2017). Finding the remedy: Measure for measure, puns, rules. *Shakespeare Quarterly, 68*(4), 374-392.
40	Lite 201710	Hopsch, L.,&Lilja, E. (2017). Embodied rhythm in space and time: A poem and a sculpture. *Style: A Quarterly Journal of Aesthetics, Poetics, Stylistics, and Literary Criticism, 51*(4), 413-441.
41	Lite 201601	Young, R. J. C.,&Jean-François, E. B. (2016). That which is casually called a language. *PMLA/Publications of the Modern Language Association of America, 131*(5), 1207-1221.
42	Lite 201602	Bell, A. (2016). Interactional metalepsis and unnatural narratology. *Narrative, 24*(3), 294-310.
43	Lite 201603	Walsh, R. (2016). The fictive reflex: A fresh look at reflexiveness and narrative representation. *Neohelicon, 43*(2), 379-389.
44	Lite 201604	Grossman, S. J. (2016). Ugly data in the age of weather satellites. *American Literature: A Journal of Literary History, Criticism, and Bibliography, 88*(4), 815-837.
45	Lite 201605	Halsall, F. (2016). Actor-network aesthetics: The conceptual rhymes of Bruno Latour and contemporary art. *New Literary History: A Journal of Theory and Interpretation, 47*(2-3), 439-461.
46	Lite 201606	Johns-Putra, A. (2016). "My job is to take care of you": Climate change, humanity, and Cormac McCarthy's *The Road*. *MFS: Modern Fiction Studies, 62*(3), 519-540.
47	Lite 201607	Armillas-Tiseyra, M. (2016). Afronauts: On science fiction and the crisis of possibility. *The Cambridge Journal of Postcolonial Literary Inquiry, 3*(3), 273-290.
48	Lite 201608	Erney, H.-G. (2016). Dodging pitfalls in *Dodgy Autorickshaws with Amitava Kumar*. *ARIEL: A Review of International English Literature, 47*(4), 71-102.
49	Lite 201609	Smith, I. (2016). We are Othello: Speaking of race in early modern studies. *Shakespeare Quarterly, 67*(1), 104-124.
50	Lite 201610	von Contzen, E. (2016). The limits of narration: Lists and literary history. *Style, 50*(3), 241-260.

Appendix 2: ERAs in the refined corpus

Linguistics sub-corpus

Year	Number
2020	01, 04, 05, 06, 07, 08 ,09, 10
2019	01, 04, 05, 06, 07, 08, 10
2018	01, 04, 05, 06, 07, 08, 09, 10
2017	05, 06, 07, 08, 09, 10
2016	01, 06, 07, 08, 09, 10

Physics sub-corpus

Year	Number
2020	0102, 0103, 01, 02, 03, 04, 05, 06, 07, 08, 09, 10
2019	0102, 01, 02, 03, 04, 05, 06, 07, 08, 09
2018	03, 04, 05, 06, 07, 08, 09, 10
2017	03, 04, 05, 06, 07

Literature sub-corpus

Year	Number
2020	01, 02, 03, 05, 06, 09
2019	01, 02, 03, 04, 05, 06, 07, 08
2018	02, 03, 04, 05, 06, 08, 10
2017	01, 02, 03, 04, 05, 06, 08, 10
2016	01, 02, 03, 04, 05, 06

Appendix 3: CRAs

1	王毓琦 . 二语坚毅与交际意愿的关系探究——外语愉悦与焦虑的中介效应 [J]. 现代外语 ,2023,46(01):42−55.DOI:10.20071/j.cnki.xdwy.2023.01.012.
2	李绍鹏 , 于涵静 , 胡越竹 , 等 . 二语水平和隐喻类型对二语写作隐喻产出过程的影响 [J]. 现代外语 ,2023,46(05):664−675.DOI:10.20071/j.cnki.xdwy.20230620.007.
3	郑咏滟 , 李慧娴 . 复杂动态系统理论视角下二语写作发展的变异性研究 [J]. 现代外语 ,2023,46(05):650−663.DOI:10.20071/j.cnki.xdwy.20230620.006.
4	胡春雨 , 徐奕琳 . 基于语料库的企业身份建构话语 − 历史研究 [J]. 现代外语 ,2023,46(04):464−477.DOI:10.20071/j.cnki.xdwy.20230420.009.
5	张凯 , 李玉 , 陈凯泉 . 情绪体验与互动模式对合作学习情感投入的作用机理 [J]. 现代外语 ,2023,46(03):371−383.DOI:10.20071/j.cnki.xdwy.20230221.010.
6	马利红 , 李斑斑 , 焦雨虹 , 等 . 思辨能力与外语愉悦对外语成绩的影响路径研究 [J]. 现代外语 ,2023,46(05):676−687.DOI:10.20071/j.cnki.xdwy.20230620.008.
7	张洁 , 王敏 , 陈康 . 体裁对读后续写中协同效应和写作质量的影响 [J]. 现代外语 ,2023,46(02):259−269.DOI:10.20071/j.cnki.xdwy.20230104.003.
8	黄菁菁 , 李可胜 . 文旅新媒体宣传中身份建构的人际语用研究 [J]. 现代外语 ,2023,46(03):345−357.DOI:10.20071/j.cnki.xdwy.20230221.003.
9	惠良虹 , 冯晓丽 . 心理弹性对在线英语学习投入的影响——交互距离的中介作用 [J]. 现代外语 ,2023,46(04):552−562.DOI:10.20071/j.cnki.xdwy.20230420.006.
10	李梦骁 , 张会平 . 研究生介入评价使用的发展特征研究 [J]. 现代外语 ,2023,46(01):56−68.DOI:10.20071/j.cnki.xdwy.2023.01.011.
11	惠晓萌 , 冯晓丽 . 第二外语法语在线学习投入内在作用机制研究——网络自我效能的调节作用 [J]. 外语教学与研究 ,2023,55(03):385−396+479.DOI:10.19923/j.cnki.fltr.2023.03.010.
12	穆从军 . 读后创写思辨能力培养模式及其有效性研究 [J]. 外语教学与研究 ,2023,55(02):225−237+319−320.DOI:10.19923/j.cnki.fltr.2023.02.005.
13	吴继峰 , 刘康龙 , 胡韧奋 , 等 . 翻译汉语和原创汉语句法复杂度对比研究 [J]. 外语教学与研究 ,2023,55(02):264−275+320−321.DOI:10.19923/j.cnki.fltr.2023.02.011.
14	刘雪卉 , 文秋芳 . 概念化迁移的判断方法框架：基于认知对比分析的运动事件眼动研究 [J]. 外语教学与研究 ,2023,55(02):212−224+319.DOI:10.19923/j.cnki.fltr.2023.02.006.
15	苏雯超 , 李德凤 . 技术辅助下新型同声传译的认知负荷与译文质量研究 [J]. 外语教学与研究 ,2024,56(01):125−135+161.DOI:10.19923/j.cnki.fltr.2024.01.012.
16	纪晓丽 , 张辉 , 李爱军 . 显、隐性训练方式对二语学习者英语语调习得的影响 [J]. 外语教学与研究 ,2023,55(01):66−78+159−160.DOI:10.19923/j.cnki.fltr.2023.01.012.
17	杨颖莉 , 高子涵 . 学习者个体差异因素对二语写作表现影响的追踪研究 [J]. 外语教学与研究 ,2024,56(01):113−124+161.DOI:10.19923/j.cnki.fltr.2024.01.013.
18	冯学芳 , 刘洁 . 中国初、高中英语学习者二语词汇语义网络结构比较研究 [J]. 外语教学与研究 ,2023,55(03):397−409+479−480.DOI:10.19923/j.cnki.fltr.2023.03.013.

续表

19	王华 . 中国英语学习者不同体裁口头表达句法复杂度的对比研究 [J]. 外语教学与研究 ,2023,55(04):544−555+640.DOI:10.19923/j.cnki.fltr.2023.04.009.
20	安颖 . 中国英语学习者口语发展中的词汇及句法变异实证研究 [J]. 外语教学与研究 ,2023,55(02):251−263+320.DOI:10.19923/j.cnki.fltr.2023.02.008.
21	韦晓保 , 彭剑娥 , 秦丽莉 , 等 . 课堂环境、二语坚毅与英语学业成绩的关系——学业情绪的中介作用 [J]. 现代外语 ,2024,47(01):89−100.DOI:10.20071/j.cnki.xdwy.20231027.005.
22	邢加新 , 赵海永 , 罗少茜 , 等 . 任务复杂度、工作记忆、任务情绪与大学生口语表现 [J]. 现代外语 ,2024,47(01):76−88.DOI:10.20071/j.cnki.xdwy.20231027.007.
23	黄恩谋 , 蒋联江 , 赖春 . 社会文化视角下的技术环境与学习者自主 [J]. 现代外语 ,2024,47(01):50−62.DOI:10.20071/j.cnki.xdwy.20231027.008.
24	于涵静 , 彭红英 , 黄婷 , 等 . 外语愉悦和学习投入的历时发展研究 [J]. 现代外语 ,2024,47(01):101−113.DOI:10.20071/j.cnki.xdwy.20231027.004.
25	韩晔 , 许悦婷 , 李斑斑 , 等 . 研究生学术论文写作与发表情境下的情绪调节策略研究 [J]. 现代外语 ,2024,47(01):114−125.DOI:10.20071/j.cnki.xdwy.20231027.003.
26	孔德亮 . 大学生学术英语学习动机量表的编制研究 [J]. 中国外语 ,2023,20(04):61−69.DOI:10.13564/j.cnki.issn.1672−9382.2023.04.002.
27	邓云华 , 邓凯方 . 动用颜色词行为全貌的动态历时演变——以"红""白""黑"为例 [J]. 中国外语 ,2023,20(01):38−47.DOI:10.13564/j.cnki.issn.1672−9382.2023.01.010.
28	刘宏刚 . 高校外语教师学术研修动机生态模型构建研究 [J]. 中国外语 ,2023,20(06):24−31.DOI:10.13564/j.cnki.issn.1672−9382.2023.06.007.
29	郑春萍 , 陈旭 , 王婧怡 . 海峡两岸大学生英语学习动机与在线自我调控学习研究 [J]. 中国外语 ,2023,20(01):64−72.DOI:10.13564/j.cnki.issn.1672−9382.2023.01.012.
30	张跃伟 , 潘宁 , 贾鹰 . 基于语料库的《红楼梦》霍译本中双及物小句句式翻译的认知语义动因研究 [J]. 中国外语 ,2023,20(04):86−94.DOI:10.13564/j.cnki.issn.1672−9382.2023.04.010.
31	张茜 , 王建华 . 教师支持与大学生外语学习投入的关系探究——学业情绪的多重中介作用 [J]. 中国外语 ,2023,20(05):69−77.DOI:10.13564/j.cnki.issn.1672−9382.2023.05.011.
32	陈雪贞 , 冯欣 . 内容依托式与项目依托式相融合的医学英语教学探究 [J]. 中国外语 ,2023,20(02):18−25.DOI:10.13564/j.cnki.issn.1672−9382.2023.02.004.
33	程英 . 体验式外语教学视阈下的同伴互评效果分析 [J]. 中国外语 ,2023,20(01):81−88.DOI:10.13564/j.cnki.issn.1672−9382.2023.01.001.
34	孙曙光 , 张虹 . 云共同体学员活动参与度提升策略研究 [J]. 中国外语 ,2023,20(06):66−72.DOI:10.13564/j.cnki.issn.1672−9382.2023.06.006.
35	卢信朝 , 李德凤 , 李丽青 . 职业译员与学员的同声传译译员能力调查研究 [J]. 中国外语 ,2023,20(04):17−27.DOI:10.13564/j.cnki.issn.1672−9382.2023.04.014.

References

[1] Abdollahpour, Z.,&Gholami, J. (2019). Embodiment of rhetorical moves in lexical bundles in abstracts of the medical sciences. *Southern African Linguistics and Applied Language Studies, 37*(4), 339-360.

[2] Abrams, Z. I.,&Byrd, D. R. (2016). The effects of pre-task planning on L2 writing: Mind-mapping and chronological sequencing in a 1st-year German class. *System*, *63*, 1-12.

[3] Accurso, K. (2020). Bringing a social semiotic perspective to secondary teacher education in the United States. *Journal of English for Academic Purposes, 44*, Article 100801. https://doi.org/10.1016/j.jeap.2019.100801

[4] Adam, J-M. (2011). *A linguística textual: Introdução àanálise textual dos discursos [Textual linguistics: An introduction to textual analysis of discourse*s]. São Paulo: Cortez Editora.

[5] Afros, E.,&Schryer, C. F. (2009). Promotional (meta)discourse in research articles in language and literary studies. *English for Specific Purposes, 28*(1), 58-68. https://doi.org/10.1016/j.esp.2008.09.001

[6] Alenezi, H., Cam, M. E.,&Edirisinghe, M. (2019). Experimental and theoretical investigation of the fluid behavior during polymeric fiber formation with and without pressure. *Applied Physics Reviews*, *6*(4), 041401.

[7] Algee-Hewitt, M. (2017). Distributed Character: Quantitative Models of the English Stage, 1550-1900. *New Literary History: A Journal of Theory and Interpretation*, *48*(4), 751-782.

[8] Ansarifar, A., Shahriari, H.,&Pishghadam, R. (2018). Phrasal complexity in academic writing: A comparison of abstracts written by graduate students

and expert writers in applied linguistics. *Journal of English for Academic Purposes, 31*, 58-71. https://doi.org/10.1016/j.jeap.2017.12.008

[9] Ariely, M., Livnat, Z.,&Yarden, A. (2019). Analyzing the language of an adapted primary literature article: Towards a disciplinary approach of science teaching using texts. *Science&Education, 28*(1-2), 63-85.

[10] Aristotle. (1920). *On the art of poetry* (translated by Ingram Bywater). Clarendon Press.

[11] Arizavi, S.,&Choubsaz, Y. (2021). Citation practices in research article introductions: The interplay between disciplines and research methodologies. *International Journal of Applied Linguistics*. https://doi.org/10.1111/ijal.12337

[12] Askehave, I.,&Swales, J. M. (2001). Genre identification and communicative purpose: A problem and a possible solution. *Applied Linguistics, 22*(2), 195-212.

[13] Astone, P., Cerdá-Durán, P., Di Palma, I., Drago, M., Muciaccia, F., Palomba, C.,&Ricci, F. (2018). New method to observe gravitational waves emitted by core collapse supernovae. *Physical Review D, 98*(12), 122002.

[14] Austin, J. L. (1962). *How to do things with words.* Harvard University Press.

[15] Baicchi, A.,&Erviti, A. I. (2018). Genre as cognitive construction: An analysis of discourse connectors in academic lectures. *Pragmatics&Cognition, 25*(3), 576-601.

[16] Bakhtin, M. M. (1986). The Problem of Speech Genres. In M. M. Bakhtin, *Speech genres and other late essays* (translated by V. McGee) (pp. 60-102). University of Texas Press.

[17] Barnes, M. (2017). Washback: Exploring what constitutes “good” teaching practices. *Journal of English for Academic Purposes, 30*, 1-12.

[18] Barthes, R. (1977). *Image, music, text.* Fontana.

[19] Bax, S. (2011). *Discourse and genre: Analysing language in context.* Palgrave Macmillan.

[20] Bazerman, C. (1988). *Shaping written knowledge: Genre and activity of the*

experimental article in science. The University of Wisconsin Press.

[21] Bazerman, C. (2019). A? Developmental? Path? To? Text? Quality? *Journal of Literacy Research, 51*(3), 381-387.

[22] Bazerman, C., Simon, K., Ewing, P.,&Pieng, P. (2013). Domain-specific cognitive development through written genres in a teacher education program. *Pragmatics&Cognition, 21*(3), 530-551.

[23] Benelhadj, F. (2019). Discipline and genre in academic discourse: Prepositional phrases as a focus. *Journal of Pragmatics, 139,* 190-199.

[24] Berkenkotter, C. (2001). Genre systems at work-DSM-IV and rhetorical recontextualization in psychotherapy paperwork. *Written Communication, 18*(3), 326-349.

[25] Berkenkotter, C. (2009). A case for historical "wide-angle" genre analysis: A personal retrospective. *Iberica (18),* 9-21.

[26] Berkenkotter, C.,&Hanganu-Bresch, C. (2011). Occult Genres and the Certification of Madness in a 19th-Century Lunatic Asylum. *Written Communication, 28*(2), 220-250.

[27] Berkenkotter, C.,&Huckin, T. N. (1993). Rethinking genre from a sociocognitive perspective. *Written Communication, 10*(4), 475-509.

[28] Bernstein, B. (1996). *Pedagogy, symbolic control and identity: Theory, research, critique.* London: Taylor&Francis.

[29] Bernstein, B. (1999). Vertical and horizontal discourse: An essay. *British Journal of Sociology of Education, 20* (2), 157-173.

[30] Bhatia, A. (2012). The corporate social responsibility report: The hybridization of a "confused" genre (2007-2011). *Ieee Transactions on Professional Communication, 55*(3), 221-238.

[31] Bhatia, A. (2013). International genre, local flavour: Analysis of PetroChina's corporate and social responsibility report. *Revista Signos, 46*(83), 307-331.

[32] Bhatia, V. K. (1993). *Analyzing genre: Language use in professional settings.* Longman.

[33] Bhatia, V. K. (2004). *Worlds of written discourse.* Continuum International

Publishing Group.

[34] Bhatia, V. K. (2010). Interdiscursivity in professional communication. *Discourse&Communication, 4*(1), 32-50.

[35] Bhatia, V. K. (2017). *Critical genre analysis: Investigation interdiscursive performance in professional practice*. Routledge.

[36] Biber, D. (1988). *Variation across speech and writing*. Cambridge University Press.

[37] Biber, D. (1995). *Dimensions of register variation: A cross-linguistic perspective*. Cambridge University Press.

[38] Biber, D. (2009). *Register, genre, and style* (first edition). Cambridge University Press.

[39] Biber, D. (2019). *Register, genre, and style* (second edition). Cambridge University Press.

[40] Biber, D., Egbert, J., Keller, D.,&Wizner, S. (2021). Towards a taxonomy of conversational discourse types: An empirical corpus-based analysis. *Journal of Pragmatics, 171*, 20-35.

[41] Biber, D., Gray, B., Staples, S.,&Egbert, J. (2020). Investigating grammatical complexity in L2 English writing research: Linguistic description versus predictive measurement. *Journal of English for Academic Purposes, 46*, 100869. https://doi.org/https://doi.org/10.1016/j.jeap.2020.100869

[42] Brisk, M. E., Tian, Z.,&Ballard, E. (2021). Autobiography writing instruction: The journey of a teacher participating in a systemic functional linguistics genre pedagogy professional development. *System, 97*, Article 102429. https://doi.org/10.1016/j.system.2020.102429

[43] Bronckart, J-P. (1999). *Atividades de linguagem, textos ediscursos–Por um interacionismo sócio-discursivo [Language activities, texts and discourses for a social discursive interactionism]*. São Paulo: Educ.

[44] Burdiles Fernandez, G. (2016). Clinical case study genre: Rhetorical organization of the macromove case report in Chilean medical journals. *Revista Signos, 49*(91), 192-216.

[45] Cargill, M.,&O'Connor, P. (2009). *Writing scientific research articles: Strategy and steps*. Wiley-Blackwell.

[46] Cavallaro, C. J.,&Sembiante, S. F. (2021). Facilitating culturally sustaining, functional literacy practices in a middle school ESOL reading program: A design-based research study. *Language and Education, 35*(2), 160-179.

[47] Chandler, J. (2009). Introduction: doctrines, disciplines, discourse, dcpartmcnts. *Critical Inquiry, 35*, 729-746.

[48] Chen, C. H.,&Zhang, L. J. (2017). An intercultural analysis of the use of hedging by Chinese and Anglophone academic English writers. *Applied Linguistics Review, 8*(1), 1-34. https://doi.org/10.1515/applirev-2016-2009

[49] Cheng, A. (2019). Examining the "applied aspirations" in the ESP genre analysis of published journal articles. *Journal of English for Academic Purposes, 38*, 36-47. https://doi.org/10.1016/j.jeap.2018.12.005

[50] Cheng, F. W.,&Unsworth, L. (2016). Stance-taking as negotiating academic conflict in applied linguistics research article discussion sections. *Journal of English for Academic Purposes, 24*, 43-57. https://doi.org/10.1016/j.jeap.2016.09.001

[51] Christie, F. (1997). Curriculum macrogenres as forms of initiation into culture. In F. Christie&J. R. Martin (Ed.). *Genre and institutions: Social processes in the workplace and school* (pp. 134-160). Cassell Academic.

[52] Christie, F. (2002). *Classroom discourse analysis: A functional perspective*. Continuum.

[53] Christie, F. (Ed.). (1999). *Pedagogy and the shaping of consciousness: Linguistic and social processes*. Cassell.

[54] Christie, F.,&Maton, K. (2011). Why disciplinarity? In F. Christie&K. Maton (Eds.), *Disciplinarity: Functional linguistic and sociological perspectives* (pp. 1-9). Continuum.

[55] Christie, F.,&Maton, K. (Eds.). (2011). *Disciplinarity: Functional linguistic and sociological perspective*. Continuum.

[56] Cortes, V. (2013). The purpose of this study is to: Connecting lexical bundles

and moves in research article introductions. *Journal of English for Academic Purposes, 12*(1), 33-43. https://doi.org/10.1016/j.jeap.2012.11.002

[57] Cotos, E., Huffman, S.,&Link, S. (2017). A move/step model for methods sections: Demonstrating rigour and credibility. *English for Specific Purposes, 46*, 90-106.

[58] Crane, C.,&Malloy, M. (2021). The development of temporal-spatial meaning in personal recounts of beginning L2 writers of German. *System, 99,* Article 102498. https://doi.org/10.1016/j.system.2021.102498

[59] Crompton, P. (1997). Hedging in academic writing: Some theoretical problems. *English for Specific Purposes, 16*, 271–287.

[60] Crosby, S. L.,&Willow, A. J. (2020). Indigenous-Washing and the Petro-Hero in Genre Fictions of the North American Oil Boom. *MFS: Modern Fiction Studies*, *66*(1), 78-100.

[61] Crosthwaite, P. (2016). A longitudinal multidimensional analysis of EAP writing: Determining EAP course effectiveness. *Journal of English for Academic Purposes, 22*, 166-178. https://doi.org/10.1016/j.jeap.2016.04.005

[62] Cummings, M. (2016). Genre and register hybridization in a historical text. In D. R. Miller&P. Bayley (Eds.), *Hybridity in systemic functional linguistics* (pp.268-285). Equinox.

[63] Dafouz-Milne, E. (2008). The pragmatic role of textual and interpersonal metadiscourse markers in the construction and attainment of persuasion: A crosslinguistic study of newspaper discourse. *Journal of Pragmatics, 40*(1), 95-113.

[64] Dimroth, C. (2018). Beyond statistical learning: Communication principles and language internal factors shape grammar in child and adult beginners learning Polish through controlled exposure. *Language Learning*, *68*(4), 863-905.

[65] Doran, Y. J. (2018). *The discourse of physics*. Routledge.

[66] Doran, Y. J. (2021). Multimodal knowledge: using language, mathematics and images in physics. In K. Maton, J. R. Martin,&Y. J. Doran (Eds.),

Teaching science: Knowledge, language, pedagogy (pp. 162-184). Routledge.

[67] Doran, Y. J.,&Martin, J. R. (2021). Field relation: understanding scientific explanations. In K. Maton, J. R. Martin,&Y. J. Doran (Eds.), *Teaching science: Knowledge, language, pedagogy* (pp. 105-133). Routledge.

[68] Du-Babcock, B.,&Feng, H. (2018). Culture and identity on intercultural business requests: A genre-based comparative study. *Iberica (35)*, 171-199.

[69] El-Dakhs, D. A. S. (2018). Why are abstracts in PhD theses and research articles different? A genre-specific perspective. *Journal of English for Academic Purposes, 36*, 48-60. https://doi.org/10.1016/j.jeap.2018.09.005

[70] Feng, D. (2019). Interdiscursivity, social media and marketized university discourse: A genre analysis of universities' recruitment posts on WeChat. *Journal of Pragmatics, 143*, 121-134. https://doi.org/10.1016/j.pragma.2019.02.007

[71] Feng, Y., Jiang, T., Liang, X., An, J.,&Wang, Z. L. (2020). Cylindrical triboelectric nanogenerator based on swing structure for efficient harvesting of ultra-low-frequency water wave energy. *Applied Physics Reviews, 7*(2), 021401.

[72] Fenwick, L.,&Herrington, M. (2021). Teacher use of genre pedagogy: engaging students in dialogue about content area language during text deconstruction. *Language and Education*. https://doi.org/10.1080/09500782.2021.1912082

[73] Friginal, E.,&Mustafa, S. S. (2017). A comparison of US-based and Iraqi English research article abstracts using corpora. *Journal of English for Academic Purposes, 25*, 45-57. https://doi.org/10.1016/j.jeap.2016.11.004

[74] Gao, X. (2020). A comparable-corpus-based study of informal features in academic writing by English and Chinese scholars across disciplines. *Iberica,* (39), 119-140.

[75] Ge, Y. F.,&Wang, H. (2019). Understanding the discourse of Chinese civil trials: The perspective of Critical Genre Analysis. *Journal of Pragmatics, 152*, 1-12. https://doi.org/10.1016/j.pragma.2019.07.024

[76] Georgiou, H. (2016). Putting physics knowledge in the hot seat: The semantics of student understanding of thermodynamics. In K. Maton, S. Hood,&S. Shay (Eds.), *Knowledge-building: Educational studies in legitimation code theory* (pp. 176-192). Routledge.

[77] Ghosh, S., Brüser, V., Kaplan-Ashiri, I., Popovitz-Biro, R., Peglow, S., Martínez, J. I., Alonso, J. A.,&Zak, A. (2020). Cathodoluminescence in single and multiwall WS2 nanotubes: Evidence for quantum confinement and strain effect. *Applied Physics Reviews*, *7*(4), 041401.

[78] Golparvar, S. E.,&Barabadi, E. (2020). Key phrase frames in the discussion section of research articles of higher education. *Lingua, 236*, Article 102804. https://doi.org/10.1016/j.lingua.2020.102804

[79] Gonzalez Riquelme, C.,&Burdiles Fernandez, G. (2018). Rhetorical organization of the genre Financial Stability Report: A contrast between the report of the Central Bank of Chile and the German Federal Bank. *Circulo De Linguistica Aplicada a La Comunicacion (73)*, 145-160.

[80] Graham, S., Woore, R., Porter, A., Courtney, L.,&Savory, C. (2020). Navigating the challenges of L2 reading: Self-Efficacy, self-regulatory reading strategies, and learner profiles. *The Modern Language Journal*, *104*(4), 693-714.

[81] Guan, X., Wang, Y., Lin, C.-H., Hu, L., Ge, S., Wan, T., Younis, A., Li, F., Cui, Y., Qi, D.-C., Chu, D., Chen, X. D.,&Wu, T. (2020). A monolithic artificial iconic memory based on highly stable perovskite-metal multilayers. *Applied Physics Reviews*, *7*(3), 031401.

[82] Halliday, M. A. K. (1978). *Language as social semiotic: The social interpretation of language and meaning*. Edward Arnold.

[83] Halliday, M. A. K. (1992a). Corpus studies and probabilistic grammar. In K. Aijmer,&B. Altenberg (Eds.), *English corpus linguistics: Studies in honor of Jan Svartvik* (pp.30-43). Longman. Reprinted in J. J. Webster (Ed.), (2005). *Computational and quantitative studies. Volume 6* in *The collected works of M. A. K. Halliday* (pp. 63-75). Continuum.

[84] Halliday, M. A. K. (1994). *An introduction to functional grammar* (2nd ed.). Edward Arnold.

[85] Halliday, M. A. K.,&Hasan, R. (1985). *Language, context and text: Aspects of language in a social-semiotic perspective*. Deakin University Press.

[86] Halliday, M. A. K.,&Matthiessen, C. M. I. M. (1999). *Construing experience through meaning: A language-based approach to cognition*. Cassell.

[87] Halliday, M. A. K.,&Matthiessen, C. M. I. M. (2014). *Halliday's introduction to functional grammar (4th ed.)*. Routledge.

[88] Hao, J. (2020). *Analyzing scientific discourse from a systemic functional perspective: A framework for exploring knowledge building in biology*. Routledge.

[89] Hao, J. (2021). Building taxonomies: A discourse semantic mode of entities and dimensions in biology. In J.R. Martin&Y. J. Doran (Eds.), *Teaching science: Knowledge, language, and pedagogy* (pp. 134-161). Routledge.

[90] Hardy, J. A.,&Römer, U. (2013). Revealing disciplinary variation in student writing: A multi-dimensional analysis of the Michigan Corpus of Upper-level Student Papers (MICUSP). *Corpora, 8*(2), 183-207.

[91] Harwood, N. (2005a). 'Nowhere has anyone attempted ... In this article I aim to do just that': A corpus-based study of self-promotion *I* and *we* in academic writing across four disciplines. *Journal of Pragmatics, 37*(8), 1207-1231.

[92] Harwood, N. (2005b). 'We do not seem to have a theory ... The theory I present here attempts to fill this gap': Inclusive and exclusive pronouns in academic writing. *Applied Linguistics, 26*(3), 343-375.

[93] Hasan, R. (1984). The nursery tale as a genre. *Nottingham Linguistics Circular, 13,* 71-102.

[94] Hasan, R. (1989). The structure of a text. In M.A.K. Halliday&R. Hasan, *Language, context and text: Aspects of language in a social semiotic perspective*. Oxford University Press.

[95] Hasan, R. (2009). The place of context in a systemic functional model. In M. A. K. Halliday&J. J. Webster (Eds.), *Continuum companion to systemic*

functional linguistics (pp. 166-189). Continuum.

[96] Hasan, R. (2014) Towards a paradigmatic description of context: Systems, metafunctions, and semantics. *Functional Linguistics, 1(*1), 9. https://doi.org/10.1186/s40554-014-0009-y

[97] Hill, C., Khoo, S.,&Hsieh, Y.-C. (2020). An investigation into the learning transfer of English for specific Academic Purposes (ESAP) writing skills of students in Singapore. *Journal of English for Academic Purposes*, *48*, 100908.

[98] Hood, S. (2010). *Appraising research: Evaluation in academic writing.* Palgrave Macmillan.

[99] Hood, S. (2011). Writing disciplines: Comparing inscriptions of knowledge and knowers in academic writing. In F. Christie&K. Maton (Eds.), *Disciplinarity: Functional linguistic and sociological perspectives* (pp. 106-128). Continuum.

[100] Hood, S. (2016). Ethnographies on the move, stories on the rise: Methods in the humanities. In K. Maton, S. Hood,&S. Shay (Eds.), *Knowledge-building: Educational studies in legitimation code theory* (pp. 117-137). Routledge.

[101] Hood, S. (2021). Live lectures: The significance of presence in building disciplinary knowledge. In J. R. Martin, K. Maton&Y. J. Doran (Eds.), *Accessing academic discourse: Systemic functional linguistics and legitimation code theory* (pp. 211-235). Routledge.

[102] Hu, G.,&Liu, Y. (2018). Three minute thesis presentations as an academic genre: A cross-disciplinary study of genre moves. *Journal of English for Academic Purposes, 35*, 16-30. https://doi.org/10.1016/j.jeap.2018.06.004

[103] Hu, G.,&Cao, F. (2015). Disciplinary and paradigmatic influences on interactional metadiscourse in research articles. *English for Specific Purposes, 39*, 12-25. https://doi.org/10.1016/j.esp.2015.03.002

[104] Huang, J. C. (2018). Marine engineering and sub-disciplinary variations: A rhetorical analysis of research article abstracts. *Text&Talk, 38*(3), 341-363.

[105] Huckin, T. (2002). Textual silence and the discourse of homelessness.

Discourse&Society, 13(3), 347-372.

[106] Hunston, S. (1993). Professional conflict: Disagreement in academic discourse. In M. Baker, G. Francis,&E. Tognini-Bonelli (Eds.), *Text&technology: In honor of John Sinclair* (pp. 115-133). John Benjamins.

[107] Hyland, K. (2005). *Metadiscourse: Exploring interaction in writing.* Continuum.

[108] Hyland, K.,&Jiang, F. (2018). "In this paper we suggest": Changing patterns of disciplinary metadiscourse. *English for Specific Purposes, 51,* 18-30.

[109] Hyland, K.,&Zou, H. (2020). In the frame: Signalling structure in academic articles and blogs. *Journal of Pragmatics, 165*, 31-44.

[110] IBM Corp. (2017). IBM SPSS Statistics for Windows, Version 25.0. Armonk, NY: IBM Corp.

[111] Ignatieva, N. (2021). Ideational and interpersonal analysis of student history texts in Spanish within the systemic framework. *Revista Signos, 54(105)*, 169-190.

[112] Jalilifar, A., Soltani, P.,&Shooshtari, Z. G. (2018). Improper textual borrowing practices: Evidence from Iranian applied linguistics journal articles. *Journal of English for Academic Purposes, 35*, 42-55.

[113] Jiang, F.,&Hyland, K. (2017). Metadiscursive nouns: Interaction and cohesion in abstract moves. *English for Specific Purposes, 46*, 1-14.

[114] Jordens, C. F. C.,&Little, M. (2004). 'In this scenario, I do this, for these reasons': Narrative, genre and ethical reasoning in the clinic. *Social Science&Medicine, 58*(9), 1635-1645.

[115] Jordens, C. F. C., Little, M., Paul, K.,&Sayers, E.-J. (2001). Life disruption and generic complexity: A social linguistic analysis of narratives of cancer illness. *Social Science&Medicine, 53*(9), 1227-1236.

[116] Jose Serrano, M. (2017). A variable cognitive and communicative resource in Spanish: The first-person plural subject and object. *Journal of Pragmatics, 108*, 131-147.

[117] Karimnia, A.,&Jafari, F. M. (2019). A sociological analysis of moves in the

formation of Iranian epitaphs. *Semiotica, 229*, 25-39.

[118] Kashiha, H.,&Marandi, S. (2019). Rhetoric-specific features of interactive metadiscourse in introduction moves: A case of discipline awareness. *Southern African Linguistics and Applied Language Studies, 37*(1), 1-14.

[119] Kasten, M.,&Gruenler, C. (2011). The point of the plow: Conceptual integration in the allegory of Langland and Voltaire. *Metaphor and Symbol, 26*(2), 143-151.

[120] Kawase, T. (2015). Metadiscourse in the introductions of PhD theses and research articles. *Journal of English for Academic Purposes, 20*, 114-124. https://doi.org/10.1016/j.jeap.2015.08.006

[121] Kelly-Laubscher, R. F., Muna, N.,&van der Merwe, M. (2017). Using the research article as a model for teaching laboratory report writing provides opportunities for development of genre awareness and adoption of new literacy practices. *English for Specific Purposes*, *48*, 1-16.

[122] Khany, R.,&Kafshgar, N. B. (2016). Analyzing texts through their linguistic properties: A cross-disciplinary study. *Journal of Quantitative Linguistics, 23*(3), 278-294. https://doi.org/10.1080/09296174.2016.1169848

[123] Khedri, M.,&Kritsis, K. (2020). How do we make ourselves heard in the writing of a research article? A study of authorial references in four disciplines. *Australian Journal of Linguistics, 40*(2), 194-217.

[124] Kim, D. Y. (2020). Translations and ghostings of History: The novels of Han Kang. *New Literary History: A Journal of Theory and Interpretation, 51*(2), 375-399.

[125] Kindenberg, B. (2021). Narrative and analytical interplay in history texts: Recalibrating the historical recount genre. *Journal of Curriculum Studies*. https://doi.org/10.1080/00220272.2021.1919763

[126] Kithulgoda, E.,&Mendis, D. (2020). From analysis to pedagogy: Developing ESP materials for the Welcome Address in Sri Lanka. *English for Specific Purposes, 60*, 140-158.

[127] Kress, G.,&Van Leeuwen, T. (1996/2006). *Reading images: The grammar of*

visual design. Routledge.

[128] Kwan, B. S. C.,&Chan, H. (2014). An investigation of source use in the results and the closing sections of empirical articles in information systems: In search of a functional-semantic citation typology for pedagogical purposes. *Journal of English for Academic Purposes, 14*, 29-47.

[129] Kyle, K.,&Crossley, S. (2016). The relationship between lexical sophistication and independent and source-based writing. *Journal of Second Language Writing, 34*, 12-24. https://doi.org/https://doi.org/10.1016/j.jslw.2016.10.003

[130] Labov, W.,&Waletsky, J. (1967). Narrative analysis: Oral versions of personal experience. In J. Helm (Ed.), *Essays on the verbal and the visual arts* (pp. 3-38), University of Washington Press.

[131] Lai, C. C.-T., Law, S.-P.,&Kong, A. P.-H. (2017). A quantitative study of right dislocation in Cantonese spoken discourse. *Language and Speech, 60*(4), 633-642.

[132] Le, T. N. P.,&Pham, M. M. (2020). Genre practices in mechanical engineering academic articles: Prototypicality and infra-disciplinary variation. *Iberica* (39), 243-266.

[133] Lee, D.,&Swales, J. (2006). A corpus-based EAP course for NNS doctoral students: Moving from available specialized corpora to self-compiled corpora. *English for Specific Purposes, 25*(1), 56-75.

[134] Lee, J. J. (2016). “There’s intentionality behind it...”: A genre analysis of EAP classroom lessons. *Journal of English for Academic Purposes, 23*, 99-112.

[135] Lester, J. D.,&Lester, J. D. (2006). *Writing research papers in the social sciences*. Pearson/Longman.

[136] Lewin, B.A., Fine, J.,&Young, L. (2001). *Expository discourse: A genre-based approach to social science research texts*. Continuum.

[137] Li, Z. J.,&Xu, J. F. (2020). Reflexive metadiscourse in Chinese and English sociology research article introductions and discussions. *Journal of*

Pragmatics, 159, 47-59. https://doi.org/10.1016/j.pragma.2020.02.003

[138] Lim, J. M. H. (2019). Explicit and implicit justifications of experimental procedures in language education: Pedagogical implications of studying expert writers' communicative resources. *Journal of English for Academic Purposes, 37*, 34-51. https://doi.org/10.1016/j.jeap.2018.10.006

[139] Lin, L.,&Evans, S. (2012). Structural patterns in empirical research articles: A cross-disciplinary study. *English for Specific Purposes, 31*(3), 150-160.

[140] Lin, L.,&Liu, M. (2021). Towards a Part-of-Speech (PoS) gram approach to academic writing: A case study of research introductions in different disciplines. *Lingua, 254*, Article 103052. https://doi.org/10.1016/j.lingua.2021.103052

[141] Lindley, J. (2016). Literal versus exaggerated always and never: A cross-genre corpus study. *International Journal of Corpus Linguistics, 21*(2), 219-249.

[142] Lindley, J. (2020). Discourse functions of always progressives: Beyond complaining. *Corpus Linguistics and Linguistic Theory, 16*(2), 333-361.

[143] Liu, Y. (2019). Overseas translation of modern Chinese fiction via T'ien Hsia Monthly. *Neohelicon, 46*(2), 393-409. https://doi.org/10.1007/s11059-019-00503-3

[144] Liu, Y. L.,&Buckingham, L. (2018). The schematic structure of discussion sections in applied linguistics and the distribution of metadiscourse markers. *Journal of English for Academic Purposes, 34*, 97-109.

[145] Loi, C. K., Lim, J. M. H.,&Wharton, S. (2016). Expressing an evaluative stance in English and Malay research article conclusions: International publications versus local publications. *Journal of English for Academic Purposes, 21*, 1-16. https://doi.org/10.1016/j.jeap.2015.08.004

[146] Lu, X. F., Casal, J. E.,&Liu, Y. Y. (2020). The rhetorical functions of syntactically complex sentences in social science research article introductions. *Journal of English for Academic Purposes, 44*, 1-16.

[147] Lu, X. F., Yoon, J.,&Kisselev, O. (2018). A phrase-frame list for social

science research article introductions. *Journal of English for Academic Purposes, 36*, 76-85. https://doi.org/10.1016/j.jeap.2018.09.004

[148] Lu, X., Yoon, J.,&Kisselev, O. (2021). Matching phrase-frames to rhetorical moves in social science research article introductions. *English for Specific Purposes, 61*, 63-83. https://doi.org/10.1016/j.esp.2020.10.001

[149] Luo, N.,&Hyland, K. (2019). "I won't publish in Chinese now": Publishing, translation and the non-English speaking academic. *Journal of English for Academic Purposes, 39*, 37-47. https://doi.org/https://doi.org/10.1016/j.jeap.2019.03.003

[150] Maher, P.,&Milligan, S. (2019). Teaching master thesis writing to engineers: Insights from corpus and genre analysis of introductions. *English for Specific Purposes, 55*, 40-55.

[151] Marti, L., Yilmaz, S.,&Bayyurt, Y. (2019). Reporting research in applied linguistics: The role of nativeness and expertise. *Journal of English for Academic Purposes, 40*, 98-114. https://doi.org/10.1016/j.jeap.2019.05.005

[152] Martin, J. R. (1984/2012). Lexical cohesion, field, and genre: Parceling experience and discourse goals. In Z. H. Wang (Ed.), *Collected works of J. R. Martin Vol 3* (pp. 31-64). Shanghai Jiaotong University Press.

[153] Martin, J. R. (1985). Process and text: Two aspects of human semiosis. In J.D. Benson&W.S. Greaves (Eds.), *Systemic perspectives on discourse, vol 1* (pp.248-274). Ablex.

[154] Martin, J. R. (1992). *English text: System and structure*. John Benjamins.

[155] Martin, J. R. (1994/2012). Macro genres: The ecology of the page. In Z. H. Wang (Ed.), *Collected works of J. R. Martin Vol 3* (pp.78-126). Shanghai Jiaotong University Press.

[156] Martin, J. R. (1995). Text and clause: Fractal resonance. *Text, 15*(1), 5-42.

[157] Martin, J. R. (1996). Register and genre: Modelling social context in functional linguistics: narrative genres. *Discourse analysis: Proceedings of the international conference on discourse analysis,* University of Lisbon, Portugal, Colibri/Portuguese Linguistics Association.

[158] Martin, J. R. (1999/2012). Modelling context: A crooked path of progress in contextual linguistics. In Z. H. Wang (Ed.), *Collected Works of J. R. Martin Vol 3* (pp.222-247). Shanghai Jiaotong University Press.

[159] Martin, J. R. (2002/2012). A universe of meaning-how many practices? In Z. H. Wang (Ed.), *Collected Works of J.R. Martin Vol 3* (pp. 303-313). Shanghai Jiaotong University Press.

[160] Martin, J. R. (2008). Innocence: Realization, instantiation and individuation in a Botswanan town. In A. Mahboob&N. Knight (Eds.), *Questioning linguistics* (pp.32-76). Cambridge Scholars Publishing.

[161] Martin, J. R. (2011). Bridging troubled waters: Interdisciplinarity and what makes it stick. In F. Christie&K. Maton (Eds.), *Disciplinarity: Functional linguistic and sociological perspectives* (pp. 35-61). Continuum.

[162] Martin, J. R. (2020). Revisiting field: specialized knowledge in secondary school science and humanities discourse. In J. R. Martin, K. Maton&Y. J. Doran (Eds.), *Accessing academic discourse: Systemic functional linguistics and legitimation code theory* (pp. 114-148). Routledge.

[163] Martin, J. R.,&Rose, D. (2003). *Working with Discourse: Meaning beyond the clause*. Continuum.

[164] Martin, J. R.,&Rose, D. (2007). *Working with discourse* (2nd ed). Continuum.

[165] Martin, J. R.,&Rose, D. (2008). *Genre relations: Mapping culture*. Equinox.

[166] Martin, J. R.,&Rose, D. (2012a). *Genre relations: Mapping culture*. Foreign Language Teaching and Research Press.

[167] Martin, J. R.,&Rose, D. (2012b). *Learning to write, reading to learn: Genre, knowledge and pedagogy in Sydney school*. Equinox.

[168] Martin, J. R.,&White, P. (2005). *The language of evaluation: Appraisal in English*. Palgrave Macmillan.

[169] Martin, J., Maton, K.,&Matruglio, E. (2010). Historical cosmologies: Epistemology and axiology in Australian secondary school history discourse. *Revista Signos*, *43*(74), 433-463. https://doi.org/10.4067/S0718-09342010000500003

[170] Martin, J.R.,&Rose, D. (2014). *Working with discourse* (2nd ed). Peking University Press.

[171] Martin, L. J. (2016). Musicality and musicianship: Specialization in jazz studies. In K. Maton, S. Hood,&S. Shay (Eds.), *Knowledge-building: Educational studies in legitimation code theory* (pp. 193-213). Routledge.

[172] Maton, K. (2000). Languages of legitimation: The structuring significance for intellectual fields of strategic knowledge claims. *British Journal of Sociology of Education, 21*(2), 147-167.

[173] Maton, K. (2007). Knowledge-knower structures in intellectual and educational fields. In F. Christie&J. R. Martin (Eds.), Language, knowledge and pedagogy (pp.87-108). Continuum.

[174] Maton, K. (2009). Cumulative and segmented learning: Exploring the role of curriculum structures in knowledge-building. *British Journal of Sociology of Education, 30*(1), 43-57.

[175] Maton, K. (2014). *Knowledge and knowers: Towards a realist sociology of education*. Routledge.

[176] Maton, K.,&Doran. Y. J. (2021). Constellating science: How relations among ideas help build knowledge. In K. Maton, J. R. Martin,&Y. J. Doran (Eds.), *Teaching science: Knowledge, language, pedagogy* (pp. 49-75). Routledge.

[177] Maton, K., Martin, J. R.&Matruglio, E. (2016). LCT and systemic functional linguistics: Enacting complementary theories for explanatory power. In K. Maton, S. Hood,&S. Shay (Eds.), *Knowledge-building: Educational studies in legitimation code theory* (pp. 93-114). Routledge.

[178] Matthiessen, C. M. I. M. (2015). Register in the round: Registerial cartography. *Functional Linguistics*, *2*(1), 9. https://doi.org/10.1186/s40554-015-0015-8

[179] Matthiessen, C. M. I. M. (2019). Register in Systemic Functional Linguistics. *Register Studies, 1:1,* 10-41.

[180] Matthiessen, C. M. I. M.,&Pan, J. (2019). Expounding Knowledge through explanations: Generic types and rhetorical-relational patterns. *Semiotica,*

227:31-76.

[181] Matthiessen, C. M. I. M.,&Teruya, K. (2016). Registerial hybridity: Interdeterminacy among fields of activity. In D. R., Miller&P. Bayley (Eds.), *Hybridity in systemic functional linguistics* (pp.205-239). Equinox.

[182] Matthiessen, C. M. I. M., Teruya, K.&Lam, M. (2016). *Key terms in systemic functional linguistics.* Foreign Language Teaching and Research Press.

[183] Maxim, H. H. (2021). A longitudinal case study of curriculum-based L2 writing development. *System, 96*, Article 102397.

[184] May, L., Crisp, T., Bingham, G. E., Schwartz, R. S., Pickens, M. T.,&Woodbridge, K. (2020). The durable, dynamic nature of genre and science: A purpose-driven typology of science trade books. *Reading Research Quarterly, 55*(3), 399-418. https://doi.org/10.1002/rrq.274

[185] Miller, C. R. (1984). Genre as social action. *Quarterly Journal of Speech, 70:*2, 151-167

[186] Miller, C. R. (2014). Gene as social action (1984), revisited 30 years later. *Letras&Letras, 31* (3), 56-72.

[187] Miller, C. R., Devitt, A. J.,&Gallagher, V. J. (2018). Genre: Permanence and Change. *Rhetoric Society Quarterly, 48*(3), 269-277.

[188] Miller, D. R.,&Bayley, P. (2016). *Hybridity in systemic functional linguistics: Grammar, text and discursive context*. Equinox.

[189] Mitchell, T. D., Pessoa, S.,&Gomez-Laich, M. P. (2021). Know your roles: Alleviating the academic-professional tension in the case analysis genre. *English for Specific Purposes, 61*, 117-131.

[190] Moreno, A. I.,&Swales, J. M. (2018). Strengthening move analysis methodology towards bridging the function-form gap. *English for Specific Purposes, 50*, 40-63. https://doi.org/10.1016/j.esp.2017.11.006

[191] Moyano, E. I. (2019). Knowledge construction in discussions of research articles in two disciplines in Spanish: The role of resources of APPRAISAL. *Journal of Pragmatics, 139*, 231-246. https://doi.org/10.1016/j.pragma.2018.09.011

[192] Muller, J. (2007). On splitting hairs: Hierarchy, knowledge and the school curriculum. In F. Christie,&J. Martin (Eds.), *Language, knowledge and pedagogy: Functional linguistics and sociological perspectives* (pp. 65-86). Continuum.

[193] Muller, J. (2011). Through others' eyes: the fate of disciplines. In F. Christie&K. Maton (Eds.), *Disciplinarity: Functional linguistic and sociological perspectives* (pp. 13-34). Continuum.

[194] Muntigl, P. (2006). Macrogenre: A multiperspectival and multifunctional approach to social interaction. *Linguistics and the Human Sciences 2*(2), 233-256.

[195] Mwinlaaru, I. N. I. (2017). Bridging boundaries across genre traditions: A Systemic functional account of generic patterns in biodata. *Functions of Language, 24*(3), 259-293. https://doi.org/10.1075/fol.15017.mwi

[196] Negretti, R.,&McGrath, L. (2018). Scaffolding genre knowledge and metacognition: Insights from an L2 doctoral research writing course. *Journal of Second Language Writing, 40*, 12-31.

[197] Neiderhiser, J. A., Kelley, P., Kennedy, K. M., Swales, J. M.,&Vergaro, C. (2016). 'Notice the similarities between the two sets…': Imperative usage in a corpus of upper-level student papers. *Applied Linguistics, 37*(2), 198-218.

[198] Nelson, I. (2019). Poetics of the rule: Form, biopolitics, lyric. *New Literary History: A Journal of Theory and Interpretation*, *50*(1), 65-89.

[199] O'Donnell, M (2022). UAM CorpusTool version 6.2e. Retrieved April 13, 2022, from http://www.corpustool.com/

[200] O'Donnell, M. (2021). UAM CorpusTool version 3.3w. Retrieved August 1st, 2021, from http://www.corpustool.com/

[201] Oakey, D. (2020). Phrases in EAP academic writing pedagogy: Illuminating Halliday's influence on research and practice. *Journal of English for Academic Purposes*, *44*, Article 100829.

[202] Omidian, T., Shahriari, H.,&Siyanova-Chanturia, A. (2018). A cross-disciplinary investigation of multi-word expressions in the moves of research

article abstracts. *Journal of English for Academic Purposes, 36*, 1-14.

[203] Paltridge, B. (1997). *Genre, frames and writing in research settings*. Benjamins.

[204] Papi, M. B. (2018). Satire as a genre. *Pragmatics&Cognition, 25*(3), 459-482.

[205] Parkinson, J. (2011). The discussion section as argument: The language used to prove knowledge claims. *English for Specific Purposes, 30*(3), 164-175. https://doi.org/10.1016/j.esp.2011.03.001

[206] Parodi, G. (2016). A genre-based study across the discourses of undergraduate and graduate disciplines: Written language use in university setting. In N. Aremeva&A. Freedman (Eds.), *Genre studies around the globe: Beyond the three traditions* (pp. 165-207). Trafford Publishing.

[207] Parviz, M., Jalilifar, A.,&Don, A. (2020). Phrasal discourse style in cross-disciplinary writing: A comparison of phrasal complexity features in the results sections of research articles. *Circulo De Linguistica Aplicada a La Comunicacion, 83,* 191-204. https://doi.org/10.5209/clac.70573

[208] Peacock, M. (2002). Communicative moves in the discussion section of research articles. *System, 30*, 479-497.

[209] Plato. (1961). The Republic. (trans. Paul Shorey). In E. Hamilton&C. Huntington (Eds.), *The collected dialogues of Plato* (pp. 576-844). Princeton University Press.

[210] Pun, J. K. H. (2019). Salient language features in explanation texts that students encounter in secondary school chemistry textbooks. *Journal of English for Academic Purposes, 42*, Article 100781.

[211] Qian, Y. B. (2020). A critical genre analysis of MD&A discourse in corporate annual reports. *Discourse&Communication, 14*(4), 424-437.

[212] Qiu, X. Y.,&Ma, X. H. (2019). Disciplinary enculturation and authorial stance: Comparison of stance features among master's dissertations, doctoral theses, and research articles. *Iberica, 38,* 327-348.

[213] Ramirez, A. (2020). The case for Culturally and Linguistically

Relevant Pedagogy: Bilingual Reading to learn for Spanish-Speaking immigrant mothers. *System*, *95*, Article 102379. https://doi.org/10.1016/j.system.2020.102379

[214] Ren, W., Bhatia, V. K.,&Han, Z. (2020). Analyzing interdiscursivity in legal genres: The case of Chinese lawyers' written opinions. *Pragmatics and Society, 11*(4), 615-639. https://doi.org/10.1075/ps.17030.han

[215] Rose, D. (1997). Science, technology and technical literacies. In F. Christie&J. R. Martin (Eds.), *Genre and institutions: Social processes in the workplace and school* (pp. 40-72). London: Cassell.

[216] Rose, D. (2005). Democratising the classroom: A literacy pedagogy for the new generation. *Journal of Education, 37*, 127-64.

[217] Rose, D. (2007). Towards a reading-based theory of teaching. Plenary paper in Proceedings 33rd International Systemic Functional Congress. Sao Paulo: PUCSP.

[218] Rose, D. (2008). Writing as linguistic mastery: The development of genre-based literacy pedagogy. In R. Beard, D. Myhill, J. Riley&M. Nystrand (Eds.), *Handbook of writing development* (pp. 151-166). Sage.

[219] Rose, D. (2011). Beyond literacy: Building an integrated pedagogic genre. *Australian Journal of Language and Literacy, 34*(1), 81-97.

[220] Rose, D. (2012). Genre in the Sydney school. In J. P. Gee&M. Handford (Eds.), *The Routledge handbook of discourse analysis* (pp.209-225). Routledge.

[221] Rose, D. (2020a). Building a pedagogic metalanguage I: Curriculum genres. In J. R. Martin, K. Maton&Y. J. Doran (Eds.), *Accessing academic discourse: Systemic functional linguistics and legitimation code theory* (pp. 236-267). Routledge.

[222] Rose, D. (2020b). Building a pedagogic metalanguage II: Knowledge genres. In J. R. Martin, K. Maton&Y. J. Doran (Eds.), *Accessing academic discourse: Systemic functional linguistics and legitimation code theory* (pp. 268-302). Routledge.

[223] Rose, D.,&Martin, J. R. (2012). *Learning to write, reading to learn: Genre, knowledge and pedagogy in the Sydney School.* Equinox.

[224] Rothery, J. (1989). Learning about language. In R. Hasan&J. R. Martin (Eds.), *Language development: Learning language, learning culture* (pp. 199-256). Ablex.

[225] Rothery, J. (1994). *Exploring literacy in school English (write it right resources for literacy and learning)*. Sydney: Adult Migrant Education Service, Sydney: Metropolitan East Disadvantaged Schools Program.

[226] Ruan, Z. L. (2018). Structural compression in academic writing: An English-Chinese comparison study of complex noun phrases in research article abstracts. *Journal of English for Academic Purposes, 36*, 37-47.

[227] Ryshina-Pankova, M., Barthold, W.,&Barthold, E. (2021). Enhancing the content- and language-integrated multiple literacies framework: Systemic functional linguistics for teaching regional diversity. *System, 96, Article 102403*.

[228] Sadeghi, K.,&Alinasab, M. (2020). Academic conflict in Applied Linguistics research article discussions: The case of native and non-native. *English for Specific Purposes, 59*, 17-28. https://doi.org/10.1016/j.esp.2020.03.001

[229] Samraj, B. (2013). Form and function of citations in discussion sections of master's theses and research articles. *Journal of English for Academic Purposes, 12*(4), 299-310. https://doi.org/10.1016/j.jeap.2013.09.001

[230] Samraj, B. (2016). Discourse structure and variation in manuscript reviews: Implications for genre categorization. *English for Specific Purposes, 42*, 76-88.

[231] Sauer, L.,&Ellis, R. O. D. (2019). The social lives of adolescent study abroad: Learners and their L2 development. *The Modern Language Journal, 103*(4), 739-762.

[232] Shahmirzadi, A. A. (2019). "Where is the friend's home?": New world landscapes in Sohrab Sepehri's *Poetic Geography. The Cambridge Journal of Postcolonial Literary Inquiry*, *6*(3), 313-328.

[233] Sheldon, E. (2018). Dialogic spaces of knowledge construction in research article Conclusion sections written by English L1, English L2 and Spanish L1 writers. *Iberica, 35*, 13-39.

[234] Sheldon, E. (2019). Knowledge construction of discussion/conclusion sections of research articles written by English L1 and L2 and Castilian Spanish L1 writers. *Journal of English for Academic Purposes, 37*, 1-10.

[235] Shen, Q.,&Tao, Y. (2021). Stance markers in English medical research articles and newspaper opinion columns: A comparative corpus-based study. *Plos One*, *16*(3), Article e0247981. https://doi.org/10.1371/journal.pone.0247981

[236] Shi, L., Baker, A.,&Chen, H. (2019). Chinese EFL teachers' cognition about the effectiveness of genre pedagogy: A case study. *Relc Journal, 50*(2), 314-332.

[237] Stosic, D. (2021). Persuasion strategies for demonstrating topic significance in reports of randomised controlled trials. *English for Specific Purposes, 62,* 1-14.

[238] Su, H.,&Zhang, L. (2020). Local grammars and discourse acts in academic writing: A case study of exemplification in linguistics research articles. *Journal of English for Academic Purposes, 43*, Article 100805.

[239] Swales, J. M. (1990). *Genre analysis: English in academic and research settings*. Cambridge University Press.

[240] Swales, J. M. (2004). *Research genres: Explorations and applications*. Cambridge University Press.

[241] Swales, J. M. (2019). The futures of EAP genre studies: A personal viewpoint. *Journal of English for Academic Purposes, 38*, 75-82.

[242] Swales, J. M.,&Post, J. (2018). Student use of imperatives in their academic writing: How research can be pedagogically applied. *Journal of English for Academic Purposes, 31*, 91-97.

[243] Swales, J. M., Ahmad, U. K., Chang, Y. Y., Chavez, D., Dressen, D. F.,&Seymour, R. (1998). Consider this: The role of imperatives in scholarly

writing. *Applied Linguistics, 19(1)*, 97-121.

[244] Swales, J. M., Barks, D., Ostermann, A. C.,&Simpson, R. C. (2001). Between critique and accommodation: Reflections on an EAP course for Masters of Architecture students. *English for Specific Purposes, 20*, 439-458.

[245] Szenes, E. (2017). *The linguistic construction of business reasoning: Towards a language-based model of decision-making in undergraduate business.* Unpublished Ph.D. Thesis. University of Sydney, Australia.

[246] Szücs, T., Mohr, P., Gyürky, G., Halász, Z., Huszánk, R., Kiss, G. G., Szegedi, T. N., Török, Z.,&Fülöp, Z. (2019). Cross section of α-induced reactions on ^{197}Au at sub-Coulomb energies. *Physical Review C, 100*(6), 065803.

[247] Tanko, G. (2017). Literary research article abstracts: An analysis of rhetorical moves and their linguistic realizations. *Journal of English for Academic Purposes, 27*, 42-55. https://doi.org/10.1016/j.jeap.2017.04.003

[248] Tardy, C. M., Sommer-Farias, B.,&Gevers, J. (2020). Teaching and researching genre knowledge: Toward an enhanced theoretical framework. *Written Communication, 37*(3), 287-321. https://doi.org/10.1177/0741088320916554

[249] Thompson, G. (2016). Hybridisation: How language users graft new discourses on old root stock. In D. R. Miller&P. Bayley (Eds.), *Hybridity in systemic functional linguistics* (pp. 181-204). Equinox.

[250] Tiller, E. (2020). Humanist transfer of knowledge from foreign lands: Modes of cognitive perception of the world among Florentine travelers to America between 1490 and 1530. *Neohelicon, 47*(2), 357-378.

[251] Torsello, C. T. (2016). Woolf's lecture/novel/essay a room of one's own. In D. R. Miller&P. Bayley (Eds.), *Hybridity in systemic functional linguistics* (pp. 240-267). Equinox.

[252] Townley, A.,&Jones, A. (2016). The role of emails and covering letters in negotiating a legal contract: A case study from Turkey. *English for Specific Purposes, 44*, 68-81.

[253] Triki, N. (2019). Revisiting the metadiscursive aspect of definitions in academic writing. *Journal of English for Academic Purposes, 37*, 104-116.

[254] Troyan, F. J. (2021). "Alors, on va faire une activite": An SFL perspective on student engagement in contextualized world language instruction. *System, 98, Article 102483*. https://doi.org/10.1016/j.system.2021.102483

[255] Troyan, F. J., Sembiante, S. F.,&King, N. (2019). A case for a functional linguistic knowledge base in world language teacher education. *Foreign Language Annals, 52(3)*, 644-669.

[256] Tseng, M. Y. (2018). Creating a theoretical framework: On the move structure of theoretical framework sections in research articles related to language and linguistics. *Journal of English for Academic Purposes, 33*, 82-99. https://doi.org/10.1016/j.jeap.2018.01.002

[257] Uzun, K.,&Zehir Topkaya, E. (2020). The effects of genre-based instruction and genre-focused feedback on L2 writing performance. *Reading&Writing Quarterly, 36*(5), 438-461.

[258] Van Compernolle, R. A. (2019). Constructing a second language sociolinguistic repertoire: A sociocultural usage-based perspective. *Applied Linguistics*, *40*(6), 871-893.

[259] Vandertop, C. (2018). "The earth seemed unearthly": Capital, world-ecology, and enchanted nature in Conrad's *Heart of Darkness*. *MFS: Modern Fiction Studies*, *64*(4), 680-700.

[260] Veel. R. (1997). Learning how to mean—scientifically speaking: Apprenticeship into scientific discourse in the secondary school. In F. Christie&J. R. Martin (Eds.), *Genre and institutions: Social processes in the workplace and school* (pp. 161-195). Cassell.

[261] Vian Jr., O. (2016). Beyond the three traditions in genre studies: A Brazilian perspective. In N. Aremeva&A. Freedman (Eds.), *Genre studies around the globe: Beyond the three Traditions* (pp. 141-164). Trafford Publishing.

[262] Wang, Q.,&Hu, G. (2023). Disciplinary and gender-based variations: A frame-based analysis of interest markers in research articles. *English for*

Specific Purposes, *70*, 177-191. https://doi.org/https://doi.org/10.1016/j.esp.2022.12.006

[263] Wang, W. H.,&Yang, C. S. (2015). Claiming centrality as promotion in applied linguistics research article introductions. *Journal of English for Academic Purposes, 20*, 162-175. https://doi.org/10.1016/j.jeap.2015.05.002

[264] Wang, Y.,&Liu, H. (2017). The effects of genre on dependency distance and dependency direction. *Language Sciences, 59*, 135-147.

[265] Weissberg, R.,&Buker, S. (1990). *Writing up research: Experimental research report writing for students of English.* Prentice-Hall Regents.

[266] Wignell, P. (1994). Genre across the curriculum. *Linguistic and Education 6*, 355-72.

[267] Wignell, P., Martin, J. R.&Eggins, S. (1989). The discourse of geography: Ordering and explaining the experiential world. *Linguistics and Education 1*(4), 359-92.

[268] Wulfert, R., Seifert, U.,&Speck, T. (2017). Nonequilibrium depletion interactions in active microrheology. *Soft Matter, 13(48)*, 9093-9102.

[269] Wulff, S., Swales, J. M.,&Keller, K. (2009). "We have about seven minutes for questions": The discussion sessions from a specialized conference. *English for Specific Purposes, 28(2)*, 79-92.

[270] Xu, X. Y.,&Nesi, H. (2019a). Differences in engagement: A comparison of the strategies used by British and Chinese research article writers. *Journal of English for Academic Purposes, 38*, 121-134.

[271] Xu, X. Y.,&Nesi, H. (2019b). Evaluation in research article introductions: A comparison of the strategies used by Chinese and British authors. *Text&Talk, 39*(6), 797-818. https://doi.org/10.1515/text-2019-2046

[272] Yang, R. Y.,&Allison, D. (2003). Research articles in applied linguistics: Moving from results to conclusions. *English for Specific Purposes, 63*(6), 735-736. https://doi.org/10.1016/S0889-4906(02)00026-1

[273] Yang, R. Y.,&Allison, D. (2004). Research articles in applied linguistics: Structures from a functional perspective. *English for Specific Purposes,*

23(3), 264-279. https://doi.org/10.1016/s0889-4906(03)00005-x

[274] Ye, Y. P. (2019). Macrostructures and rhetorical moves in energy engineering research articles written by Chinese expert writers. *Journal of English for Academic Purposes, 38*, 48-61. https://doi.org/10.1016/j.jeap.2019.01.007

[275] Yeh, H.-C. (2015). Facilitating metacognitive processes of academic genre-based writing using an online writing system. *Computer Assisted Language Learning, 28*(6), 479-498.

[276] Yoon, J.,&Casal, J. E. (2020). Rhetorical structure, sequence, and variation: A step-driven move analysis of applied linguistics conference abstracts. *International Journal of Applied Linguistics, 30*(3), 462-478.

[277] Young, H.&Freedman, R. (2012). *University physics* (13th Edition). Addison Wesley.

[278] Young, L. (1990). *Language as behaviour, language as code: A study of academic English*. John Benjamins.

[279] Zhang, R., Chen, T.,&Wang, X.-B. (2017). Deterministic quantum controlled-PHASE gates based on non-Markovian environments. *New Journal of Physics*, *19*(12), 123001.

[280] Zhang, Y.,&Pramoolsook, I. (2019). Generic complexity in bachelor's theses by Chinese English majors: An SFL perspective. *Journal of Language Studies, 19*(4), 304-326. https://doi.org/10.17576/gema-2019-1904-16

[281] Zou, H.,&Hyland, K. (2020a). Managing evaluation: Criticism in two academic review genres. *English for Specific Purposes, 60*, 98-112.

[282] Zou, H.,&Hyland, K. (2020b). "Think about how fascinating this is": Engagement in academic blogs across disciplines. *Journal of English for Academic Purposes, 43*, 100809. https://doi.org/https://doi.org/10.1016/j.jeap.2019.100809

[283] 程乐、裴佳敏 . 2018. 未保价快递限额赔偿格式条款效力之体裁检视 [J]. 浙江工商大学学报 , 151(04): 78-89.

[284] 邓庆环 .2012. 英语限定性小句复合体与知识建构——以大学教科书为例 [D]. 厦门 : 厦门大学博士学位论文 .

[285] 韩宝成、魏兴 . 2021. 整体外语教学视域下的大学英语论说语类教学探讨 [J]. 外语教学 , 42(04): 50-56.

[286] 赖良涛 . 2012. 基于目的论的语类分析模式——以公司网站语类为例 [M]. 厦门 : 厦门大学出版社 .

[287] 赖良涛、王任华 . 2018. 语言学期刊研究论文的语类布局策略 [J]. 外语教学 , 39(06): 39-43.

[288] 李小坤 . 2017. 英语学位论文的语类特征 : 文本、语境与批评分析 [M]. 南京 : 南京师范大学出版社 .

[289] 李志君 . 2021. 中英社会科学期刊论文标题的词汇句法特征比较 [J]. 华侨大学学报 (哲学社会科学版), 143(02): 154-164.

[290] 卢楠、袁传有 . 2022. 司法意见书的语类嵌入结构探析 [J]. 外国语 , 45(03): 34-47.

[291] 庞继贤、陈珺、程乐 . 2021. 英语学术论文语篇的话语策略研究 [M]. 杭州 : 浙江大学出版社 .

[292] 汪燕华 .2012. 语类的多模态分析——以英语心理学教材为例 [D]. 厦门 : 厦门大学博士学位论文 .

[293] 王薇 . 2019. 学术英语写作学习者的元认知与体裁习得研究 [J]. 外语教育研究前沿 , 2(02): 73-80+93.

[294] 武建国、牛振俊、黄泽文 . 2018. 微信公众号中广告话语的批评性体裁分析 —— 以三大外资超市为例 [J]. 山东外语教学 , 39(04): 30-37.

[295] 夏中华 . 2009. 现代语言学引论 [M]. 上海 : 学林出版社 .

[296] 徐燕、冯德正 . 2020. 新媒体商务话语中的多模态体裁互文 : 语域类型学视角 [J]. 外语教学 , 41(03): 23-28.

[297] 许家金 . 2019. 语料库与话语研究 [M]. 北京 : 外语教学与研究出版社 .

[298] 杨信彰 . 2005. 语言学概论 [M]. 北京 : 高等教育出版社 .

[299] 杨信彰 . 2018. 英语物理学语篇中的言据性动词 [J]. 英语研究 , (01):66-76.

[300] 叶斐声、徐通锵 . 2010. 语言学纲要 (修订版) [M]. 北京 : 北京大学出版社 .

[301] 叶云屏 . 2020. 体裁混合现象对大学生 EAP 教学的启示——以科学 60 秒为例 [J]. 中国 ESP 研究 , 11(01): 21-31+104.

[302] 于晖 . 2018. 功能语篇体裁分析理论与实践 [M]. 北京：外语教学与研究出版社 .

[303] 张德禄、郭恩华 . 2019. 体裁混合综合分析框架探索 [J]. 中国外语，16(01): 20-27.

[304] 张曼 . 2009. 英语学术论文摘要中的情态配置 [D]. 厦门大学博士学位论文 .

[305] 张先刚 . 2015. 语言学学术期刊论文摘要的意义生成——系统功能意义学语类分析 [J]. 当代外语研究 , 409(01):14-19.

[306] 赵清丽 . 2012. 中小学物理教科书的知识建构 [D]. 厦门大学博士学位论文 .

[307] 赵文超 . 2014. 中学科学教科书的知识表征——概念意义分形视角 [D]. 厦门大学博士学位论文 .

[308] 赵永青、刘璐达、邓耀臣、刘兆浩 . 2019. 国际文学类期刊论文英文摘要的语步——语阶序列分析 [J]. 外语研究 , 36(01): 18-23.

[309] 赵永青、刘兆浩、邓耀臣、刘璐达 . 2019. 实证类期刊论文讨论部分体裁结构的学科变异研究 [J]. 外语教学 , 40(06): 26-31.